ARABS
IN THE
AMERICAS

PETER LANG
New York • Washington, D.C./Baltimore • Bern
Frankfurt am Main • Berlin • Brussels • Vienna • Oxford

ARABS IN THE AMERICAS

Interdisciplinary Essays on the Arab Diaspora

Edited by
Darcy A. Zabel

PETER LANG
New York • Washington, D.C./Baltimore • Bern
Frankfurt am Main • Berlin • Brussels • Vienna • Oxford

Library of Congress Cataloging-in-Publication Data

Names: Zabel, Darcy A., editor.
Title: Arabs in the Americas: interdisciplinary essays on the Arab diaspora /
edited by Darcy A. Zabel.
Description: New York: Peter Lang, 2006.
Includes bibliographical references.
Identifiers: LCCN 2006022704 | ISBN 978-0-8204-8111-1 (paperback: alk. paper)
Subjects: LCSH: Arabs—America—History. | Arabs—Migrations—History.
Arabs—America—Social conditions. | Arabs—America—Intellectual life.
Ethnicity—America. | Stereotype (Psychology)—America. | America—Ethnic relations.
American literature—Arab American authors—History and criticism.
America—Intellectual life.
Classification: LCC E29.A73A73 2006 | DDC 305.892'707—dc22
LC record available at https://lccn.loc.gov/2006022704

Bibliographic information published by **Die Deutsche Nationalbibliothek**.
Die Deutsche Nationalbibliothek lists this publication in the "Deutsche
Nationalbibliografie"; detailed bibliographic data are available
on the Internet at http://dnb.d-nb.de/.

Cover design by Joni Holst

The paper in this book meets the guidelines for permanence and durability
of the Committee on Production Guidelines for Book Longevity
of the Council of Library Resources.

Printed in the United States of America

This volume is lovingly dedicated to the children and young people in our lives who represent the future and all the promise and potential the future holds:

Quinnehtukqut, Robert, Audrey, Gabriel, Liam, David, Ghada, Sham, Hisham, Juman, Patricia, Anna, Ramon, Maria, Eyas, Enal, Malik, Tariq, Katie, Rosie, Christa, Charlie, Thomas, John, and Tommy.

∞ Table of Contents ∞

Part 1: Arriving in the Americas

Part 2: The Experience of the Americas

Part 3: Assessing the Americas

Part 4: After 9/11

❧Acknowledgments ☙

I would like to thank Dr. John Yoder, Dr. Wayne Howdeshell, Constance Hope Reimer, and Max Burson and his colleagues at the Friends University library for their continued support and commitment to promoting faculty research and development.

Thank you also to Steve Cohlmia, Chris Farha, Ted, Farha, Warren Farha, Kenneth James Kallail, Rosemary Kallail, and Eric Namee for graciously allowing their stories to become a part of Kirk Scott's chapter on Arab American identity politics in the American west.

A project of this kind requires a great deal of time and emotional energy; and so I would also like to say thank you, once again, to Heidi, and to the authors who contributed to this volume, and to their families and employers, for making the time to make this project possible.

ஐIntroductionos

The Arab Diaspora in the Americas:
Latin America, the United States, and Canada

Darcy A. Zabel

Before September 11, 2001, the majority of scholarly works devoted to the study of the Arab diaspora to the Americas had, in essence, two main purposes: the first, to inform and correct misrepresentations about Arabs currently living in America and the second, to illustrate the plight of oppressed Arabs still living in the Middle East.

Immediately following what is now commonly referred to in the United States as "9/11," essay collections about the Arab American experience continued to focus attention on countering anti-Arab American stereotypes, and to do so by cataloging the long history of the Arab presence in the United States, highlighting the long-term contributions of Arab Americans to the cultural diversity and economic life of America, and the American-ness of second and third-generation Arab Americans with the hope of replacing the 9/11 negative stereotype of the Islamic fundamentalist-terrorist with an alternate image of the educated, successful, Christian, socially aware and involved Arab émigré and his or her descendents.

While these are all very important and very real contributions to the field of Arab American studies, there is still a problem with this post-9/11 agenda in that it, too, distorts a reader's understanding of the Arab presence in the Americas in three significant ways. First, to put together a collection of essays in the immediate shadow of such a political event, with the hope of shaping a reader's response to or perception of the Arabs now living in the Americas, necessarily limits the scholarly direction of the collection and just as Michael Suleiman observed about the early twentieth-century studies of Arabs in America, tends to limit scholarship to the "general, concerned largely with providing background information."[1] Thus, instead of advancing scholarship from the general to the specific, many mainstream post-9/11 collections have attempted to justify or simply celebrate the Arab American presence in

America, rather than to truly engage in scholarship about specific facets and representations of Arab culture in the Americas, which is, ultimately, the only way to advance the field of Arab American studies.

The second lacuna in the majority of pre-and post-9/11 collections of essays about Arabs in America that this collection hopes to correct is that all too often the term "America" is used to signify "the United States" thus narrowing the field of Arab American studies to just the Arab American presence in the United States, shifting attention away from both Canada and Latin America. Such a focus simply reinforces the U.S.-centric notion that the United States is the most important country in the Americas or that most members of the Arab diaspora coming to the Americas chose to settle in the United States, the fabled land of opportunity. Large numbers of immigrants did choose to settle in the United States—there are, according to the United States Census Bureau's 2000 report, which includes a voluntary declaration of ancestry, 1.2 million Arabs in the United States. According to other non-government sources, the Arab American population in the United States is actually closer to 3 to 5 million people.[2] However, despite these numbers, to use the term *America* interchangeably with the *United States*, shifts attention away from the actual settlement patterns of the members from the various waves of immigration that form the Arab diaspora.

There are, for example, far more members of the Arab diaspora who actually chose to settle in Latin America than in the United States with over 12 million people of Arab ancestry living in Latin America with large numbers of people of Arab descent to be found in Brazil, Honduras, Ecuador, Argentina, Columbia, Mexico, and many other Latin American locales.[3] Canada, too, has a thriving population of citizens of Arab ethnic origin which includes Canadian-born Arabs and both recent and non-recent Arab immigrants.[4] The Americas, plural, have long been a destination point for members of the Arab diaspora and to refer to the United States as America and to ignore the even larger number of Arab immigrants and their descendents who live in the "other" Americas is to continue to marginalize and minimize the global impact of the Arab diaspora on the Americas.

The third and final stumbling block for editors of interdisciplinary collections of essays on Arab immigrant experiences, collections put together during the time period immediately following 9/11, is that too many collections tend to focus on the "whiteness" and the educational, economic, and religious status of American Arabs as if "whiteness," education, wealth, and a particular religious creed are somehow an indication of "American-ness" or a pre-requisite for status as "American," rather than encouraging a broader, more expansive understanding of what it means to be of Arab descent and to live in the Americas. Now, several years after 9/11, it is possible to re-examine the experience of Arabs in the Americas from a variety of viewpoints and with a multitude of intentions. As Maysa Abou-Youssef Hayward notes, "politics alone" have "raised a global awareness of Arab culture" and so the purpose of interdisciplinary collections need not be simply to "introduce Western readers" to the fact that Arabs and people of Arab descent live in the Americas.[5] Instead, it is possible to look at how people of Arab descent in Latin America, the United States, and Canada negotiate the "self" in the diaspora and how "hyphenated identities," (Arab American, Arab Canadian, and so on) evoke, as Heba Sharobeem describes, "questions and debates about what side of the hyphen a person belongs to."[6] It is also possible to look at Arab Studies texts that address topics that stretch beyond a U.S.-centric focus and to study their impact on the expanding field of Arab American studies.

While my original intent, as editor, was to arrange the collection chronologically according to the various waves of Arab immigration that comprise the Arab diaspora in the Americas, when the essays started to come in, I came to realize that while it is possible to limit a discussion of an event or theme to a specific time period, that to do the topic justice, often the topic itself breaks the chronological frame and insists on both a backward glance into the historical contexts of the event, and also looks forward to a hoped for or imagined future, and this is particularly true with an interdisciplinary collection of essays. With this in mind, many of the essays in this collection could be grouped into more than one section, but for the purposes of arrangement, I have, somewhat artificially, grouped the essays into four loosely thematic units.

Part 1: "Arriving in the Americas" includes essays related to early immigration to Latin America (1890s), the construction of an Arab American identity in the United States (1920s) and the impact of being an expatriate (1970s–1990s). In Part 2: "The Experience of the Americas," the essays focus on the sensation of having multiple identities, the impact of pop culture and stereotypes on one's experience of the Americas, specifically North America, and a "then and now" look at Arab experiences in Latin America. Part 3: "Assessing the Americas" discusses the cultural significance of Arab American literature, critically examines Arab American reclamation rhetoric, and looks at representations of Arabs in juvenile fiction both pre-and post-9/11 ; and Part 4: "After 9/11" invites readers to drop the purely scholarly gaze for just a moment and to ponder on a more personal level questions of identity, the post-9/11 responses of the larger community, and the situation, today, of Arabs in the Americas.

For readers unfamiliar with the history of Arab diaspora to the Americas—to Latin America, Canada, and the United States what now follows is a very brief history of the early journeys and the current situation today.

Latin America

As Theresa Alfaro Velcamp observes, "few primary sources combined with a seeming disinterest (until recently) in Middle Eastern immigration to Latin America" makes the study of Arabs in Latin America challenging.[7] Also, because Europeans, historically, were considered the "desirable" immigrants to Latin America, "immigrants that were not Anglo-Saxons, French, or North Italians" assimilated as quickly as possible, disguising their ethnic roots as part of a "whitening" process.[8] Record keeping regarding early the Arab immigration to the Americas that make up Latin America (i.e., the countries of Central and South America including Mexico, but excluding the Caribbean countries) is thus scanty indeed.

The earliest instances of Arab immigration to Latin America, according to Carol Fadda-Conrey, occurred in the earliest parts of the seventeenth century when, "in response to several Moorish uprisings. . . . King Philip II issued a royal decree in 1609 that ordered the expulsion of 300,000 Moriscos"[9] (Arabs living in Spain), an event that resulted in a ripple of forced emigration from Spain and immigration to other lands. Evidence exists that during the Spanish conquest of the New World, some of these exiles "were successful in slipping into the Americas" throughout the sixteenth century.[10] According to this reckoning, these first Arab immigrants to Latin America were thus Arabs already previously dispossessed from Arab lands who had immigrated to Spain, been forced to convert from Islam to Catholicism, and who were then still driven from Spain due to increased cultural pressure to conform to an ethnographic as well as religiously Catholic way of life. While the numbers are small, these were the first Arab immigrants to the region.

The larger better documented waves of immigration to Latin America; however, are most commonly identified as first occurring in the 1870s[11] and

1880.[12] For these immigrants, Velcamp writes, the "primary stimulus for emigration was the oppression of Christians by the Ottoman rulers."[13] Michael Humphrey, however, argues that this "common perception" that most Arab immigrants to Latin America were "overwhelming Christians fleeing Ottoman persecution is misleading," and Humphrey states that the records indicate that during the peak period of Arab immigration, "the proportion of Muslims reached as high as 45 percent."[14] Humphrey explains that almost one-third of the Christians who fled to Latin America because of Ottoman abuses actually returned to their homelands, and that "the Ottoman government financed the repatriation of some emigrants."[15] Arab immigration records in Argentina, for example, indicate that in addition to the Maronite and Orthodox Christian Arabs who came to Argentina, "significant numbers were Sunni, Shi'ite, Alawai, as well as Jewish."[16]

During the period after World War II, or the second wave, emigration from the Middle East to Latin America was motivated primarily by a combination of economic, religious, and political considerations. As Marc Osterweil explains, during this phase of the Arab diaspora, Arab immigrants "came seeking new homes and opportunities" and the numbers of Arab immigrants increased "due to the positive experiences of their predecessors."[17] Thus, as Dario Euraque explains, while the study of "the unique presence of Arab and Jewish immigrants within the broader currents of nineteenth-and twentieth-century immigrations to Latin America is still in its infancy," it is clear that the patterns of Arab immigration to Latin America parallel Arab migrations to other destination points in the Americas.[18]

Today, it has become increasingly important to understand the role the Arab diaspora has played and continues to play in shaping Latin American culture in order to fully understand the context of political events such as the 2005 South American and Arab Nations Summit. There are, of course, important economic and political reasons for such a summit that are not predicated on the existence of a large Arab population in Latin America, but such a summit did result in increased attention regarding contributions to Latin American culture by Arab immigrants. While the summit included sessions on trade and the Israel–Palestine situation,[19] and a move to "criticize U.S. economic sanctions against Syria and question Britain's claim to the Falkland Islands" that resulted in a draft statement to be signed by leaders from thirty-three South American and Arab nations,[20] according to Mario Osava of the Global Information Network, the summit's organizers also created "parallel events" such as "photography and film exhibits" to "highlight the influence of Arab immigrants in South America, which is home to around 17 million people of Arab descent."[21] Though the historical record may be difficult to read regarding the impact of early Arab immigration to Latin America, with 17 million people of Arab descent now living in that region, the need for further study and appreciation of that history becomes clear.

The United States

As in Latin America, Arab immigration to the United States also occurred primarily during two periods of time with the first wave of immigration taking place between 1870 and the 1920s (with immigration numbers waning in 1924 when the immigration laws in the United States changed and became more restrictive), and the second wave beginning in the late 1940s (after World War II).[22] As Köszegi and Melton observe, scholars who study the Arab diaspora and immigration patterns to the United States disagree about the impetus for Arab immigration, citing both "push and pull factors."[23] Many scholars assert that Arabs were pushed into the diaspora by "a desire to flee sectarian and political conflict" with "tensions accompanying economic and social transformation; the imposition of conscription; the spread of foreign education; the improvement of transportation, and the massacres of 1860."[24] Others argue that the United States as a destination was the product of a specific economic choice, and the first wave of Arab immigration to the United States was not intended to be a permanent resettling. These scholars argue that Arab immigrants were not pushed from their homelands and instead were simply drawn to the United States by "its accelerating urbanization and industrialization," and that these immigrants only came for "a two-or-three year sojourn to make money and return to the homeland, where most had left their families," and they did not leave because of "religious persecution or economic oppression," but money was, "the dominant attraction."[25] They were, Suleiman argues, "sojourners staying in the United States on a temporary basis with the primary or sole purpose of making a fortune they could enjoy back home."[26]

Regarding the second wave of immigration to the United States, however, scholars are largely in agreement. The reason for the second wave of immigration, which scholars identify as any immigration occurring after 1950, was war. Immigration was slow throughout the 1950s and 1960s, and these members of the Arab diaspora were early arrivals of immigrants fleeing what they saw as clear signs of impending war. The floodgates opened in the late 1960s and throughout the 1970s. Some cite the Arab-Israeli conflict (1967) as the primary cause of the second wave of the diaspora; others reference the violent civil war in Lebanon (1975-1976),[27] and the "brutality of the Assad regime, whose crushing of Islamic fundamentalist rebels at Hama in 1982 caused the death of 20,000 civilians," or the "continuing unanswered occupations by Israel."[28] War and the political, social, and religious unrest caused by war is clearly the motivating factor for migration during this second wave of migration.

At present, Arabs and United States citizens of Arab descent officially make up approximately 1% of the entire population of the United States, where they are not classified as an official ethnic or minority group.[29] There are an estimated 3 to 5 million Americans of Arab descent. Of those United States citizens who identify themselves as Arab American, 47% are from Lebanon, 15% from Syria, 9% from Egypt, 6% from Palestine, and 23% are from 18 other countries.[30] Forty-two percent of these Arab Americans identify themselves as Catholic, 23% percent are Muslim, another 23% percent are Eastern Orthodox, and 12% are Protestant.[31] However, as Michael Suleiman explains, even "after more than a century of immigration . . . true integration and full assimilation have eluded them," the "them" being Arabs of the Arab diaspora and their descendents.[32] Suleiman believes that this is a result of "the hostility of the host society" and that to succeed in America, Arab immigrants and their descendents are expected to "de-emphasize or deny" their Arab background and to refrain from "strong or vocal support of Arab or Arab nationalist causes." After 9/11, as Steven Salaita observes, this expectation became even more pronounced, creating a "domestic environment" in which many Arab Americans kept "away from politics" to avoid "harassment, complaints of anti-Americanism, or, worse, accusations of anti-Semitism."[33] While in the immediate aftermath of 9/11 political figures such as United States President George W. Bush and the United States media urged citizens to refrain from racial violence against citizens of Arab descent, scholars continue to debate the long-term impact of the Domestic Security Enhancement Act (also known as the Patriot Act) on Arab Americans in the United States today. Political situations such as this continue to affect the Arab American experience of the Americas and one's sense of what it means to be a member of the Arab diaspora.

Canada

While headlines such as the *Wall Street Journal*'s July 2002, "Is Canada a Launching Pad for Terror?"[34] suggest that there are large numbers of Arab immigrants in Canada, in fact, the while the percentage number is slightly higher than, for example, in the United States, the actual number of Canadians of Arab descent is far smaller than the numbers in either the United States or Latin America. According to the 1991 Canadian Census data, there are approximately 200,000 Arabs living in Canada, [35] though according to more recent nongovernmental sources, that number is now closer to "375,000 Canadians of Arab origin, or 1.3 percent of Canada's total population."[36] Immigration to Canada, again, follows the same basic two-wave pattern of the Arab diaspora found in Latin America and the United States, although the dates of arrival differ by approximately 15 years for the initial wave, and the second wave having a period of intensity in the early 1960s not duplicated in the United States or Latin America.

The first officially recorded Arab immigrants to Canada arrived in 1892, and from the 1890s onward, there was a steady increase of Arab immigrants until the approach of World War I when the Canadian government began to restrict and then halt the immigration of those "who did not come to Canada by direct and continuous journey from their homeland," a statute meant to stem the tide of immigration from Asian and Arab lands.[37] After World War II, the immigration law regarding the continuous journey regulation was repealed, and the Canadian government ruled that "the citizens of most Middle Eastern countries" would henceforth "be treated as Europeans rather than Asians."[38] The 1967 Canadian Immigration Act thus permitted Arabs to apply for immigration on the basis of a point system based on education, training, and skills, status as a refugee based on humanitarian grounds, or as sponsored applicants of existing Canadian relatives.[39] The most substantial increase of Arab immigration occurred in the early 1960s, and followed a different pattern than that of Latin America or the United States. In Canada, "a large portion of these post-war wave Arab immigrants were from North Africa (57%), hence French-oriented."[40]

In the 1990s, the pattern of immigration again shifted with 60% of the present Arab population in Canada self-identifying as recent immigrants, with the largest number of recent immigrants hailing from Lebanon, Morocco, Algeria, Kuwait, Jordan, Saudi Arabia, the United Arab Emirates, Egypt, and

Somalia; and with 62% of Arab Canadians self-identifying as Christian, and 32% self-identifying as Muslim.[41]

According to Baha Abu-Laban, "Canada's ethnic kaleidoscope" has always been able to embrace both "the Eastern Christian and Islamic traditions," and Arab Canadian immigrants and their descendents "maintain frequent social and cultural links with [their] Eastern heritage."[42] He cites the Canadian government's "policy of multiculturalism and the relatively tolerant public attitude towards ethnic difference" as important elements aiding in the "preservation of ethnic identity without diminishing loyalty to Canada as the chosen land." In the years following 9/11, however, T. Y. Ismael and John Measor note that mainstream Canadian media sources rapidly increased their "volume of anti-Arab, anti-Muslim, and anti-dissent materials" and that Canadian media coverage of the "Islamic world" presents Arabs as "collectively engaged in a war against Western interests and values."[43] The sentiments stirred up against Arabs and Muslims in Canada has had an impact on Canadian immigration regulations including a tightening up of immigration policy, new legislation defining terrorism, Canadian bill C-36, and the deportation of "those deemed a threat" (para. 52). These policy changes continue to affect the Canadian Arab experience of the Americas.

As Michael Humphrey explains, the contemporary use of the term *Arab diaspora* refers to so much more than just a sense of displacement from one's country of origin; rather, its usage has moved from simply identifying a specific moment of "an historical experience" of migration to a statement of "an existential condition" or "a metaphor" for the sense of "uncertainty, displacement and fragmented identity" many Arab Americans and their descendents still feel today.[44] Others embrace a diasporic identification because of what Humphrey calls a "desire" to "reanchor their identity" in "the legacy of past and continuing personal suffering." Thus, in this post-9/11 interdisciplinary collection of essays on Arabs in the Americas and the Arab diaspora, the authors seek, in a variety of ways, and through the lenses of their own disciplines, to advance a definition of the Americas and American-ness that focuses on the fusion, rather than the fragmentation of identities. As they discuss the immigration of Arabs to the Americas, the experiences of these immigrants their descendents in the Americas, and the embracing of past legacies and the impact of present political situations, the focus of this collection is not simply on the past or continuing personal sufferings or on simply celebrations of or introductions to Arab American history, but rather, as John Tofik Karam concludes in his essay included in this collection, the focus is on how reflective scholarship, combined with personal memory can shape "the theater of the past" and how "its margins can also be used for the construction of a more just future."

Notes

1. Michael Suleiman's preface to *Arabs in America: Building a New Future* (Philadelphia: Temple University Press, 1999), xi.
2. See Sarah Freeman's "Census: More Arabs Live in U.S." *CBS News.com*, December 4, 2003 available online at http://www.cbsnews.com/ Stories /2003 /12 /04 /national /printable 586895.shtml (accessed November 6, 2005); The Prejudice Institute's "Arab Americans: Factsheet," available online at http:// www.prejudiceinstitute.org /Factsheets5- Arab Americans.html (accessed November 6, 2005); Michael Suleiman's *Arabs in America: Building a New Future* (1999); Michael Kőszegi and J. Gordon Melton's *Islam in North America: A Sourcebook* (1992); Ernest McCarus's *The Development of Arab American Identity* (New York: Garland., 1992); Gregory Orfalea's *Before the Flames: A Quest for the History of Arab Americans* (Austin: University of Texas Press, 1988); James Zogby's *Arab America Today* (Washington, DC: The Arab American Institute, 1990); James Zogby, Pat Aufderheide, and Anne Mooney's *Taking Root and Bearing Fruit* (Washington, DC: The American-Arab Anti Discrimination Committee, ADC Research Institute/International Graphics, 1984); Philip Harsham's "Arabs in America," *Aramco World Magazine* 26, no. 2 (March/April, 1975), http: //www.saudiaramcoworld.com/index/BackIssues1970.aspx (accessed February 22, 2006).
3. See Ignacio Klich and Jeff Lesser's *Arab and Jewish Immigrants in Latin America: Images and Realities* (Portland, OR: Frank Cass, 1998); and Larry Luxner's "The Arabs of Honduras," *Saudi Aramco World*, 52 4 (2001): 46-51; and Albert Pozo's "Arabs from the Earliest Times: Havana," Embassy of Cuba in the Syrian Arab Republic, 2004, http:// embacubasiria.com/ a000035e.html (accessed February 22, 2006).
4. For more background on the numbers of Arabs in Canada, see the Canadian Arab Federation's "A Profile of Arabs in Canada" (1999), http:// ceris.metropolis.net/ Virtual%20Library/community/ Arabs1/arab1.html; and Baha Abu-Laban's *An Olive Branch on the Family Tree: The Arabs in Canada* (Toronto: McClelland and Stewart in Association with the Multiculturalism Directorate, Department of the Secretary of State and the Canadian Government Publishing Centre, Canada, 1980).
5. Maysa Abou-Youssef Hawyard's "Introduction" to "Arabesque: Arabic Literature in Translation and Arab Diasporic Writing," *Studies in the Humanities* 30.1-3 (June-December 2003): 6.
6. See "The Hyphenated Identity and the Question of Belonging: A Study of Samia Serageldin's *The Cairo House*," by Heba M. Sharobeem in "Arabesque: Arabic

Literature in Translation and Arab Diasporic Writing," *Studies in the Humanities,* 30 1-2 (June–December 2003): 25.

7. See Theresa Alfaro Velcamp's "The Historiography of Arab Immigration to Argentina: The Intersection of the Imaginary and Real Country," in *Arab and Jewish Immigrants in Latin America: Images and Realities,* eds. Ignacio Klich and Jeffrey Lesser (Portland, OR: Frank Cass, 1998), 227.

8. Velcamp, "The Historiography of Arab Immigration to Argentina: The Intersection of the Imaginary and Real Country," 232.

9. Fadda-Conrey, "The Passage from West to South: Arabs between the Old and New World," in chapter one of this collection.

10. Fadda-Conrey, "The Passage from West to South: Arabs between the Old and New World," chapter one of this collection.

11. Velcamp, "The Historiography of Arab Immigration to Argentina: The Intersection of the Imaginary and Real Country," 233. In her essay, Velcamp cites earlier studies by Marta A. Saleh de Canuto and Susana Budeguer on Arab immigration, setting the earliest official date of immigration as 1871, and the earliest Arab immigrants as Christians fleeing Muslim oppression.

12. See Karam, "Margins of Memory on the *Rua 25 de Marco*: Constructing the Syrian-Lebanese Past in Sao Paulo, Brazil," in this collection. See also Ignacio Lich and Jeff Lesser's *Arab and Jewish Immigrants in Latin America: Images and Realities* (1998) and Larry Luxner's "The Arabs of Honduras" (2001).

13. Velcamp, "The Historiography of Arab Immigration to Argentina: The Intersection of the Imaginary and Real Country," 233.

14. Humphrey, "Ethnic History, Nationalism and Transnationalism in Argentine Arab And Jewish Cultures," in *Arab and Jewish Immigrants in Latin America: Images and Realities,* ed. Ignacio Klich and Jeffrey Lesser (Portland, OR: Frank Cass, 1998), 167-88.

15. Humphrey, "Ethnic History," 170.

16. Humphrey, "Ethnic History," 169.

17. Humphrey, "Ethnic History," 148.

18. Dario Euraque, "The Arab-Jewish Presence in San Pedro Sula, the Industrial Capital of Honduras: Formative Years, 1880s–1930s," in *Arab and Jewish Immigrants in Latin America: Images and Realities,* eds. Ignacio Klich and Jeffrey Lesser (Portland, OR: Frank Cass, 1998), 116.

19. See Mario Osava's report "South America: First Summit with Arab Nations to Focus on Trade," *Global Information Network,* New York: May 10, 2005, 36 paragraphs. Available from Proquest online database at Friends University, http:// www. libary.friends.edu (accessed November 13, 2005). Osava discusses both the draft declaration delegates planned to sign condemning Israel's part in the Israeli-Palestinian conflict and the actual document signed which "goes no further" than supporting resolutions approved by the UN (para 8).

20. Though they were expected to be formally approved on the third day of the conference, these draft statements ultimately were not signed. For a more in-depth discussion of the issues in the draft proposals, see Raymond Colitt's "Latin America Politics: S.

Americans, Arab Nations Meet," *The Economist Intelligence Unit ViewsWire*, May 11, 2005, available from Proquest Online database at Friends University, http:// www.library.friends.edu (accessed November 13, 2005).

21. Osava further discusses the exhibit stating that it "showcases" the Arab influence in Latin American architecture, customs, cuisine, and daily life. He also discusses trade between the area and the twenty-two countries of the Arab League. Brazil alone engages in trade with the Arab world to the tune of $8.19 billon a year (para. 28). See Mario Osava's report "South America: First Summit with Arab Nations to Focus on Trade," *Global Information Network*, May 10, 2005, available online through the Proquest Online database at Friends University, http:// www. libary.friends.edu (accessed November 13, 2005).

22. See Alixa Naff's "The Early Arab American Experience," in *The Development of Arab American Identity*, ed. Ernest McCanus (Ann Arbor: University of Michigan Press, 1994); Michael Suleiman's *Arabs in America: Building a New Future* (Philadelphia: Temple University Press, 1999); Michael Kőszegi and J. Gordon Melton's, *Islam in North America: A Sourcebook* (New York: Garland., 1992); and Gregory Orfalea's *Before the Flames: A Quest for the History of Arab Americans* (Austin: University of Texas Press, 1988).

23. Kőszegi and Melton's *Islam in North America*, 50–53.

24. See Kőszegi and Melton's *Islam in North America: A Sourcebook*, 50, for a brief summary of the "push" and "pull" factors and their conclusion that "the pull factors were perhaps more important" (50). See Gregory Orfalea's *Before the Flames: A Quest for the History of Arab Americans*, 51–53, where he discusses Naff and Kayal's argument that immigration was a result of economic and political conflict and Issawi's theory that immigration was sparked by massacres, periodic famines, insect blights, and droughts that caused massive and widespread starvation.

25. Naff, "The Early Arab Immigrant Experience," 24.

26. Suleiman, 9.

27. Kőszegi and Melton, 51.

28. Orfalea, 177-78.

29. See the CIA World Factbook "United States" 2005, section 3, para 1, http:// www. cia. gov/ cia/ publications/factbook/geos/us.html (accessed November 10, 2005); and also the Prejudice Institute's "Arab Americans: Factsheet," 2005, para. 5, http://www.prejudiceinstitute.org/ Factsheets5-ArabAmericans.html (accessed November 6, 2005).

30. The Prejudice Institute, para. 10.

31. The Prejudice Institute, para. 10.

32. Suleiman, 15-16.

33. Steven Salaita's "Ethnic Identity and Imperative Patriotism: Arab Americans before and After 9/11," *College Literature*, 32 2 (2005), 48 paragraphs. Available from Proquest online database, Friends University, Wichita, KS, para 16, http:// www. library. friends.edu (accessed February 8, 2006).

34. The actual article goes on to identify the "terrorist threat" as coming from North African-born Islamists and provides a United States example of the type of news coverage discussed by T. Ismael and John Measor in "Racism and the North American Media Following 11 September: The Canadian Setting," *Arab Studies Quarterly*, 25 1-2 (Winter 2003): 101. Available through Proquest Online database. Friends University, Wichita, KS, http:// www.friends.edu (accessed July 21, 2005).
35. The Canadian Arab Federation, "A Profile of Arabs in Canada," 1999, para 11. Available online at http:// ceris.metropolis.net/ Virtual%20Library/community/ Arabs1/ Arab1.html (accessed July 21, 2005).
36. Ibrahim Hayani, "Arabs in Canada: Assimilation or Integration," *Arabs in America: Building a New Future*, ed. Michael Suleiman (Philadelphia: Temple University Press, 1999), 284.
37. See Baha Abu-Laban's *An Olive Branch on the Family Tree: The Arabs in Canada* (Toronto: McClelland and Stewart Limited in Association with the Multiculturalism Directorate, Department of the Secretary of State and the Canadian Government Publishing Centre, Canada, 1980), 55.
38. Abu-Laban, 56.
39. Hayani, 285.
40. Hayani, 65-67.
41. The Canadian Arab Federation, paras. 16–17, 36, 49.
42. Abu-Laban, 212–14.
43. Ismael and Measor, paras. 80–81.
44. Humphrey, "Lebanese Identities," para. 3–4.

Works Cited

Abu-Laban, Baha. *An Olive Branch on the Family Tree: The Arabs in Canada*. Toronto: McClelland and Stewart in Association with the Multiculturalism Directorate, Department of the Secretary of State and the Canadian Government Publishing Centre, Canada, 1980.

Canadian Arab Federation. "A Profile of Arabs in Canada." 1999. http://ceris.metropolis.net/Virtual%20Library/community/ Arabs1/arab1.html.

Chipello, Christopher, and Dan Bilefsky. "A Global Journal Report: Is Canada a Launching Pad for Terror?" July 10, 2002. p. A10 *The Wall Street Journal* (Eastern edition). Available through Proquest Online database. Friends University, Wichita, KS. http:// www. library. friends.edu.

CIA World Factbook. "United States." 2005. Available from http://www.cia.gov/ cia/publications/factbook/geos/us.html.

Colitt, Raymond. "Latin American Politics: S. Americans, Arab Nations Meet," *The Economist Intelligence Unit ViewsWire*. NY: May 11, 2005. Available from Proquest Online database at Friends University. http:// www.library.friends.edu.

Euraque, Darío. "The Arab-Jewish Economic Presence in San Pedro Sula, the Industrial Capital of Honduras: Formative Years, 1880s-1930s." In *Arab and Jewish*

Immigrants in Latin America, eds. Ignacio Klich and Jeffrey Lesser. Portland, OR: Frank Cass, 1998.

Freeman, Sarah. "Census: More Arabs Live in U.S." *CBS News.com*. December 4, 2003. http://www.cbsnews.com/ Stories/2003/12/04/national/printable586895.shtml.

Harsham, Philip. "Arabs in America." *Aramco World Magazine*, 26 2 (1975, March-April). http://www/saudiaramcoworld.com /index/BackIssues1070.aspx.

Hayward, Maysa Abou-Youssef. "Introduction to *Arabesque: Arabic Literature in Translation and Arab Diasporic Writing*." *Studies in the Humanities*, 30 2 (June-December, 2003):1-6. Available through Blue Skyways online database service, Expanded Academic ASAP. Friends University. http:// www. library.friends.edu.

Humphrey, Michael. "Lebanese Identities: Between Cities, Nations, and Transnations." *Arab Studies Quarterly* 26 1, (2004): 31. Available through Proquest online database. Friends University,Wichita, KS. http:// www. library.friends.edu.

———. "Ethnic History, Nationalism and Transnationalism in Argentine Arab and Jewish Cultures." In *Arab and Jewish Immigrants in Latin America*, eds. Ignacio Klich and Jeffrey Lesser. Portland, OR: Frank Cass, 1998.

Ismael, T. Y., and John Measor. "Racism and the North American Media Following 11 September: The Canadian Setting." *Arab Studies Quarterly* 25 1–2 (2003): 101. Available through Proquest online database. Friends University, Wichita, KS. http:// www.library.friends.edu.

Klich Ignacio, and Jeffrey Lesser, eds. *Arab and Jewish Immigrants in Latin America*. Portland, OR: Frank Cass, 1998.

Köszegi, Michael, and J. Gordon Melton. *Islam in North America: A Sourcebook*. New York: Garland, 1992.

Luxner, Larry. "The Arabs of Honduras." *Saudi Aramco World*, 52 4 (2001): 46–51.

MacDonald, Robert. "Foreword." In *A Community of Many Worlds: Arab Americans in New York City*. New York: Syracuse University Press in Association with the Museum of the City of New York, 2002.

McCarus, Ernest, ed. *The Development of Arab American Identity*. Ann Arbor: The University of Michigan Press, 1994.

Naff, Alixa. "The Early Arab Immigrant Experience." In *The Development of Arab American Identity*, ed. Ernest McCarus. Ann Arbor: The University of Michigan Press, 1994.

Orfalea, Gregory. *Before the Flames: A Quest for the History of Arab Americans*. Austin: University of Texas Press, 1988.

Osava, Mario. "South America: First Summit with Arab Nations to Focus on Trade." *Global Information Network*. New York: May 10, 2005, 36 paragraphs. Available from Proquest Online database at Friends University. http:// www. libary.friends.edu.

Osterweil, Marc. "The Economic and Social Condition of Jewish and Arab Immigrants in Bolivia, 1890-1980." In *Arab and Jewish Immigrants in Latin America*, eds. Ignacio Klich and Jeffrey Lesser. Portland, OR: Frank Cass, 1998.

Pozo, Albert. "Arabs from the Earliest Times: Havana." Embassy of Cuba in the Syrian Arab Republic. http://embacubasiria.com/a000035e.html.

Prejudice Institute. "Arab Americans: Factsheet." 2005. Available from http:// www.prejudiceinstitute.org/Factsheets5-ArabAmericans.html.

Salaita, Steven. "Ethnic Identity and Imperative Patriotism: Arab Americans Before and After 9/11." *College Literature*, 32 2 (2005), 48 paragraphs. Available from Proquest Online database, Friends University, Wichita, KS. http:// www. library. friends.edu.

Sharobeem, Heba. "The Hyphenated Identity and the Question of Belonging: A Study of Samia Serageldin's *The Cairo House*." *Studies in the Humanities*, 30.2 (2003): 60. Available through Blue Skyways online database service, Expanded Academic ASAP. Friends University, Wichita, KS. http:// www.library.friends.edu.

Suleiman, Michael. *Arabs in America: Building a New Future*. Philadelphia: Temple University Press, 1999.

Velcamp, Theresa Alfaro. "The Historiography of Arab Immigration to Argentina: The Intersection of the Imaginary and the Real Country." In *Arab and Jewish Immigrants in Latin America*, eds. Ignacio Klich and Jeffrey Lesser. Portland, OR: Frank Cass, 1998.

Zogby, James. *Arab America Today*. Washington, DC: The Arab American Institute, 1990.

Zogby, James, Pat Aufderheide, and Anne Mooney, eds. *Taking Root Bearing Fruit: The Arab American Experience*. Washington, DC: The American-Arab Anti-Discrimination Committee, ADC Research Institute/International Graphics, 1984.

Part 1

Arriving in the Americas

1

The Passage from West to South: Arabs between the Old and New World

Carol N. Fadda–Conrey

The transnational movements of Arab populations across the globe have been going on for centuries, deeply affecting the communal and individual Arab character, and resulting in a medley of national affiliations and complex, frequently hyphenated identities. The scrutiny that Arab and Muslim groups have been subjected to in the United States after the events of September 11, 2001, often portray members of these groups as new arrivals in the United States. Such a perspective obscures the long history of Arab immigration that encompasses not only the United States but other parts of the world as well, including Latin America, Europe, Africa, and Australia.

Starting in the late nineteenth century, large groups of Lebanese and Syrians living under the Ottoman rule left their countries, searching to settle in new lands. Such large-scale movements were preceded by earlier cases of Arab immigration that constitute an important addition to the history of Arab diaspora, especially because some of these immigrations emanated from countries such as Spain, which was ruled by the Moors for around 800 years. This essay maps out the presence of Moriscos (Arab and Berber Muslims in Spain who had converted to Christianity after the Spanish Reconquista) highlighting the role that women played in resisting the Spaniards' religious and cultural impositions. By doing so, this essay highlights a specific historical experience of a group of Muslims/Arabs in geographical settings that extend beyond the Middle Eastern/U.S. framework. The essay then moves on to delineate the dispersion of Moriscos after their expulsion from Spain in 1607, relying on scattered accounts of their movement toward the New World to introduce some precursors of the numerous waves of Arab immigrants arriving in Latin America from the nineteenth century onward. Such delineation is by no means exhaustive, but it is meant to call attention to the lack of information about the presence of Muslims/Arabs in Latin America before the nineteenth century. The main aim of this essay then is to point to the complexity of Arab patterns of immigration, emphasizing the cultural and geographical relativity of notions of East and West by showing that the "West" (in this case Spain) has been historically a point of departure for Arab Muslims, and that arrival points in America are not only restricted to the United States but include Latin America as well.

Moriscas in Spain

The Muslim presence in Spain spans over nine centuries, beginning in 711 with the Muslim invasion of the Iberian Peninsula. However, with the conquest of Granada by the Christians in 1492, the Moors faced extreme persecution and were forced to convert to Christianity if they wished to remain in Spain. Referred to as Moriscos, meaning "little Moor," which pertains to their Arab or Berber ancestry, this minority for the most part succumbed to the forced Christian conversions imposed by the Spanish Inquisition (established by Ferdinand and Isabella in 1480),[1] adopting new Christian names and abandoning their Arabic language and Muslim religion. Nevertheless, there remained strong pockets of Moorish resistance throughout the Spanish world, by which Moriscos maintained their traditions and practiced their religion in secret.

In response to several Moorish uprisings that defied the restrictions of Spanish rule, King Philip II issued a royal decree in 1609 that ordered the expulsion of around 300,000 Moriscos from the country. The steady removal of Moriscos from Spain continued until 1614, by which the men and women were exiled, mainly to North Africa and European countries like France and Italy. Required to leave all their belongings behind, some Moriscos were even forced to leave their young children in Spain to be raised by Christians. Quite a few, however, managed to remain in Spain even after the expulsion, while others slipped back into their old homeland to retrieve the possessions and children they were made to abandon.[2]

The role of Morisco women in this tumultuous period was of great import, for personal homes became the primary space in which the Moriscos could practice their religion and culture without being detected. As Mary Elizabeth Perry points out, at a time when "Morisco men increasingly disappeared into death, captivity, hiding, or exile, . . . women . . . took on the major role of preserving Islam."[3] Even though "the Islamic ideal of the cloistered, sheltered woman, the woman protected in the home or the harem, continued to resonate in Iberian society, as did the strong link between female virginity and honor,"[4] Moriscas challenged and subverted these traditional mores in important ways.

In her extensive work on Morisco culture, Perry presents poignant narratives about several Moriscas who embodied such a challenge to Spanish rule, including Leonor Hernández, Fatima (also known as Ana), Madalena, and María de Aguilar. The social position of these women varied, but they were all subjected to the Spanish Inquisition for their secret adherence to Islam. Some Moriscas like Leonor Hernández endured torture and imprisonment for teaching Islam to her sons, while others such as the Muslim slave Fatima (also known by her Christian name Ana) was put on trial for denying her baptism. In contrast to the Moriscos who were forced to convert to Christianity at the beginning of the sixteenth century, Muslim slaves were allowed to preserve their religious practices. Even though conversion released many Moriscos from slavery, Fatima/Ana was adamant about not having assented to her baptism, a denial that caused her to be tried by the Inquisitors and allotted a punishment of two hundred lashes, which she survived.[5] While some Moriscas found themselves victims of the Inquisition, others like María de Aguilar, who professed that her conversion to Christianity was genuine, sought refuge in the Inquisition to escape her Muslim husband, who, she claimed, was still secretly practicing his faith and was planning on taking her to North Africa against her will. Nevertheless, the fate of María de Aguilar was not any less harsh than her Morisca counterparts, for on her way to Sanlucar, where she hoped to find protection from her husband, her ship sank and she drowned.[6]

Despite the persecution and punishment they faced for preserving their religious beliefs and cultural practices, women still comprised a large sector of Moriscos who defied the harsh edicts of the Spanish Inquisition. Some Moriscas even participated in numerous battles against Christians on Spanish soil. The Amazon Zarçamodonia, for instance, took part in the battle of Galera in the late sixteenth century between Moriscos and Christian Spaniards, even intervening to negotiate peace between the Moriscos and the Turkish allies who were assisting them in the battle.[7] Moreover, other battle accounts include stories of Moriscas joining in the fighting alongside their men, often using "stones and roasting spits" because they had no other weapons at hand.[8]

Moriscas in the New World

With the expulsion of Moriscos from Spain in 1607, the Spanish throne tried to rid itself of all Muslim subjects, whom it regarded as a threat to the kingdom's authority. Scattered around Europe and North Africa, with some exiles eventually settling in the Ottoman Empire, Moriscos were even barred from immigrating to the New World. Having enforced the conversion and the expulsion of not only the Moors, but also the Jews of Spain, the state forbade these minority groups, along with Protestants and Gypsies, from entering its colonies.[9] In this way, "[t]he obsessive Iberian requirement to maintain *limpieza de sangre* (purity of blood) and 'pride of lineage' for reasons of religious orthodoxy" depended on the "absence of Moriscos and Jews in the New World."[10] Such restrictions lasted till about 1900, with the first arrivals of emigrants from Lebanon and other neighboring countries.[11] Nevertheless, there exists some evidence that in fact Moriscos, and specifically women among them, were successful in slipping into the Americas during the Spanish Conquest of the New World, beginning with the arrival of Christopher Columbus in America in 1492 and continuing throughout the sixteenth century.

Among those believed to have succeeded in entering the New World despite their Moorish background are Beatriz la Morisca and Isabel Rodriguez, also known as "La Conquistadora."[12] Other than the fact that both women, as cited in Paul Lunde's article entitled "The Arabs of Havana," assisted Francisco Pizarro in conquering Peru, very little is known about them. The lack of documentation on Moriscos and other Muslims living in the Americas during this period can be explained by the travel constraints that barred them from entering the Spanish-controlled territories and that consequently rendered them invisible in the annals of emigrants entering the New World. According to Lyle N. McAlister, "To enforce its policies, the crown required all emigrants to obtain licenses from the *Casa de Contratación* (Royal House of Trade) in Seville, excepting clerics, soldiers, sailors, and servants." "It is likely, however," McAlister continues, "that individual initiatives and ingenuity had more to do with the quantity and quality of emigration to the Indies than did the wishes of kings."[13] Although it is estimated that a large number of illegal immigrants found ways to enter the New World, "[i]t is impossible to say how many of these were of Muslim descent."[14] What makes it even harder to pinpoint their original identities is that they traveled from a medley of Islamic areas, including Turkey and North Africa, with their links to Moorish Spain becoming less and less distinguishable with the lapse of time and with successive displacements and exiles.

Not all Morisco, as well as Jewish, women who arrived in the Americas were free. For, as Susan Migden Socolow notes in *The Women of Colonial Latin America*, "[t]he first female slaves to arrive in America came directly from Spain in the retinue of the conquistadors." Nevertheless, Socolow continues, "[m]ost black slaves . . . did not come to America from the Iberian Peninsula. Instead they were shipped from Africa, as merchandise in a trade that eventually saw 3.5 million people forceably [sic] moved across the Atlantic."[15] However, the relationship between Moriscos and African slaves, and their interaction with European Christians in the New World there should be regarded as the continuation of contacts established "hundreds of years earlier in Iberia, North Africa, and elsewhere in the Mediterranean." The Moors themselves were a "diverse assembly of differentiated unequals that included Arabs, Berbers, Arabo–Berbers, and West Africans."[16] In this way, the term *Moor* did not connote racial characteristics as much as cultural, specifically Islamic, ones. Thus the mixing of indigenous and non–indigenous cultures and races in what became known as Latin America produced multiple categories: "The so-called *mulatto* (European–African), *mestizo* (European-indigenous), and *castizo* (mestizo-European) were joined by the morisco (in this context, a 'mulatto'-European issue) and the *zambo*, the result of an indigenous and African union."[17] With such categories firmly in place, the term *Morisco* started losing its Spanish specificity in the New World, becoming more and more entrenched in hierarchical racial categorizations denoting caste and culture.

The case of Beatriz de Padilla exemplifies the changing meaning of the term Morisca in the New World and its connections to the mulatto designation. Brought to the attention of the Inquisitors in western Mexico in 1650 for allegedly poisoning one of her lovers and then driving another one to insanity with the aid of potions and spells, Beatriz de Padilla announced to her captors that she in fact "was not a mulatta but a lighter–skinned *morisca*, the daughter of a white man and a mulatta."[18] Born to don Lorenzo de Padilla and Cecilia de Alvarado, a serving woman, Beatriz inherited her mother's slave status, but they were both freed by Cecilia's employer, the parish priest Francisco Perez Rubin.[19] She defended herself in front of the Inquisitors by claiming that her townspeople were very envious of her relations with Diego Ortiz Saavedra, the priest serving as commissioner of the Holy Office in Lagos whom she was accused of poisoning, and Diego de las Marinas, the lord mayor of Juchipila whom she allegedly drove insane.

Beatriz's case exemplifies the way in which "free women of color [in the Spanish-conquered world], especially mulattas, were viewed as highly sensual temptresses who could be dangerous because they threatened the social order and morality."[20] In the same way that Moriscas were questioned and imprisoned in the Iberian Peninsula during the Spanish Inquisition, women of color were also brought under the probing eye of the state in the New World, but instead of being questioned about their cultural and religious practices, the focus shifted to their sexual and moral conduct. Beatriz nevertheless succeeded in defending herself in front of the Tribunal of the Inquisition, after which she returned to her former position at the house of Diego de las Marinas. Solange Alberro points out that such an acquittal reflects the ease with which women of color could move in colonial American societies, compared to the strict regulations and expectations imposed on the "respectable" white woman, "who was obliged to concern herself always with what others might say and to do her best to adhere to the norms of society."[21]

First Wave of Middle-Eastern Arabs Arrives in Latin America

The restricted entrance into colonial America that people of color, including Muslim and Moriscos, suffered from was not eased until 1900. In the period between the late nineteenth century and the early twentieth century, however, the first wave of immigrants from Lebanon started arriving in Latin America. This first group headed mainly to Argentina and Brazil, and was largely made up of Christians fleeing Ottoman persecution and famine. Some immigrants, mostly single men or couples with young children, arrived in the New World looking for economic advancement.[22] The presence of women among these Arab immigrants was important for creating long-lasting roots in Latin America because women "made it possible to raise families in the protective atmosphere of the community—which was the primary means of transmitting cultural and religious traditions."[23] According to Patricia Nabti, Latin America inadvertently became the final destination of many of the first Lebanese and Syrian immigrants either because they were denied entry into the United States due to health problems and opted to continue on to South America, or because they boarded the ships thinking they were headed to the United States, only to end up in Latin America.[24]

Between 1870 and 1947, around 80,000 Syrian-Lebanese arrived in Brazil, with the numbers of Middle-Eastern settlers being even higher in Argentina. These immigrants were referred to alternately as Syro-Lebanese or Turks because up till the end of World War I, Syria and Lebanon fell under the mandate of the Ottoman Empire. Even after the defeat of the Ottomans and the establishment of Lebanon and Syria as separate states, immigrants arriving in Latin America from these regions were referred to as "turcos."[25] Most often starting out as peddlers and small shop owners, many of them prospered in their adopted countries, in many cases achieving great wealth and social status, while still retaining strong ties to their mother countries.

The movement of Arabs/Muslim from the Middle East to the Americas, then, is neither a simple nor a recent one. Paralleling the history of the Moriscos who traveled to various countries (including Latin America) after their exile from Spain, the late nineteenth-, early nineteenth-century immigrants from the Middle East not only brought with them to the Americas similar stories of persecution on the hands of their Ottoman rulers, but also carried the same zeal for survival and success that characterized the Moriscos before them. Caught between two worlds, they tried to assimilate into their new cultures, while still working hard to preserve the cultures they brought with them from their original homelands. Writing about her family background, which encompasses Palestinian, Caribbean, European, North American, and Latin American heritage, contemporary poet, essayist, and activist Nathalie Handal describes the sense of uprootedness resulting from the constant movement and displacement that her family has experienced. She poignantly negotiates the widely varied parts of her identity and ruminates on her role as a female writer by stating,

> [W]e as ethnic women, as women, as feminists, we who have histories rooted in occupation, oppression, alienation—must continue remembering, acting, speaking, and writing. In the past twenty years, we have (re)constructed ourselves as women, and have translated our cultures—not rejected them but re-adapted them according to our times and our new histories. It's an endless negotiation of difference, but as long as these negotiations are articulated, adapted, and tolerated—no matter how many times they continue to shift—we women continue to participate in positive transformations.[26]

In fact, such contributions to "the negotiation of difference" are not recent, for they can be traced to a long historical female tradition spanning hundreds of years. Handal's words in fact carry within them the weight of history, including the challenges that Moriscas posed to Spanish rule in the sixteenth and early seventeenth centuries, their illegal entry into the New World, as well as communal and individual accounts of persecution and dreams of success that the immigrants of the late eighteenth-, early nineteenth-century carried with them from the Arab world to the Americas. As Handal asserts, it is with the recognition of such history that a true "negotiation of difference" can be achieved.

Notes

1. Henry Charles Lea, *The Moriscos of Spain: Their Conversion and Expulsion* (New York: Burt Franklin, 1968), 14.
2. Mary Elizabeth Perry, "Between Muslim and Christian Worlds: Moriscas and Identity in Early Modern Spain," *The Muslim World* 95 no. 2 (2005): 190.
3. Perry, "Between Muslim and Christian Worlds," 179.
4. Susan Migden Socolow, *The Women of Colonial Latin America* (Cambridge,UK: Cambridge University Press, 2000), 6.
5. Perry, "Between Muslim and Christian Worlds," 184.
6. Perry, "Between Muslim and Christian Worlds," 189-90.
7. Perry, *The Handless Maiden: Moriscos and the Politics of Religion in Early Modern Spain* (Princeton: Princeton University Press, 2005), 88.
8. Quoted in Perry, *The Handless Maiden*, 88.
9. Laura A. Lewis, *Hall of Mirrors: Power, Witchcraft, and Caste in Colonial Mexico* (Durham: Duke University Press, 2003), 23.
10. Lewis, 42; Paul Lunde, "The New World Through Arab Eyes," 43 no. 3 (May/June 1992). August 15, 2005. http://www.saudiaramcoworld.com /issue/199203/the.new. world. through.arab. eyes .htm
11. Bill Strubbe and Karen Wald, "The Arabs of Havana," *Saudi Aramco World*, 46 no. 2 (March/April 1995). June 16, 2005. http://www.saudiaramcoworld.com /issue/ 199502/ the.arabs .of.havana.htm
12. Lunde.
13. Lyle N. McAlister, *Spain & Portugal in the New World 1492-1700* (Minneapolis: University of Minnesota Press, 1984), 110.
14. Lunde.
15. Socolow, 131.
16. Michael A. Gomez, *Black Crescent: The Experience and Legacy of African Muslims in the Americas* (Cambridge, UK: Cambridge University Press, 2005), 5.
17. Gomez, 23.
18. Solange Alberro, "Juan de Morga and Gertrudis de Escobar: Rebellious Slaves," in *Struggle and Survival in Colonial America*, ed. David G. Sweet and Gary B. Nash, 248 (Berkeley: University of California Press, 1981).

19. Alberro, 248.
20. Socolow, 141.
21. Alberro, 255.
22. Liz Hamui-Halabe, "Re-creating Community: Christians from Lebanon and Jews from Syria in Mexico, 1900-1938," in *Arab and Jewish Immigrants in Latin America: Images and Realities*, ed. Ignacio Klich and Jeffrey Lesser, 130 (London: Frank Cass, 1998).
23. Hamui-Halabe, 130.
24. Nabti is quoted in Theresa Alfaro Velcamp, "The Historiography of Arab Immigration to Argentina: The Intersection of the Imaginary and the Real Country," in *Arab and Jewish Immigrants in Latin America: Images and Realities*, ed. Ignacio Klich and Jeffrey Lesser, 235 (London: Frank Cass, 1998).
25. Estela Valverde, "Integration and Identity in Argentina: The Lebanese of Tucuman," in *The Lebanese in the World: A Century of Emigration*, ed. Albert Hourani and Nadim Shehadi, 314 (London: Centre for Lebanese Studies & Tauris, 1992).
26. Nathalie Handal, "Shades of a Bridge's Breath," in *This Bridge We Call Home: Radical Visions for Transformation*, ed. Gloria E. Anzaldúa and AnaLouise Keating, 160 (New York: Routledge, 2002).

Works Cited

Alberro, Solange. "Juan de Morga and Gertrudis de Escobar: Rebellious Slaves." In *Struggle and Survival in Colonial America*, ed. David G. Sweet and Gary B. Nash, 165-88. Berkeley: University of California Press, 1981.

Gomez, Michael A. *Black Crescent: The Experience and Legacy of African Muslims in the Americas*. Cambridge: Cambridge University Press, 2005.

Hamui-Halabe, Liz. "Re-creating Community: Christians from Lebanon and Jews from Syria in Mexico, 1900-1938." In *Arab and Jewish Immigrants in Latin America: Images and Realities*, eds. Ignacio Klich and Jeffrey Lesser, 125-45. London: Frank Cass, 1998.

Handal, Nathalie. "Shades of a Bridge's Breath." In *This Bridge We Call Home: Radical Visions for Transformation*, eds. Gloria E. Anzaldúa and AnaLouise Keating, 158-65. New York: Routledge, 2002.

Lea, Henry Charles. *The Moriscos of Spain: Their Conversion and Expulsion*. New York: Burt Franklin, 1968.

Lewis, Laura A. *Hall of Mirrors: Power, Witchcraft, and Caste in Colonial Mexico*. Durham: Duke University Press, 2003.

Lunde, Paul. "The New World Through Arab Eyes." 43 no. 3 (May/June 1992). August 15, 2005. http://www.saudiaramcoworld.com/issue/199203/the.new.world.through.arab.eyes.htm

McAlister, Lyle N. *Spain & Portugal in the New World 1492-1700*. Minneapolis: University of Minnesota Press, 1984.

Perry, Mary Elizabeth. "Between Muslim and Christian Worlds: Moriscas and Identity in Early Modern Spain." *The Muslim World*, 95 no. 2 (2005): 177-98.

——. *The Handless Maiden: Moriscos and the Politics of Religion in Early Modern Spain*. Princeton: Princeton University Press, 2005.

Socolow, Susan Migden. *The Women of Colonial Latin America*. Cambridge: Cambridge University Press, 2000.

Strubbe, Bill, and Karen Wald. "The Arabs of Havana." *Saudi Aramco World*, 46 no. 2 (March/April1995).June16,2005.
    http://www.saudiaramcoworld.com/issue/199502/the.arabs.of.havana.htm

Valverde, Estela. "Integration and Identity in Argentina: The Lebanese of Tucuman." In *The Lebanese in the World: A Century of Emigration*, eds. Albert Hourani and Nadim Shehadi, 314-37. London: Centre for Lebanese Studies & Tauris, 1992.

Velcamp, Theresa Alfaro. "The Historiography of Arab Immigration to Argentina: The Intersection of the Imaginary and the Real Country." In *Arab and Jewish Immigrants in Latin America: Images and Realities*, eds. Ignacio Klich and Jeffrey Lesser, 227-47. London: Frank Cass, 1998.

2

Margins of Memory on the *Rua 25 de Março*: Constructing the Syrian–Lebanese Past in São Paulo, Brazil

John Tofik Karam

Peddling served as the livelihood par excellence of late nineteenth-century Syrian and Lebanese immigrants in the city of São Paulo, Brazil. Originally settling on the *Rua 25 de Março* (25th of March Street) in the city center, immigrants rose from peddlers to storeowners and petty manufacturers during the early twentieth century. This locale continues to be directed by second- and third-generation Syrian-Lebanese today, but it has also become home to migrants from northeast Brazil who work as street vendors. How has the memory of Syrian-Lebanese commerce been constructed in these current circumstances? Brazilians of Arab descent,[1] I endeavor to show, have referenced the peddling past as a way to fix their ethnicity to the place of *Rua 25 de Março*, but in so doing, they have sought to exclude street vendors, the "peddlers" of today.

Memory and the material-historical context in which it is claimed and contested are crucial questions raised here. As Walter Benjamin has observed, "memory is not an instrument for exploring the past but its theater."[2] In this sense, I do not construe individual or collective memories of peddling "as the way it was." Although the *mascate* (peddler) is generally represented as a pioneer by Brazilians of Arab descent today, he was a peripheral figure in the late nineteenth and early twentieth centuries. Envisioning a country composed of farm workers at this time, Brazilian elites denigrated peddlers as parasites who supposedly became rich at the expense of the nation. However, this past has been omitted from the museum exhibits and nostalgic narratives of present-day descendents. Such an occlusion strengthens Arab Brazilian ties to 25 de Março while it justifies the marginalization of street vendors today.

Ultimately, I approach the memory of the *mascate* as an expression of the current struggle between formal and informal merchants over public space in downtown São Paulo. As will be explored below, present-day street vendors, called *camelôs*, recognize the fact that Syrian-Lebanese immigrants peddled in the past. What they dispute, however, is the use of this memory to exclude or remove them from the region today. By emphasizing this perspective in my essay, I aim to put into practice another reflection made by Benjamin: the need to "cite" the past "...in all its moments."[3] In this way, I seek not to invalidate present-day Arab Brazilian claims to the place of 25 de Março, but rather to show that early twentieth-century immigrant peddlers were also marginalized by Brazilian elites. To put it another way, I seek recourse to the margins of memory in efforts to avoid repeating the exclusionary past in the present.

Mostly stemming from present-day Syria and Lebanon, 140,464 Middle Easterners immigrated to Brazil from 1880 to 1969.[4] Imagining the earliest immigrant waves today, many descendents recount the story of two Syrians, Assad Abdalla and Najib Salem, who disembarked in São Paulo in the early 1890s and soon after established a wholesale entrepot on the present-day *Rua 25 de Março*. An akin story is that of the Jafet brothers, who arrived in the same period and opened textile factories in the first decade of the twentieth century. In 1913, figures from these three families convened the "preparatory meeting" of the "Syrian Chamber of Commerce." The main speaker was the eldest Jafet brother, Nami. "The Chamber," he emphasized, "will be a lighthouse that will illuminate and orient each Syrian merchant, from the peddler with a box to the wholesaler. In this way, we will have a base of operations for large and small and we will be able to progress."[5] Though this chamber never materialized, the Abdalla, Salem, and Jafet family-run enterprises supplied goods to fellow *patrícios* (countrymen) who peddled them on urban and rural peripheries alike.

Indeed, in 1893, Arabs made up 90 percent of the *mascates* (peddlers) in the São Paulo city almanac.[6] In the 1907 edition of the almanac, there were 315 Arab–owned businesses, the majority specializing in clothing and dry goods. By 1920, their factories numbered 91 in São Paulo. At this time, Syrian-Lebanese established "factories that required a minimum amount of capital. One could install a small factory with four or five workers in a rented room, using second hand sewing machines."[7] Their forte, though, was commerce. In fact, by 1930, Syrian-Lebanese owned "468 of the listed 800 retail stores and 67 of the 136 wholesale" in São Paulo.[8]

However, this arabesque negotiated in the Brazilian economy drew the scorn of early twentieth-century national elites. The latter regarded the country as a "plantation" of exportable raw goods, namely coffee, for North America and Europe.[9] Elites often labeled Middle Easterners as *turcos* (Turks) and viewed them as innately shrewd traders. Alfredo Ellis Júnior spoke of the "syrio" as a "merchant by...inheritance... able to barter his own life, swearing to have not earned a penny."[10] Similarly, Guilherme de Almeida, a commentator in the 1930s, reflected, "What's the recipe for a Turk? Take the 25 de Março street cocktail shaker and put in a Syrian, an Arab, an Armenian, a Persian, an Egyptian, a Kurd. Shake it up really well and, boom, out comes a Turk."[11] Confirmed by Rua 25 de Março, so-called *turcos* were viewed as essentially the same in their mercantile propensity.

These immigrants were likewise assumed to use their inborn business acumen for personal enrichment at the expense of the agriculturally imagined Brazilian nation. Take for instance a participant in the 1926 National Society of Agriculture meeting who commented "we should also do everything to make difficult the immigration of Syrian elements which, far from benefiting agriculture, parasitically exploit it in the profession of false businessmen."[12] One of the most outspoken critics of Syrian immigration, Herbert Levy, wrote that "the type of immigration required by the country's needs is that of agricultural workers and the Syrians are not classified in this category," being rather "dedicated to commerce and speculative activities." He pointed out that "Syrians are not present" among the 700,000 agricultural workers tallied in São Paulo.[13] In the agricultural paradigm of Brazilian economy, Arabs were not pioneers but pariahs.

In the next few decades, however, trade and industry experienced extraordinary growth. From 1907 to 1939, industrial production expanded to more than 20 percent of the total Brazilian GNP.[14] In this historic turn, Syrian-Lebanese continued their trajectory from peddlers to proprietors and manufacturers. In 1945, they accounted for 27 percent of the firms in the spinning and weaving segments of cotton, silk, rayon, wool, and linen fabrics (112 out of 413).[15] Almost without exception, these enterprises opened in the mid-1930s, due in part to a protectionist policy that placed high tariffs on imports.[16] At this conjuncture, the *Rua 25 de Março* gained fame as a wholesale textile center in Brazil. It served as an important intermediary between domestic manufacturers and retailers in the textile market. During the next few decades, merchants on 25 de Março accounted for an estimated 60 percent of textile wholesale profits in the entire country.[17]

The rising status of Syrian-Lebanese businessmen also became evident at this time. Take for example the then head of the aforementioned Jafet family, Basílio.   Before his death, the latter oversaw the wealthiest Arab-owned enterprise with more than 2,000 workers.[18] In the late 1940s, a city council bill was proposed to rename a street near 25 de Março after him (theretofore named *Itobi*). In support of the legislation, a petition was signed by almost two hundred shop owners in the region. Justifying that the "majority of residents and established persons on Itobi Street are Syrian-Lebanese descendents," the petitioners hailed the bill as perpetuating the memory of a "Palatinus of our industry and Patriarch of the Syrian-Lebanese Community."[19] In 1949, the bill was approved and the street name was changed to "Rua Cavalheiro Basílio Jafet - Industrial."[20] In the following decades, five more laws put other Syrian-Lebanese names on several streets in the 25 de Março environs.[21] Such recognition in urban space reflected not only upward ethnic mobility, but also the novel commercial and industrial paradigm of the mid-twentieth century Brazilian nation.

So-called *turcos* thus gained greater respectability, but in ambivalent ways. On the one hand, media elites congratulated them for making 25 de Março into a "public thoroughfare of a distinguished commercial function."[22] For urban chronicler Gabriel Marques, the street "should be called *rua Sírio-Libanesa*...which merges well in São Paulo's roadway conjuncture ...and its agitated economic milieu."[23] He later noted that the "Old Road of Raw Kibe" marks "Paulista prosperity" and "symbolizes the power of a people united and strong."[24] However, the region began to make news as a hotbed for irregular fiscal activities as well. One article recounted how a team of 40 tax inspectors "conferred thousands of fiscal receipts, opened hundreds of packages, and apprehended a sizeable quantity of goods in an operation ...dubbed 'taking the pulse of trade.'"[25] Whether praised for "commercial functions" or suspected of questionable fiscal activities, *sírio-libaneses* and the *Rua 25 de Março* became intertwined with one another in the popular imagination by the mid-twentieth century.

Fifty years later, a memory of the *mascate* has materialized from this equivocal past. In 2000, the "Cultural Memorial of 25 de Março" was founded with the objective to "preserve the memory of Syrian and Lebanese immigrants in the 25 de Março region." It has two spacious rooms, elegantly exhibiting black and white photographs, antique furniture, and office equipment memorabilia. Textual banners lining the walls recount in prose and verse the shared histories of 25 de Março and Syrian-Lebanese commerce. Having fled the Ottoman empire "with 5 millennia of history to give and sell," Syrian-Lebanese are celebrated as peddlers of "a pioneering civilization" in Brazil. "The Syrian-Lebanese went through backlands, founding stores of commerce in each settlement," one banner reads. They transformed the Rua 25 de Março into "the great center of...wholesale textiles, clothing, and accessories." Constructing this memory of Syrian-Lebanese mercantilism today, descendents omitted the marginal and ambivalent status of their early twentieth-century immigrant forefathers.

The memorial is located on the second floor of a store called "O Rei do Armarinho" (King of Cabinetries). It is one of the hundreds of Middle-Eastern run enterprises that opened in the protectionist era of the Brazilian economy. In the 1930s, "O Rei do Armarinho" specialized in the wholesale commerce of ribbon, thread, and other textile products. As an intermediary between manufacturers and retailers, "O Rei do Armarinho" expanded in the following years, as did other wholesale businesses. Through post–WW II times, it bought textile stocks from national manufacturers, and later sold them to garment-makers and retailers. However, in the late 1970s, "O Rei do Armarinho" witnessed a decrease in sales. This tendency accelerated with economic liberalization in the early 1990s. In order to survive the "flood" of cheaper imports with the lowering of trade tariffs,[26] domestic manufacturers bypassed wholesalers and sold directly to retailers and customers. Once leading the distribution of textiles in the entire country, only six wholesalers, one pessimistic merchant estimated, have survived today on 25 de Março.[27]

By way of a response, some storeowners have shifted from wholesale to retail operations. Catering to everyday consumers, store shelves now carry imported goods, such as sneakers, costume jewelry, toys, and electronic goods. In fact, the 25 de Março area has become famous for cheap imports in the city of São Paulo. Announcing this transition, a 1993 news article reported that "stores from the traditional region of 25 de Março are turning into big clients of Italian, North American, Korean, Chinese enterprises."[28] A similar observation was made by Beto, the president of the commercial association of the 25 de Março, himself a third-generation Syrian-Lebanese. On 25 de Março, he began, "any store that you enter today has....half imported products, not less than that." Beto continued:

The local economy is supplied with a lot of stuff from abroad. You have many stores that sell articles from abroad, from Asia, from China. Gifts, toys, and such...You enter, for example, in a costume jewelry store, there's a lot of stuff that comes from abroad. You enter into a toy store, there's a lot of stuff from abroad. You enter into a garment store, the same thing. So today, the commerce here is really dependent on importation.

Today run by second-generation Syrian-Lebanese cousins, the aforementioned "King of Accessories" store reflects this transition as well. One of the cousins, Rodolfo, explained that his firm now imports 80 percent of its merchandise from Italy, China, the United States, and elsewhere. He and his partners have even renovated their four-story complex as a retail space. Originally a textile wholesale warehouse, their building now caters to low- and middle-class shoppers. As we walked through its aisles and staircases, Rodolfo noted the change in decor. A room originally used for shipping wholesale orders, for instance, was remodeled in the image of a turn-of-the-century German train station. With "European" wooden benches amidst shelves stocked with plastic flowers, baskets, and other imports from China, I imagined that a worldly shopping experience has been promoted in more ways than one.

Overseeing the renovations that marked the store's shift to retail operations, Rodolfo commented on an initial dilemma concerning his father and uncle's old-fashioned office space on the second floor. Evocative of good memories, the antiquated area garnered some black and white photographs of his family, antique typewriters and cash registers, as well as classic wooden furniture and book cases. Instead of razing this space of nostalgia, Rodolfo recalled, he decided to transform it into the Memorial da 25 de Março as a tribute to his father, uncles, and Syrian-Lebanese like them. As the one-time wholesale warehouse was renovated as a retail store for Italian lace, German beads, and Chinese decorations, its second floor was also remodeled for the exhibition of the memory of Syrian-Lebanese commerce.[29]

Such nostalgia is part of the ethnic economic transition on 25 de Março. A small but significant number of Syrian-Lebanese have sold their storefronts and rented out the property today. In 1995, a news article related that 5 percent of the enterprises on 25 de Março were doing so.[30] The point has been echoed by third-generation Syrian-Lebanese Fernando, who explained that "the real-estate itself has not left Arab hands...It could even be that they're

not operating [a store]...they sold it, but continue being the real–estate owner."
This Arab-owned real–estate, however, has been rented by recent Chinese,
Taiwanese, and Korean immigrants. In fact, Asian newcomers have been
called by one street vendor as "the renters of the Arabs."

The *Rua 25 de Março* has also become home to an estimated 1,000
stationary *camelôs* (street vendors) today.[31] After being legitimated in legislation
in 1989, informal street vending flourished in the region. [32] Although some
camelôs stem from other South American countries, the majority have
migrated from the underdeveloped *nordeste* (Northeast) of Brazil. Selling
garments, jewelry, pirated music CDs, and other knickknacks, street vendors
set up their tables in front of busy stores specializing in the same merchandise.
For established proprietors, *camelôs* embody unwanted competition and
threaten property values. From 1989 until today, almost daily confrontations
have erupted between municipal or state police forces, established merchants,
real-estate owners, and street vendors.

Tracing their origins to the Middle East, East Asia, and Northeast Brazil,
informal and formal business persons on 25 de Março have been supplied
through importation. Their goods, however, have been often deemed
"irregular" by state fiscal agents, allegedly smuggled into Brazil through
Paraguay. Indeed, when the borders between the two countries were
temporarily closed in early 2001, storeowners and street vendors lacked items
on stands and shelves.[33] In these circumstances, surprise inspection or search
and seizure operations, called *blitzes*, have been regularly carried out from
1999 to 2001.[34] At times weighing more than a ton, goods without proper
documentation were apprehended from street vendors and storeowners alike.
At one point, Beto, the aforementioned third-generation Syrian Lebanese, was
visited by inspectors, much to the vaunting of street vendors. Not unlike their
early and mid- twentieth–century forbearers, present-day Arab Brazilians hold
an ambivalent place in the city and nation.

In efforts to maintain their dominance in the changing ethnic economy of
25 de Março, landlords and importers of Syrian-Lebanese descent have
frequently criticized the street vending of today through their own mythic past
of peddling. The second–generation Syrian sr. Nagib, for instance, stressed
that in contrast to present-day *camelôs* who set up tables on sidewalks, Syrian-
Lebanese peddlers were forced to remain walking with a trunk of goods on
their backs. Even if Syrian Lebanese wanted to rest for a moment, concluded
sr. Nagib, they had to give their trunks to friends in order to not remain

stationary, for this would draw quick retribution from the police. A similar view was expressed by sr. Sami, another older businessman who operates a successful men's clothing store in the region. Having worked as an itinerant salesman during his youth, the latter claimed to never have had the luxury "to stop in any place," but was forced to remain circulating with his wares. Though sr. Nagib rents out his property and sr. Sami imports clothing, each uses the memory of the *mascate* to further advance middle-class livelihoods.

These claims have been further legitimated in mainstream newspaper representations of the history of 25 de Março. The title from a 1999 article captures the still intricate association between this urban space and Arab ethnicity: "25 de Março turns 140 years old and preserves its memory: 'Little Baghdad' owes the commercial tradition to the *mascates*."[35] Another headline and byline from a 2000 article alludes to the present-day predicament of the locale and its alleged ethnic founders: "On this road the Arabs resist shopping centers. And street vendors: Coming from Syria and Lebanon, they turned the Rua 25 de Março into one of the most prosperous wholesale centers of Latin America. Now they struggle to survive against modern and entrenched enemies."[36] Not coincidentally, both articles made references to the aforementioned "Cultural Memorial of 25 de Março" which mythologizes the Syrian-Lebanese peddler. Strengthening Arabs' own quest to spatialize their ethnicity on 25 de Março, these popular representations have been used to put into check the position of *camelôs*.

For their part, street vendors do not challenge the memory of the *mascate* nor its link to the history of 25 de Março. Rather *camelôs* question the way it has been used to exclude them. Alberto, the president of a street vendor association, remarked that "90% of them ('Turks') who have a store on 25 de Março...were once walking salesmen. If you go to speak with them...you are going to see that the father was a peddler, selling...those things on 25 de Março. Now they are real-estate owners." Arabs' past as walking salesmen, explained Alberto, is why they harbor such antagonistic sentiments toward present-day street vendors. For this syndicate leader, Arabs seek to "overrun" those who today exercise the peddling profession of their fathers or grandfathers precisely because of these shared histories. Alberto reflected that *camelôs* "have an experience like this, the citizen who was once a street vendor and gets himself established, he doesn't like the street vendor." Arab merchants' intention to strengthen their ethnic place constitutes the ideological fodder for *camelôs* to challenge them.

In the struggle for public space on 25 de Março, formal and informal merchants found themselves in a stalemate increasingly intermediated by city government. During the 2001 annual commemoration of the *Rua 25 de Março*, for instance, city officials introduced an urban renewal proposal to businessmen, street vendors, and laypersons. Designed to invite citizen involvement, the project of the *nova 25 de Março* was proposed in a local Lebanese restaurant, called "Mount Lebanon." Six architectural depictions of this "new" 25th of March Street were taped on the walls around the restaurant. Two television crews were on the scene as well, not only interviewing partisan representatives, but also filming the beautiful tables filled with Lebanese delicacies. The cuisine lent a colorful legitimacy to the region's Arab elite.

Aside from two token Asians, second- and third-generation Arabs composed the majority of attendees. Others present included the architect of the project, members of the research team, and city officials. Announcing that the event served to "open a discussion about a disputed area," one authority stressed that the government wants to aid "all the actors who participate." With similar language, the architect explained his goal for "a renovation, a reactivation of the area. A transformation that is democratic and not exclusionary." Seeking to "benefit" both established businessmen and street vendors, the architect and city officials proposed to relocate the majority of *camelôs* to a "boulevard of informal commerce" outside the immediate vicinity of 25 de Março, and in their place, construct a wide sidewalk with benches and trees. Although promises were made to integrate street vendors, one could not help but notice that *camelôs* would be removed from the main area of commerce. Indeed, a headline in that morning's *Folha de São Paulo* newspaper read, "Project of the New 25 de Março excludes street vendors."[37]

The event's ensuing discussion revolved around *camelôs*. Landlords and storeowners asked if officials could guarantee that street vendors would not return to the region. Although the project was alleged to be nonexclusionary, that is precisely what storeowners demanded: the once and for all removal of street vendors. At one hectic point, a man in his seventies, sr. Salomão, loudly called out to make known his own view. As the room quieted down, the elder clamored that he worked on 25 de Março for 67 years and that "we made 25 de Março and we want it to continue the way it was." Ironically, sr. Salomão has made a modest middle-class living from a retail clothing and accessory shop rented from wealthier brethren. However, by using the pronoun "we" and referring to our past, the older merchant invoked the rights of Arabs to continue doing business on 25 de Março without street vending. There again, though, erupted a cacophony of dissonant voices that stressed the need to "integrate" street vendors. As descendents ethnically claimed the sole right to use the 25 de Março space, their reference to a pioneering past has also been used to marginalize the *camelôs*, the "peddlers" of today.

Mostly landlords and importers of Syrian-Lebanese descent have constructed the memory of the *mascate* and the merchant as a way to fix their ethnicity to a one-time wholesale textile center in downtown São Paulo. However, this memory has also been evoked to subtly or explicitly invalidate the right of street vendors to work in that same urban space today. This politics of memory on 25 de Março has developed during Brazil's economic liberalization in the 1990s. During this period, many Syrian-Lebanese family enterprises were closed or restructured, a museum-like exhibition of the almost mythic origins of Syrian-Lebanese commerce was opened, and *camelôs*, the "peddlers" of today, emerged on the urban scene. As the conflict for the right to public space has intensified during this material-historical moment, the memory of the *mascate* has reflected the struggle between established businessmen, mostly of Syrian-Lebanese descent, and street vendors who have migrated from Northeast Brazil. What is rarely remembered in this often tense debate, however, is that the early twentieth-century Arab peddler was denigrated by Brazilian elites as a parasite of national agricultural wealth, in ways that parallel the present-day exclusion of the *camelô* throughout the city of São Paulo. However, if memory is the "theater" of the past, its margins can also be used for the construction of a more just future.

Notes

This essay is based on research supported by a Fulbright-Hays Doctoral Dissertation Award in 2000–2001 and the Sultan Postdoctoral Fellowship at the Center for Middle Eastern Studies at the University of California, Berkeley, in 2005. An earlier version was presented in the research forum, "A pesquisa antropológica e o futuro das populações com quem se trabalha: Uma reflexão crítica," at the 24th meeting of the Brazilian Anthropological Association (ABA) in Recife, PE, in June 2004. I want to especially thank the two coordinators of the forum, O. Hugo Benavides and Telma Camargo da Silva, for insightful and encouraging comments. I am also grateful to Jeff Lesser for his path-breaking work on immigrant ethnicity in Brazil.

1. I use the labels of Syrian Lebanese, Syrian, Lebanese, Turk, and/or Arab according to the specific context or text in this essay. "Middle Eastern" is employed as a blanket, etic

term. For the most part, however, my own tendency is to use the labels *sírio-libanês* (Syrian Lebanese) and *árabe* (Arab) interchangeably, as do most Brazilians of Middle Eastern descent. To a degree, these references to Middle Eastern immigrants and descendents are fluid in Brazil.

2. Walter Benjamin, *Reflections: Essays, Aphorisms, Autobiographical Writings*, ed. Peter Demetz (New York: Schocken, 1978), 25-26.

3. Walter Benjamin, *Illuminations: Essays and Reflections*, ed. Hannah Arendt (New York: Schocken, 1968), 254.

4. Jeffrey Lesser, *Negotiating National Identity: Immigrants, Minorities, and the Struggle for Ethnicity in Brazil* (Durham: Duke University Press, 1999), 8. Despite these estimates from the mid-twentieth century, news reportage has estimated that there are six to ten million Syrian and Lebanese descendents in present-day Brazil. The *Folha de São Paulo*, for instance, proposed that there are nine million Arab immigrants and descendents ("Brasil recebe árabes desde o século 19," December, 14, 1997, 1:29). The magazine, *Veja*, judged that there are seven million Syrian and Lebanese descendents that make up four percent of the "Brazilian population" (Flávia Varella, "Dinheiro, Diploma e Voto..." October 4, 2000: 122-29). Most recently, the *Revista da Folha* stated that there are seven million Lebanese and three million Syrian immigrants and descendents in Brazil (Yuri, Débora,"O nosso lado árabe," November 23, 2001, 8). These exaggerated estimates speak to the greater recognition of Arab Brazilians today. See John Tofik Karam, "Distinguishing Arabesques: The Politics and Pleasures of Being Arab in Neoliberal Brazil" (Ph.D. diss., Syracuse University, 2004).

5. Nami Jafet, *Ensaios e discursos* (São Paulo: Editora S/A, 1947), 304.

6. Charles Knowlton, *Sírios e libaneses em São Paulo* (São Paulo: Editora Anhembi, 1961), 23. Oswaldo Truzzi, *Patrícios: sírios e libaneses em São Paulo* (São Paulo: Editora Hucitec, 1997), 49.

7. Knowlton, *Sírios e libaneses em São Paulo*, 143.

8. Knowlton, *Sírios e libaneses em São Paulo*, 143.

9. Warren Dean, *The Industrialization of São Paulo, 1880-1945* (Austin: University of Texas Press, 1969). Thomas Holloway, *Immigrants on Land: Coffee and Society in São Paulo, 1886-1930* (New York: Routledge, 1980). Barbara Weinstein, *The Amazon Rubber Boom* (Cambridge: Harvard University Press, 1980).

10. Cited in Lesser, 64. Lesser has related that Ellis Júnior was the descendent of confederate military men who fled the United States to Brazil upon their defeat in the Civil War. He followed his father into Brazilian politics and became an essayist of daily life in São Paulo.

11. Cited in Jeffrey Lesser, "(Re)Creating Ethnicity: Middle Eastern Immigration to Brazil," *Americas: A Quarterly Review of Inter-American Cultural History*, 53 no. 1 (1996): 58.

12. Sociedade Nacional de Agricultura, *Immigração: Inquérito promovido pela Sociedade Nacional de Agricultura* (Rio de Janeiro: Villani e Barbero, 1926), 359.

13. Amarilio Júnior, *As vantagens da imigração syria no Brasil* (Rio de Janeiro: s.n., 1935), 39, 41-42.

14. Maria Antoineta Leopoldi, *Política e interesses na industrialização brasileira: As associações industriais, a política econômica e o Estado* (São Paulo: Paz e Terra, 2000), 69, 231. While agricultural growth rates hovered between .5 and 3 percent per year in the 1940s and 1950s, industrial production witnessed annual increases of more than 10 percent in the 1930s, falling slightly to 5 percent in the early 1940s, and again rising to nearly 10 percent through 1961. Werner Baer, *The Brazilian Economy: Growth and Development* (Westport: Praeger, 1983), 49.

15. Departamento Estadual da Estatística, *Catálogo das indústrias do município da Capital, 1945* (São Paulo: Rothschild Loureiro e Cia, 1947).

16. Stanley Stein, *The Brazilian Cotton Manufacture: Textile Enterprise in an Underdeveloped Area, 1850-1950* (Cambridge: Harvard University Press, 1957). Textile industrialists, wholesalers, and garment-makers were "protected by extremely high tariffs against imported textiles" that reached almost 280 percent as late as the 1960s (Joel Bergsman, *Brazil: Industrialization and Trade Policies* (New York: Oxford University Press, 1970), 137; cited in Peter Evans, *Dependent Development: The Alliance of Multinational, State, and Local Capital in Brazil* (Princeton: Princeton University Press, 1979), 133.

17. "Comércio atacadista desaparece da cadeia têxtil," *Gazeta Mercantil,* August 25, 2000.

18. Departamento Estadual da Estatística, *Catálogo das indústrias do município da Capital, 1945* (São Paulo: Rothschild Loureiro e Cia, 1947).

19. Câmara Municipal de São Paulo (CMSP). Seção do Protocólo e Arquivo (SPA). Processo no. 2.937 de 1948, Folhas 1-14.

20. Câmara Municipal de São Paulo (CMSP). Lei número 3.736 de 3 de janeiro de 1949. Let it be added that the honorific title, "Cavalheiro," literally, "gentleman," had been previously awarded to Basílio Jafet by the Brazilian and French governments. Basílio Jafet, *A supremâcia reconhecida* (São Paulo: Editora Esphinge, 1935).

21. Câmara Municipal de São Paulo (CMSP), "Rua Comendador Assad Abdalla," in Lei no. 5.234 de 21 de junho de 1957. "Rua Comendador Affonso Kherlakian," in Decreto no. 9.545 de 30 de junho de 1971. "Travessa Serop Kherlakian," in Decreto no. 13.967 de 11 de novembro de 1976. "Rua Comendador Abdo Schahin" in Decreto no. 12.854 de 26 de abril de 1976. "Praça Ragueb Chohfi," in Decreto no. 22.728 de 8 de setembro de 1986. These decrees and laws only refer to the region of 25 de Março. The names of Middle Eastern business and liberal professionals were granted to many other streets throughout São Paulo in the next thirty years as well.

22. "As ruas e sua história: A Rua Vinte e Cinco de Março," *A Nação,* October 9, 1963.

23. Gabriel Marques, "Rua Vinte e Cinco de Março: O rio das sete voltas," *Folha da Noite,* May 2, 1957. Gabriel Marques, "Rua Vinte e Cinco de Março: As chacras recuaram," *Folha da Noite,* May 3, 1957. Gabriel Marques, "Rua Vinte e Cinco de Março: O outro Harun Al-Rachid," *Folha da Noite,* May 6, 1957. See also Marques, 1966.

24. Gabriel Marques, "A velha rua do quibe cru. I," *O Estado de S. Paulo.* June 12, 1960. Gabriel Marques, "A velha rua do quibe cru. II," *O Estado de S. Paulo,* June 19, 1960. Raw Kibe, or "kibi ni'yi" (in Arabic) is a mix of raw lamb meat and wheat bulgar, often

served with fresh mint leaves, green onions, and olive oil. Not coincidentally, the best kibi that I was treated to in contemporary São Paulo was in the 25 de Março region.

25. "'Comandos' fiscais em ação na 25 de Março," *O Estado de S. Paulo,* June 28, 1960.

26. Although then President Fernando Collor de Mello lifted import tariffs in 1991, importation rates significantly increased only from 1994 onwards (especially due to the stabilization of the national monetary system by then President Fernando Henrique Cardoso).

27. "Comércio atacadista desaparece da cadeia têxtil," *Gazeta Mercantil,* August 25, 2000. This is an overstatement, but nonetheless telling in itself.

28. Wanise Ferreira, "25 de Março vira pólo de importados: Lojas de armarinhos e distribuidores de aviamentos importam a maioria dos produtos oferecidos," *O Estado de S. Paulo,* April 2, 1993. More recently in 2000, the 25 de Março region was labeled as the prime place to obtain pirated garments, sunglasses, and tennis sneakers. Fátima Fernandes, "Piratas roubam mercado de empresas e US$ 10 bi do país," *Folha de São Paulo,* September 3, 2000.

29. This placement of the Arab Brazilian past in São Paulo can be further highlighted by way of a comparison with Arab American history in New York City. Atlantic Avenue in Brooklyn, for instance, was once home to Syrian and Lebanese families whose livelihoods were tied to small-scale textile businesses on Washington Street in early twentieth-century Manhattan. From the 1970s onward, they were displaced by Jordanian, Palestinian, and Yemeni immigrants (Orfalea, 1988, 224–25). Today, recent immigrant waves stitched over the memory of early Arab American lives spun between Brooklyn and Manhattan. The Arabness of contemporary Atlantic Avenue in Brooklyn has become popularly identified with late twentieth-century immigrants, and not necessarily second-and-third generation Arab-Americans and their memory of early twentieth-century immigrant parents and grandparents. In contrast, the public memory of Arabness on *Rua 25 de Marco* in São Paulo has been identified with second-and-third generation Arab Brazilians.

30. Márcia de Chiara, "Vendas caem e lojistas já 'passam pontos,'" *Folha de São Paulo,* July 5, 1995. In Portuguese, this procedure is colloquially known as *passar o ponto* (passing the point-of-sales). Bichara, a second-generation Syrian Brazilian who owns a realty agency in the region remarked that around 70 percent of the properties on 25 de Março are still held by Arabs.

31. Alesandra Zapparoli, "Vaivém sem fim: Prefeitura faz nova tentativa de tirar os camelôs da região da 25 de Março," *Veja São Paulo,* November 8, 1999. The nongovernmental organization "Viva O Centro" estimated that there are more than 7,000 street vendors in downtown São Paulo (Viva O Centro, 1994).

32. I consider street vending to be part of the expansive informal economy today. Officials in the Secretariat of Regional Administrations of the São Paulo mayoral administration have estimated that 30,000 citizens work in the informal economy today. The *Sindicato dos Trabalhadores em Economia Informal,* however, states that there are no less than 170,000 workers in the informal economy in São Paulo (Viva o Centro, 1994).

33. Michele Oliveira, "Bloqueio no Paraguai afeta negócios na Rua 25 de Março," *Gazeta Mercantil*, September 26, 2001. The article states "the closing of the Ponte da Amizade that connects Foz do Iguaçu to Ciudad del Leste, in Paraguay, has had an impact on the region of 25 de Março... Known for imported products, the region already suffers from the lack of." various goods.

34. For example, see Alesandra Zapparoli, "Vaivém sem fim: Prefeitura faz nova tentativa de tirar os camelôs da região da 25 de Março," *Veja São Paulo*, August 11, 1999. Rossi, Valéria, "Blitz anticamelô toma 25 de Março de madrugada," *Jornal da Tarde*, June 30, 2000. Bárbara Souza, "Guardas e camelôs confrontam-se no centro," *O Estado de S. Paulo*, October 7, 2000. José Gonçalves Neto, "Região da 25 de Março é alvo de blitz," *O Estado de S. Paulo* October 12, 2000. Meire Furuno, "'Camelôdromo' da 25 segue intocável," *Jornal da Tarde*, January 20, 2001. Liliana Ciardi, "Blitz tira camelôs da Rua 25 de Março," *Jornal da Tarde* March 24, 2001.

35. Marcus Lopes, "25 de Março faz 140 anos e preserva memória: 'Pequena Bagdá' deve tradição comercial aos mascates ...," *O Estado de São Paulo*, August 16, 1999.

36. Gilberto Padilha, "Nesta rua os árabes resistem aos shoppings E aos camelôs: Vindos da Síria e do Líbano, eles tornaram a Rua 25 de Março um dos centros atacadistas mais prósperos da América Latina. Agora lutam para sobreviver contra inimigos modernos e atrevidos," *Jornal da Tarde*, June 18, 2000.

37. Sérgio Duran, "Projeto da nova 25 de Março exclui camelôs: Proposta que será apresentada hoje prevê a presença de 400 ambulantes; hoje, 5.000 atuam na região *Folha de São Paulo*," March 24, 2001. Though critical of the project, the article did not dismiss it but rather stated that the number of camelôs in the region would be drastically reduced from 5,000 to 400 subjects.

Works Cited

Archives
CMSP: Câmara Municipal de São Paulo.
    BG: Biblioteca Geral.
    SPA: Seçao do Protocólo e Arquivo.

Books and Articles
Baer, Werner. *The Brazilian Economy: Growth and Development.* Westport: Praeger, 1983, 1995.
Benjamin, Walter. *Illuminations: Essays and Reflections*, ed. Hannah Arendt. New York: Schocken, 1968.
———. *Reflections: Essays, Aphorisms, Autobiographical Writing*, ed. Peter Demetz. New York: Schocken, 1978.
Bergsman, Joel. *Brazil: Industrialization and Trade Policies.* New York: Oxford University Press, 1970.

Dean, Warren. *The Industrialization of São Paulo, 1880-1945.* Austin: University of Texas Press, 1969.

Departamento Estadual da Estatística. *Catálogo das indústrias do município da Capital, 1945.* São Paulo: Rothschild Loureiro e Cia, 1947.

Evans, Peter. *Dependent Development: The Alliance of Multinational, State, and Local Capital in Brazil.* Princeton: Princeton University Press, 1979.

Holloway, Thomas. 1980. *Immigrants on Land: Coffee and Society in São Paulo, 1886-1930.* New York: Routledge, 1980.

Jafet, Basílio. *A supremácia reconhecida.* São Paulo: Editora Esphinge, 1935.

Jafet, Nami. *Ensaios e discursos.* São Paulo: Editora S/A, 1947.

Júnior, Amarilio. *As vantagens da imigração syria no Brasil.* Rio de Janeiro: (s.n), 1935.

Karam, John Tofik. 2004. *Distinguishing Arabesques: The Politics and Pleasures of Being Arab in Neoliberal Brazil.* Ph.D. diss., Syracuse University, 2004.

Knowlton, Charles. *Sírios e libaneses em São Paulo.* São Paulo: Editora Anhembi, 1961.

Leopoldi, Maria Antoineta. *Política e interesses na industrialização brasileira: As associações industriais, a política econômica e o Estado.* São Paulo: Paz e Terra, 2000.

Lesser, Jeffrey. "(Re)Creating Ethnicity: Middle Eastern Immigration to Brazil." *Americas:A Quarterly Review of Inter-American Cultural History,* 53 no. 1 (1996): 45-65.

——. *Negotiating National Identity: Immigrants, Minorities, and the Struggle for Ethnicity in Brazil.* Durham: Duke University Press, 1999.

Marques, Gabriel. *Ruas e tradicões de São Paulo: Uma história em cada rua.* São Paulo: Conselho Estadual de Cultura, 1966.

Sociedade Nacional de Agricultura. *Immigração: Inquérito promovido pela Sociedade Nacional de Agricultura.* Rio de Janeiro: Villanie Barbero, 1926.

Stein, Stanley. *The Brazilian Cotton Manufacture: Textile Enterprise in an Underdeveloped Area, 1850-1950.* Cambridge: Harvard University Press, 1957.

Truzzi, Oswaldo. *Patrícios: sírios e libaneses em São Paulo.* São Paulo: Editora Hucitec, 1997.

Viva O Centro. *Camelôs: Subsídios para o equacionamento do problema do comércio informal de rua e sua solução.* São Paulo: Associação Viva o Centro, 1994.

Weinstein, Barbara. *The Amazon Rubber Boom.* Cambridge: Harvard University Press, 1980.

3

The *Syrian World* in the New World: The Contextual Beginnings of Arab American Literature and the Part It Played in Identity Formation

Hani Ismaeal Elayyan

Print literacy played an important role in creating a sense of minority identity among Arab immigrants to the United States in the period between the two world wars. The contributions of one publication, the *Syrian World* journal 1926–1935, to the discourse of identity were immense. Studying this publication helps us examine how the Arab American community forged a national identity for itself. It will be clear that the contribution of the ethnic press was crucial to that process.

Scholars have theorized a role for print in various institutions and areas. For example, Benedict Anderson in his groundbreaking book, *Imagined Communities*, established a role for the printing press in the emergence of nationalism in its modern form.[1] This article is informed further by the theoretical developments in the field of print culture studies or "History of the Book," a field that, according to Robert Darnton, seeks to "understand how ideas were transmitted through print and how exposure to the printed word affected the thought and behavior of mankind during the last five hundred years."[2]

Identity is a process not a product. It is to be created, maintained, and promoted through several institutions that help make it practicable and clear to those who hold it. The early Arab immigrants were granted a "racial" identity, in accordance with the official United States government classification. They, however, started a struggle to negotiate that formal classification into a solid identity that would facilitate their acceptance by American society and in accord with their self-image. To that end, they established churches, social clubs, and newspapers that served as ready sites for the formation of the new identity, largely championed by the intellectual elite.

The *Syrian World* was the major English-language journal published by Syrian immigrants to the United States in the first part of the twentieth century. It was important in the development of identity in the community because it started two years after the Immigration Act of 1924, which limited the number of Syrian immigrants to the United States to a mere hundred a year. That act marked the moment when the community had begun to stabilize for the lack of new immigrants. The target audience for the journal, therefore, was the second generation of Syrian immigrants. It was thus crucial in promoting a sense of identity among children of immigrants who had not known the home country. The journal used English, which made it accessible to the second generation, as well as to many of the first generation who knew the language. Of course, there is no reason to suppose that all readers accepted the ideas expressed in the journal. Nevertheless, it kept a sense of community alive. In particular, the letters to the editor are crucial documents to discover how the readership responded to topics discussed in the journal. The editor, Salloum Mokarzel (1881–1952), was interested in presenting a good image of the Syrians to their society. He usually raised certain issues and asked the readers to respond to them.

However, the journal was not merely an objective historical record of events in the lives of Arab Americans. On the contrary, the *Syrian World* was an active participant in creating that community. Studying the ideological configurations in its nine-year life brings to light the changes that took place in the community's self-perception at the time. A glance at the wide range of topics discussed in articles, editorials, poems, and short stories reveals the concerns of the readership and the conflicts among different generations over the identity of the community which was fluid because of the various waves of immigrants.

Arabic Culture in the *Syrian World*

The *Syrian World* contained poems translated from Arabic, together with Arabic proverbs and stories. There were also writings in English that evoked Arabic themes and topography. One can discern three uses of these topics and references: in one context, Arabic poems were cited for their references to exotic places and culture, with the objective of adding a romantic aura to the journal. The experiences described in those poems were alternative lifestyles that had become irrelevant to Syrian Americans. In other contexts, the journal gave samples of Arabic poetry portraying episodes in the life of the Middle

East as oppositional models to be avoided and condemned. The third category of Arabic culture presented positive examples that gave a good impression of Arab wisdom and showed its universal appeal. The great variety in how Arabic culture was presented in the journal stemmed from ideological differences among contributors.

Exotic poems were the most abundant in the *Syrian World*. In those poems, Arab countries were the location of strange, dream-like events that resembled *Arabian Nights* stories. Many were written by non-Syrian poets who imagined the Middle East to be a place of romance and adventure. The names of those poets indicate they were of European origins. The editors usually encouraged such poets to contribute to the journal because they gave it a cosmopolitan appeal. In such writings the Middle East region was, to use Edward Said's term, "Orientalized."[3] The representation did not correspond to the real Middle East but to what the poets wanted it to be, which was independent of the original. The lives of people who inhabited the region at that time were not as important as the romantic ancient history. For example, the ancient history and romance of Egypt was a popular topic in the journal, as the titles of the following poems show: "The Egyptian Violets" and "A Legend of the Nile" by Dr. Salim Y. Alkazin[4] and "Egypt" by Toufik Moufarrige.[5]

The last poem, by a Lebanese resident of Egypt, was first published in Arabic and then in English in the *London Graphic*. What is notable about the poem is that the poet saw Egypt in the same light as proponents of the Phoenician ideology imagined Lebanon: an ancient country with a great civilization, with its Arabic identity as just another foreign conquest that could not change its inherent self:

> The caravan of days and generations has passed her by, from
> Nations, played with them, but herself kept changeless.

Even Lebanon was sometimes seen as a very exotic place. "As I Came Down from Lebanon," a poem by Clinton Scollard, contains a catalog of exotic images. The speaker comes down from Lebanon "like Lava in the dying glow." Then he witnesses:

> Sweet sheiks from distant Samarcand
> With precious spices they had won[6]

The poem combines images of magic and natural beauty with the traditional sheiks. In contrast to the fast movement expressed in the lava and the river that "runs," those sheiks move at a much slower pace. They are stationary and unchanging, presumably like the cultures from which they come. Those guests are allowed into the city but only after long waiting and scrutiny. That city, just as all nations, has a system of opening and closing. It is a city rich in orchards and water, unlike the desert beyond its walls. It follows that desert dwellers would like to come to it. However, in order to be granted access they should be sweet and rich. They should bring to the nation commodities they have won, not stolen.

The process of Orientalizing the Middle East involved portraying unchanging colored people inhabiting remote locales. The journal published a poem entitled "The Arabian Nights" by Don C. Seitz, who used foreign-sounding words such as "Scanderoon," "Abyssinians," and "sheiks." "Swart Syrian sheiks" in those remote places are notable for their cruelty and uncivilized life:

> Dark Abyssinians, and the lords
> Who rule in terror over Sinai's hordes[7]

Notice that there are no individuals in this poem. "Orientals" are seen only in groups as "travelers," "sheiks," "Abyssinians," "lords," and "hordes." These masses of humanity are denied any individual characteristics. They are multitudes of dark, exotic peoples who need some strong lords to rein them in. The speaker denies Arabic literature the ability to evolve. The *Arabian Nights* are taken as the ultimate example of Arab contributions to world literature. The lives of modern Syrians, on the other hand, are seen to be no different from that of their forefathers. The desert life, many poets argued, determined the emotional life of Arabs and made them very intense. Consequently, they loved and hated passionately.

In "Bushru's Encounter with the Lion," a poem by Bushr Ibn 'Awna, translated by Dr. N. A. Katibah, the poet tells his sister of how he killed a fierce lion to give its head to his fiancée as a dowry:

> When lo, a lion from his lair
> Your brother, Bushru, met[8]

The poem is typical of Arabic genre of self-praise. The poet addresses a female relative to convey the good news to her. He establishes the valor of his foe, so as to exaggerate the greatness of his achievement. The translator captures that sense of valor and exoticism. The name Fatima, Prophet Mohammad's daughter, was probably known among some young Syrians, because, in the 1920s, it was the name of a brand of cigarettes in America.[9] Such connections probably contributed strongly to the orientalizing of the Syrian cultural heritage in the readers' minds.

Another example of such valorous lovers is Antar, a famous Arab knight and poet. In "The Spirit of Antar," Dr. N. A. Katibah translated a very well-known poem in which Antar addressed his beloved and boasted of his courage in war:

> When the swords (how they flashed!) entwisted and clashed
> I bethought me the while that each gleam was a smile[10]

Neither the translator nor the editor mentions anything about the complexity of the love story behind the poem. Antar was the son of an Arab man and an African slave, which meant, according to the habit of the day, that his father did not acknowledge him as his son. Consequently, Antar had to struggle to distinguish himself in order to be recognized. He was a great warrior and poet. He loved his cousin but agreed to defend the tribe only for her sake. However, the potential political uses of the poem, and any possible application to the situation of African Americans, or to American social issues, is totally obscured by this translation.

At other times the emotional intensity of desert people was used to draw negative conclusions about Arabs and their culture. Some poems and stories portrayed Arabs as very cruel people, and the desert as a harsh environment that drove its inhabitants to commit horrible acts. Mitchell Ferris describes this environment in a poem entitled "The Desert":

> Bare rocks and burning sands
> A barren land of dread[11]

The words are harsh; they have to do with death and fear. The first thing one thinks of is to escape such a harsh environment that involves death in life. The landscape is so cruel and devastating. It affects the mind, as "Love and War in the Desert" shows. This story, subtitled "An Actual Love Drama among the Bedouins and Its Sequel," tells of the love between a young sheik and a beautiful woman of another tribe whom he has kidnapped. That incident leads to a ferocious war in the desert. The story opens with a view that reflects the philosophy of geographical determinism:

The eternal forces of love and hatred, of injury and revenge, as intense and relentless as the heat of the desert sun, still exercise their sway among the Bedouin Arabs as in the remotest times of the past. Just as the mode of life of these sons of Ishmael has not changed for countless centuries, so have their characteristics, born of the hard life of their inhospitable surroundings, remained immutable.[12]

Those images of fixity stand in sharp contrast to the West, a culture of change and progress. The East is described with superlative terms: it is "remotest" from the West in every aspect; it is "relentless" in its feelings of love and hatred. The writer claims to know the East and decides to describe it to the readers. Such an authoritative attitude is typical of Orientalist discourse which, according to Edward Said, dominates the East by "making statements about it, authorizing views of it, describing it, by teaching it, settling it, ruling over it."[13] A similar story is told in the February 1932 issue about a modern love tragedy. Entitled "Blue Blood: A Recent Tragedy of Love and Death Caused by a Breach of a Social Tradition among the Arabs,"[14] it tells of a tribesman in Iraq who has killed a man of a lesser tribe for daring to marry into his.

As for proverbs and verses from Arabic, Mokarzel relegated them to bottoms of pages, and left them without explanation of who said them and on what occasions. Sometimes, he only mentioned the name of the author, but at other times he even ignored to mention that. One can find a popular saying together with verses from the Koran or *Hadith* (Prophet Mohammad's sayings). Thus, those examples of Arab culture were universalized and given as alternative outlooks on life. They did not necessarily advocate a significant part of the Syrian cultural heritage.

For example, in the September 1928 issue under the title "Arab Wisdom," there are five short quotations that consist of three anecdotes, one proverb, and a verse of poetry rendered in prose. No contexts are provided, and it is hardly likely that Young Syrian Americans knew who "Muhammad Ibn 'Ubaidallah" was, or any one of the other characters mentioned in the section.[15]

In addition to examples of classical Arabic literature, the journal published a series of traditional Syrian songs. The original Arabic text is usually provided next to the translation. Those songs were probably targeted toward the older generation who remembered and enjoyed them. Most of the poems had a festive mood, and were appropriate to the times when the Depression hit America hard. The poetry editor, Barbara Young, acknowledged the importance of poetry in giving readers a sense of relief, especially under harsh conditions. Young asked, "may not poetry refresh and renew the courage of the beaten and the disillusioned in the day's debacle? The answer is, it can and it does."[16] Her words show that middle-class sensibility always called for a practical end behind all activities. Many of the poems and stories in the journal, especially those appearing in the thirties, tended to focus on the futility of wealth and security and called readers to prefer things of eternal value, such as ethics, beauty, and family. For example, "Ya Baity" (My House), celebrates the humble residence as a refuge from cruel times:[17]

> Home, my unpretentious humble home,
> To you to hide my faults I come[18]

One wonders what kind of faults the speaker wanted to hide. Are they the faults of being poor and lacking in luxury? The mention of "drink" and "eat" indicates that the home is a private space where one can live on simple food without bothering about what the community thinks. Such poems were not escapist but aimed at comforting the immigrants under such difficult economic conditions.

Literature, then, was an integral part of the *Syrian World*. It was the site where narratives about the community were made and challenged. Consequently, no informed probe into this history of the community can succeed without a careful study of the literature it produced, high or low. Some readers might tend to dismiss the literature in the journal as amateurish and unskilled. However, one can witness in those apparently simple poems some attempts at creating a minor literature that would work within the English language. For example, in their reading of Franz Kafka, Gilles Deleuze and Felix Guattari point out that a minor literature is characterized by the deterritorialization of language. A Czech Jew writing in German, Kafka's contribution was "to challenge the language and [make] it follow a sober revolutionary path."[19] The authors mentioned that African Americans deterritorialized the English language in the same manner. In the following short poem entitled "Her Choice," one can notice a similar process at work. The speaker addresses a woman who smokes a cigarette set "within tight-lipped rosette."

He declares that this rosette "of marble blonde" is too small and insignificant:

> Henceforth I'll swear devotion
> To a thoroughbred arkhelee[20]

The Syrian poet leads the reader through the first three lines without any verbs. One expects to hear something about this cigarette which is described in detail. The rhyming "light-tipped" and "tight-lipped" give the reader a sense of order and harmony. However, the phrase "I criticize you freely" breaks the pattern. The reader becomes more curious to know why the speaker criticizes the cigarette. Order resumes with the rhyming "notion," "motion," and "devotion." Let's suppose that a non-Syrian is looking at this poem. The reader knows by now that the speakers prefer something else but will probably wonder, "a thoroughbred *what?*" In making the punch line in the poem a foreign word (Hookah) the writer manages to deterritorialize the English language. The American reader is at a loss because the word does not exist in the dictionary. However, it rhymes with "freely." The English language has been appropriated by the poet. He manages to establish the differences between his old and new cultures through the use of a single word. Syrian culture is ancient and "thoroughbred." Age has lent it a distinctive taste from the colorful but young American culture. Thus, this literary experiment and others like it laid the foundations for an Arab American minor literature. It matured at the hands of the third–generation Arab Americans who managed to find a voice of their own.

Conclusion

In a letter to the *Syrian World*'s editor, A. T. Olmstead, a professor of history at the University of Illinois, wrote:

> One of the greatest difficulties to be faced by the future historian of America is the writing up of the history of its foreign born citizens. Thanks to your *Syrian World*, it will be easy for the future historian to depict the part played by the Syrians and no doubt will result in their being given their due place in this history. [21]

Professor Olmstead's words are proving to be truly prophetic. Because Arab Americans now come from most Arab countries, and because some have long been part of the mainstream culture, the community is losing track of its Syrian beginnings. The new immigrants hold ideologies and adopt agendas drastically different from those of their predecessors. Therefore, it is important to understand the historical processes that have contributed to making the community. Such understanding will give Arab American institutions a good sense of why some ethnic organizations succeed while others have failed. They will learn to respond to changes in American policies, and become an integral part of American society.

Agency is not limited to those in power because common people often manage to participate in the dialogue about how their lives are run. Culture consists in material practices at both the individual and collective levels that contribute to shaping daily life in communities. Reading is one of the most common of such practices. It is an important tool in education, which is basic for promoting dominant ideologies. However, reading is just as indispensable in acts of dissent and social change. Therefore, print culture of immigrant groups gives us insights into how they see themselves, how they contribute to shaping their futures in the new environment, and how they cope with the culture of the majority. This critical approach refuses the image of power as monolithic, one way from top to bottom. The *Syrian World* is a valuable source for studying the changing history of Arabs in America. It records their struggles and dreams, their concerns and obsessions. Often, it offers contradictory self-images of a group in the process of redefining itself.

The intellectuals of the *Syrian World* were not simple recorders of the group's history but were active participants in making it as well. They mediated between the community and other American intellectuals, thus helping both sides understand one another. Salloum Mokarzel was the usual host to all visitors to the Syrian quarters, such as the Reconciliation Trips organized by the Federal Council of the Churches of Christ in America.[22] A designated spokesman for the group, he proved always a vigilant defender of its reputation.

During its short life, the *Syrian World* underwent major transformations that reveal the rapid changes the Syrians experienced between the two world wars. From thinking of themselves as sojourners who were in America but for a short while, the Syrians became aware that they were in America to stay. They were impotent witnesses to the partitioning of their old homeland into four distinct countries (Syria, Lebanon, Palestine, and Jordan) by the Western powers after World War I, and felt the isolation of their adopted homeland when the Immigration Act of 1924 reduced the number of Syrians admitted to the United States to a trickle. In its nine years of publication, the *Syrian World* served as a site of contested identities among Syrians. Changes in its appearance and content offer us a precise image of the paradigm shifts in the community's agenda, as well as the new concerns that arose among its members.

For many years, the residual Arabist tradition existed side by side with the dominant Phoenician tradition. However, both ideologies had to make way for the emergent voice of a younger generation, who pushed the community farther away from its Syrian identity, whether Arabist or Phoenician, until it assimilated itself almost completely by the end of World War II. It took the Six Days War of 1967 to awaken the community to its historical roots.

One can see the schism that developed between the immigrants and their homeland in the shift of focus from the journal to the newspaper. Whereas the journal targeted both parents and children, the newspaper targeted the young generation as its main audience. It addressed readers primarily as Americans. One advertisement read, "The faithful, loyal friends of the *Syrian World* are a legion of intelligent readers and progressive American citizens. Pay your $3.00 and join them!"[23] Katibah dedicated large space to addressing issues of relevance to Syrian Americans, such as the bankruptcy case of Faour Bank, which affected many Syrians, as shown by the list of depositors.[24]

The visual aspects of the newspaper reflect the changes that took place after 1932 as well. The newspaper contained more pictures than the journal, and those had a clearly popular appeal. The journal contained mainly pictures from Syrian cities and ruins of archaeological sites as well as pictures of prominent Syrian Americans. The newspaper, on the other hand, kept some of those but added more pictures that would appeal to the younger generation. For example, one issue contained a picture of Edmund Zenni, a Lebanese wrestler who arrived in New York for a visit. The picture shows the naked upper half of his body as he is posing for the camera.[25] Such less austere iconography show that the newspaper was loosening the traditional restrictions in the community. It was becoming part of the mainstream, rather than keeping its conservative ethnic features.

The newspaper also printed, for the first time, political cartoons about conditions in America. "An Old Time Figure"[26] showed a man opening the door to a closet to reveal a big man with a sack of dollars for a head. The man opening the door is labeled "Senate Investigation," whereas the closet is called "Our Financial Closet" and the man inside it is "The Money Trust." Another cartoon entitled "The Able Pilot"[27] showed Franklin Delano Roosevelt sailing down a very steep river with a lot of rocks in the stream that are called "These Perilous Times." Such cartoons brought the newspaper further into the mainstream. They appealed to young Syrians both in subject matter and form as well. It seems Roosevelt was a popular figure among Syrians. One cartoon entitled "The Cry from the Bleachers"[28] showed him as a batter holding a bat labeled "Currency Reform." One person stood up among the crowds and shouted, "Another Homer Frank." Baseball had never been a popular sport in Syria. The journal used it primarily to engage the younger generation in the United States.

Advertisements also changed in the newspaper. Instead of the few ones that were confined to the beginning and ending of the journal, the newspaper included more ads throughout that covered a wider variety of activities. For example, the March 9, 1934 issue contained two ads one for "Novelty Dance" and the other about a farce by the Syrian Junior League.[29]

Despite all the changes in the form of the newspaper, the younger generation was not impressed. H. Katibah related in one article that younger Syrians usually refused to subscribe to the newspaper and answered his appeals by arguing, "Why should I subscribe to a small Syrian paper when I can buy the *Times* or *World Telegram*?"[30] Katibah urged agents, "waste no time with such persons."

One of those unsatisfied young readers wrote a letter to the editor in which he argued that the newspaper reminded him "of a Kansas High School paper edited by a 100 per cent American sophomore who has been to New York a couple of times."[31] He continued to call the newspaper "pathetically provincial." As for the Arabian folklore specials, he argued they "seem just a bit goody-goody, singularly failing to evoke any romance or glamour. Similarly, your Arabic proverbs are wordy and their wit, at best, heavy." Such harsh attacks show that the Syrian youths were getting alienated from their heritage because, according to the writer of the letter, it "perpetuates in the minds of young American Syrians a sense of a harshly alien descent." The emerging voice of the younger generation was overwhelming the older generation, even the most open-minded among them. Young Syrians took what the elders preached to an extreme, and sought to be "good" Americans by severing all links to any other heritage.

The English language greatly influenced the *Syrian World* and contributed to its assimilationist stance. Using English meant that the publication was no more a private business among the community. Other Americans were included as a possible audience. Consequently, self-censorship became a more influential factor because the editors wanted to make a good impression on any reader who might happen to see it. This situation determined the content of the journal. It also put the journal under the pressure of competing with other mainstream publications. Because the use of the native language is the most distinguishing feature of an ethnic press, using English eventually would make the journal not very different from others. The newspaper ceased publication in 1935 and left a vacuum that has not been filled since then. Its fine intellectual tone and the serious discussions of Syrian affairs have not been paralleled by many publications. In its precise delineation of the immigrant discourse of identity, the *Syrian World* remains a valuable resource for the study of the contextual beginnings of Arab American literature.

Notes

1. Benedict Anderson, *Imagined Communities: Reflections on the Origin and Spread of Nationalism*, rev. ed. (London: Verso, 1983).
2. Robert Darnton, *The Kiss of Lamourette: Reflections in Cultural History* (New York: Norton,1990), 107.
3. Edward Said, *Orientalism* (New York: Vintage, 1979).
4. Salim Y. Alkazin, "The Egyptian Violet," *Syrian World*, February 1928, 17; "A Legend of the Nile," *Syrian World*, November 1929, 29-31.
5. Toufik Moufarrage, " Egypt," *Syrian World*, January 1931, 28-9, L 4,7.
6. Clinton Scollard, "As I Came Down from Lebanon," *Syrian World* October 1926, 27,L 16-17.
7. Don C. Seitz, "The Arabian Nights," *Syrian World* February, 1931, 35, L 9-10.
8. Bushr Ibn 'Awna, " Bushru's Encounter with the Lion," Trans. N. .A. Katibah, *Syrian World*, September 1927, 32-34.
9. Holly Edwards, ed., *Noble Dreams, Wicked Pleasures: Orientalism in America, 1870–1930* (Princeton University Press, 2000), 204.
10. Antar, "The Spirit of Antar," trans. N.A. Katibah, *Syrian World*, February 1927, 45.
11. Mitchell Ferris, "The Desert," *Syrian World*, October 1928, 37, L 1, 4.
12. Habib Katibah, "Love and War in the Desert," *Syrian World*, December 1930, L 5,8.
13. Said, *Orientalism*.

14. Habib Katibah, " Blue Blood: A Recent Tragedy of Love and Death Caused by a Breach of a Social Tradition among the Arabs," *Syrian World*, February 1932.

15. *Syrian World*, "Arab Wisdom," September 1928, 20.

16. Barbara Young, "Is Poetry a Business?" *Syrian World*, October 1931, 21-2.

17. See also M. J. Naimy,"The Endless Race," April 1928, 17, and Edna Saloomy, "Paradox," June 1931, 29.

18. *Syrian World*, "Ya Baity," Trans. Salim Y. Alkazin, February 1932, 13, L 1,4.

19. Gilles Deleuze and Felix Guattari, "What Is a Minor Literature?" in *Falling into Theory: Conflicting Views on Reading Literature*, ed. David H. Richter. (Boston: Bedford, 2000), 167-74.

20. Assid C. Corban, "Her Choice," *Syrian World*, January 1928, 23.

21. A. T. Olmstead, "Easing the Historian's Task," Letter, *Syrian World*, February, 1928, 45.

22. James Myers, "Discovering the Syrians," *Syrian World*, March 1929, 30-32.

23. *Syrian World*, "The Faithful, Loyal Friends of the *Syrian World*," Advertisement, November 1, 1935, 5.

24. *Syrian World*, "Faour Deposits Principally Small Thrift Accounts," May 5, 1933, 1.

25. *Syrian World*, Edmund Zenni. Photograph, July 21, 1933, 3.

26. *Syrian World*, "An Old Figure Brought to Life, Cartoon," June 2, 1933, 4.

27. *Syrian World*, "The Able Pilot, Cartoon," May 19, 1933, 4.

28. *Syrian World*, "The Cry from the Bleachers, Cartoon," May 5, 1933, 4.

29. *Syrian World*, "Dying to Live by the Syrian Junior League, Advertisement," April 21, 1934, 6.

30. Habib Katibah, "Objectives II: Preservation of Syrian Culture and traditions,"   Editorial, *Syrian World*, January 19, 1934, 4.

31. M.Y., "This Writer Fulminates in a Fit of Intolerant Intellectualism," Letter, *Syrian World*, December 29, 1933, 4-5.

Works Cited

Alkazin, Salim Y. "The Egyptian Violet," *Syrian World*, February 1928, 17.

———. "A Legend of the Nile," *Syrian World*, November 1929, 29-31.

Anderson, Benedict. *Imagined Communities: Reflections on the Origin and Spread of Nationalism*. Rev. ed. London: Verso, 1983.

Antar. " The Spirit of Antar" Trans. N.A. Katibah. *Syrian World*, February 1927, 45.

'Awna, Bushr Ibn. "Bushru's Encounter with the Lion," Trans. N. A. Katibah, *Syrian World*, September 1927, 32-34.

Corban, C. Assid. "Her Choice," *Syrian World*, January 1928, 23.

Darnton, Robert. *The Kiss of Lamourette: Reflections in Cultural History*. New York: Norton, 1990.

Deleuze, Gilles, and Felix Guattari. "What Is a Minor Literature?" In *Falling into Theory: Conflicting Views on Reading Literature*. Ed. David H. Richter. Boston: Bedford, 2000.

Edwards, Holly, ed. *Noble Dreams, Wicked Pleasures: Orientalism in America, 1870 –1930*. Princeton: Princeton University Press, 2000.

Ferris, Mitchell. "The Desert," *Syrian World*, October 1928, 37.

Katibah, Habib. "Blue Blood: A Recent Tragedy of Love and Death Caused by a Breach of a Social Tradition among the Arabs," *Syrian World*, February,1932, 23-27.

——. "Objectives II: Preservation of Syrian Culture and traditions." Editorial. *Syrian World*, January 19, 1934, 4.

——."Love and War in the Desert," *Syrian World*, December 1930.

Moufarrige, Toufik. " Egypt," *Syrian World*, January 1931, 29-31.

Myers, James. "Discovering the Syrians." *Syrian World*, March 1929, 30-32.

Naimy, M. J. "The Endless Race." *Syrian World*, April 1928, 17.

Olmstead, A.T. "Easing the Historian's Task." Letter. *Syrian World*, February 1928.

Said, Edward. *Orientalism*. New York: Vintage, 1979.

Saloomey, Edna K. "Paradox." *Syrian World* June 1931: 29 -35.

Scollard, Clinton. "As I Came Down From Lebanon," *Syrian World* October 1926, 27.

Seitz, Don C. "The Arabian Nights," *Syrian World*, February 1931, 35.

Syrian World, "The Able Pilot, Cartoon," May 19, 1933, 4.

Syrian World, "Arab Wisdom," September 1928, 20.

Syrian World, "The Cry from the Bleachers, Cartoon," May 5, 1933, 4.

Syrian World, "Dying to Live by the Syrian Junior League, Advertisement," April 21, 1934, 6.

Syrian World, "An Old Figure Brought to Life, Cartoon," June 2, 1933, 4.

Syrian World, "Faour Deposits Principally Small Thrift Accounts," May 5, 1933, 4.

Syrian World, "Ya Baity," Trans. Salim Y. Alkazin. February 1932, 13.

Young, Barbara. "Is Poetry a Business?" *Syrian World*, October 1931, 21-22.

Part 2

The Experience of the Americas

4

Multiple Identities: Lebanese Arab Christians in the American West

Kirk Scott

The Orthodox Christian descendants of immigrants to Kansas from Arabic-speaking lands in what is now Lebanon are part of, and witness to, a century-long process of shifting and conflicting ethnic and national self-identity. These identities are often, it seems, predicated on political, social, and cultural developments external to the Lebanese Orthodox community itself. The earliest Arabic speaking immigrants to Kansas in the 1890s were from the village of Ayn-Arab and the village of J'daidat near the city of Marj'ayoun, south of the Bekaa valley in present-day Lebanon.[1] They were part of a larger emigration of Arabic-speaking Christians from the Ottoman-ruled areas of what is now Syria and Lebanon. This emigration itself had its roots in political events in the historical region of Mount Lebanon and in the Ottoman Empire as a whole, as well as in the broader international relations between the Ottomans, the British, the Russians, the Austrians, and the French. Local as well as global events began a process that moved these communities into a culture that demanded of them, and continues to demand, an "ethnic identity" beyond the web of family, community, and religion that had served as points of identity in the Arabic speaking lands of the Ottoman Empire. The concepts of "Arab," "Arab American," "Syrian," and "Lebanese" are once again being shaped in response to outside events.

The attacks on the World Trade Center and the Pentagon on September 11, 2001, and the subsequent "War on Terror" have triggered the most recent attention to Arab ethnicity and to the self-perception of members of this community. This essay will explore the conflicted and changing identities in the face of external pressure of established, assimilated grandchildren of these early Arabic-speaking Christian immigrants to Kansas. These conflicting identities will be explored, as well, in the context of the historical development of identity among the broader Arabic-speaking Christian immigrant community.

Background

Changes in political circumstances in modern times for Arabic-speaking Christians under Ottoman rule began during the period of Ottoman history referred to as the *Tanzimat*, or reorganization. The *Tanzimat* brought about bureaucratic and legal reforms meant to "modernize" the Ottoman system. Two royal decrees in particular, those of 1839 and 1856, were meant to give equal status to non-Muslim religious minorities in matters of military conscription, state employment, and admission to state schools. Before the *Tanzimat* period, Ottoman rule of religious minorities was carried out under the *millet* system that allowed recognized Christian and Jewish communities a measure of autonomy, the ability to administer their own religious laws, and to collect their own taxes.[2] The *millet* system appears to have been an adaptation of the *dhimma* treaties used by the early Muslim caliphates to control the status of their non-Muslim populations. The *dhimmi* appear to derive from the pre-Islamic, Byzantine Christian codes that determined the state of pagans and Jews under the rule of the eastern Roman Empire. These codes were passed along from one bureaucracy to the next to reinforce the power of the official religion. Under the political direction of their community, religious authorities of Christian and Jewish communities under the Ottoman *millet* system maintained a measure of self-rule, but always at the expense of equality of status with Muslim subjects and of access to positions of power.[3]

As civil and secular matters were determined according to the laws of one's religious community, religion itself came to be viewed as the form and substance of nationality. "For Christians, Muslims and Jews from the Middle East, one's religious affiliation determines one's identity."[4] Even to the end of the nineteenth century, Orthodox Christians were "referred to solely as *Greeks*. The assimilation of these Christians to Arabism has its roots in historical myths of modern nationalism."[5]

The reforms of the *Tanzimat* encouraged Christians, and in particular the Maronite Catholics[6] of Mt. Lebanon, to pursue wider economic contacts and educational opportunities in a manner their Sunni Muslim and Druze neighbors found threatening.[7] Resulting massacres of Christian communities of Mt. Lebanon and Damascus in 1860 led, under pressure of European powers, to the creation of the *mutasarrifiya*, a semiautonomous administrative governorship surrounding Mt. Lebanon and guaranteed by Christian European authorities. Many surrounding Christian communities, Greek Catholic and Greek Orthodox worked for inclusion in the privileged Maronite Christian *mutasarrifiya*.[8] "Lebanon" began to be synonymous with "Christian," even though rivalry and tension particularly with the Lebanese Druze community persisted.

The intervention of European powers in the affairs of the Ottoman "Sick Man of Europe" brought increasing contact between Western missionaries and agents and "Syrian" Christians. The French had a long historical relationship with their coreligionists, the Maronite Catholics, and Russia saw itself as the supporter and defender of their coreligionists, the Orthodox Christians. This European influence, and the influence of American Presbyterian missionaries, brought about not only international contacts, but also increased tensions between the Arabic-speaking Christian communities and their Muslim neighbors. The Christian communities outside the *mutasarrafiya* continued to experience insecurity and violence and many Orthodox families sought safety by leaving the areas under Ottoman domination.[9] This group included the original immigrants to Kansas from Marj'ayoun. Marj'ayoun itself actually fell outside the boundaries of the semi-autonomous *mutasarrafiya*, the inhabitants thus more vulnerable to the Muslim majority.[10]

Immigration to the newly opened prairie lands of the United States began during the 1870s. It is estimated that between 1890 and 1920, "100,000 Syrian Greek Orthodox were among [the] masses migrating to the United States."[11] As members of the Greek Orthodox *millet*, early Arabic speaking immigrants to the United States viewed themselves in the limited context of religion and family. Bureau of Immigration officials, prior to 1899, referred to these immigrants, who thus identified as "Turks" or "Asiatics." After 1899, Christian immigrants from the Ottoman empire lacked an accepted nationality, as originating in "Turkey in Asia." Many who were originally from the Ottoman Empire, in reference to the historical geographic area, were given the classification "Syrian."[12] Thus, the "Syrian" national identity carried by the early immigrants was imposed from without, but accepted by the immigrants as a way of identifying themselves to their new communities. "Americans understood nationalities not millets, and the Syrians learned to accommodate their hosts."[13] However, although the "Syrians" may have identified themselves as such to outsiders, "the most meaningful and reflexive identity factors which Syrians used among themselves were family name, religion and place of origin."[14]   One need only recall the character Ali Hakim in the musical *Oklahoma* to realize the extent to which the traveling "Middle Eastern trader" entered the popular imagination of the prairie west.[15]   Syrian Christian establishments in Kansas began through a documented model of the traveling peddler, selling dry goods and notions on the prairie. By the early 1900s, individuals such as Nemtallah Farha, E. G. Stevens, A. G. Samara, and Samuel Ojile, who began establishing wholesale warehouse businesses in Wichita, Kansas, previously, worked peddling routes. As families became established, other members followed from Marj'ayoun, in a pattern reminiscent of other immigrant groups.[16]   Those who first arrived spoke Arabic, picking up English to the extent needed in their commercial relations. The desire to assimilate, however, was intense. Joining civic groups, enrolling their American-born children in school, and insisting on their speaking English exclusively are but a few of the ways this goal was to be accomplished. Anglicizing names was another. As Caswell points out, "Layoun and Habeeb became Lee and Harry, while Thoma and Eid were phonetically translated to Tom and Ed."[17]

The primary institution that maintained the communal traditions of the Syrian Christians was, of course, the Church. In 1918, the St. George Syrian-Greek Orthodox Catholic society of Wichita, Kansas, was established. "The first resident, priest, Fr. Elias El-Khouri, a native of J'daidat, Marjayoun, served the St. George Parish until 1925."   After an interim visiting priest from Oklahoma, Fr. George Cohlmia, also a native of J'daidat, Marj'ayoun, served from 1934. The fact that the priests were natives of the village from which the immigrants had come served as a tie to values of the village community. An incident that began in 1930 illustrates the extent to which identity remained a nexus of "religion, family and a place of origin." A debate over whether or not to build a new church to accommodate the members of the congregations, who numbered nearly 400 by 1930, split the families of J'daidat, who favored a new building, from the families of Ayn-Arab who were opposed. Ironically, the Ayn-Arab families left St. George to create St. Mary's Men's Club, eventually establishing St. Mary's American Syrian Orthodox Greek Catholic Church a mere four blocks from St. George. St. Mary's even placed itself under the jurisdiction of a completely different archdiocese.[18] Philip Kayel writes that "A people organized socially around their religion and village, express most of their values in relation to family life."[19]   Kinship and communal ties, removal of a powerful force, trumping "nationality," even in the face of immigration to a new land. "Because of the Middle Eastern organizational mode that inextricably intertwined the family system with the religious...Syrian-Americans would not easily merge into a single, integrated nationality group."[20]

The period after World War I saw the creation of an autonomous, enlarged Lebanon, under French mandatory authority; a Lebanon that now included Marj'ayoun. The creation of Lebanon and, in particular, the full independence of Lebanon from French authority following the establishment of the independent states of Syria and Lebanon after World War II, resulted in a confusion of identity for "Syrian Christians" in the United States. "Syrian Christians" in America began to move toward a "Lebanese" identity.[21] Many factors contributed to this: Mt. Lebanon's long history of Western, French influence through their Maronite clients; Lebanon's semiautonomous Christian character particularly after the establishment of the *mutasarffiya* in 1860; Lebanon's new status as an independent "Christian" nation among the newly independent Muslim nations of the Middle East.

During the mid-1940s, "Syrian community organizations in the US were often forced to change their names from 'American Syrian' clubs to 'Lebanese–Syrian–American' clubs. Syrian priests were surprised to find themselves with 'Lebanese' congregations and 'Syrian food' became 'Lebanese' food...Lebanese were sensitive to being identified as Syrians."[22] The identifier "Syrian," imposed by U.S. Immigration officials and gladly taken on by early Christian immigrants as a way of identifying themselves to Anglo-American and others, had now become a misnomer. Marj'ayoun, as was pointed out earlier, actually lay outside of the Lebanese *mutasarrafiya* that existed from 1860 through 1920. The Kansas community, however, was sensitive to the new international developments and readily accepted the new "Lebanese" identity.

In Wichita, Kansas, following a national trend in the 1920s and 1930s, younger Orthodox Christians began forming "city-wide and region-wide federations that, unlike those of their elders focused on Lebanese ethnic heritage, on a specific religious preference of family clan. Anyone of Arabic heritage could join the City Federation regardless of family or church affiliation." In the 1930s, material from the St. Mary's Mediterranean dinner referred to "oriental dishes" and debated the terms "Arabic people" and

"Syrian people." By the time that the St. George Annual dinner began in 1946, it was simply and clearly "Lebanese."[23]

To some extent, "Lebanese" was a new and significant manner of expressing one's identity to the outside world. In another way, it also became a way of seeing oneself in a stream of tradition larger than that of "religion, family and place of origin." "Lebanese" identity could serve as a vehicle for being part of a tradition of an Arab-speaking, Christian people with a "Western" and not an "Arab" or "Oriental" orientation. This self-identification, while expanding identity beyond the village and leadership ties, did little to create a broader "Middle Eastern" identity.

It did, in fact, "further [divide] the Arabic speaking community," by separating "Syrians" from "Lebanese." Many Syrians, who were from what was in fact now the state of Syria, began to self-identify as "Lebanese" in order to establish their credentials as Arabic speaking Western-oriented Christians. The Christian "nationality" was becoming the "Lebanese" nationality in America. The Lebanese state was often seen as a "Western outpost" in the Middle East. As late as 1975, Yasser Arafat proclaimed that the PLO was fighting "in Lebanon [for] the preservation of the country's Arab character,"[24] implying that the Christian communities with European contacts and influences represented a "non-Arab" entity. The Western influence on Lebanese Christians was seen by Muslim Arabs in the Middle East as a further sign of their "non-Arab" identity and their possible complicity with the Western powers in designs on "Arab lands."[25] The Lebanese State was becoming a new *millet* of sorts.

Ironically, Arabic–speaking Christians living in the Middle East outside of Lebanon were among the most ardent advocates for "pan-Arabism" and "Arab Nationalism." The founder of the Syrian Baath Party, Michel Aflak, was a Christian from Damascus. In the 1940s, Aflak called upon Arabic-speaking Christians to see Islam as a "national culture," "into which Christians must assimilate until they understand and love it. They will then be devoted to Islam as to the dearest as part of their Arabism."[26] The desire to bring about a pan-Arab sympathy in the Middle East may, in fact, have stemmed from a Christian desire to lessen the emphasis on religion and thus relieve their minority status among the Muslims. The creation of the "cultural Arab," as opposed to the remnants of *millet* nationalities, would have benefited Arabic speaking Christians in particular. Cultural Arabism for the

Christian, ironically, would have involved accepting the Islamic religion as a central cultural feature of a universal, almost racial, Arab identity.

To the "Lebanese" of the United States, however, the events of the late 1960s and 1970s were again to affect the self-image of a new generation. The communities of the United States inculcated a shared sense of "Arab nationality." Michael Suleiman points out that "the media images of the war," seen as "one-sided and pro-Israel" by this "third generation of Arab immigrants," wakened them "to their own identity and to see that identity as Arab and not Syrian."[27] Prejudice experienced by those with Arabic last names inspired scholars to study a specifically "Arab" experience. This period saw the creation of national organizations to further the interests of the newly described "Arab Americans," including the American–Arab Anti–Discrimination League.[28]

The 1980s saw the pervasive chaos of the Lebanese Civil War, hostage takings, Israel's invasion of Lebanon, and many hijackings and acts of violence. Popular American views of Arabs or people of Middle Eastern descent reached a new low. Acts of violence against Arab Americans reached a record in 1985 coinciding with the hijacking of TWA Flight 847 to Beirut by Lebanese Shiite gunmen. The next milestone in anti-Arab sentiments, and a new record in violence against Arab Americans, occurred during the Gulf War from the fall of 1990 to the late winter of 1991.[29] In 1995, Adele Younis speculated

> If the assimilated Syrians, and more so the Lebanese, see themselves as stereotyped again as Arabs (unassimilated immigrants, even "terrorist") and wonder if their own fate will be negatively tied up with that of the new immigrants, then all that may tie the generations and communities together might be some romantic commitment to Arab's history, culture and the generalized hostility toward all Arabs and Arab-Americans by American culture and society.[30]

As Stevens Salaita writes, "no single event shaped the destiny of Arab-Americans more than 9/11." The community was thrust into the spotlight, "and whether an outpouring of hostility or kindness," this attention created increased self-awareness and demanded that the community "define and redefine itself daily."[31] Has the climate since 9/11, increased airport security, reports of profiling, foreign invasion, and so on, accomplished just this? Has the replacement of "international communism" with "international terrorism" and "The Cold War" with the "War on Terror" affected the development of a general Arab cultural identity among the later generation of assimilated Lebanese-Americans? The following accounts of Lebanese Christian descendants of the original immigrants from Marj'ayoun to the North American prairie west shed light on the conflicted and changing feelings of this community.

Individuals

Kayal writes that "Syrian Americans come in two varieties. One type... has risen out of a certain national or ethnic past while the other... [participates] in the institutions and history of the past."[32] This statement appears to be an oversimplification. There are, in fact, those who participate fully in the institutions of the community, and yet see a weakening of ethnicity as a positive development within the institutions themselves. Chris Farha is a third-generation Lebanese American, granddaughter of Father George Cohlmia, the priest from J'daitat Marj'ayoun who served at St. George Orthodox Church after 1935. Chris is the choir director at St. George (now Cathedral) and practices the art of Byzantine chant as well. She has been involved in restaurant and food service for most of her adult life and practitioner of the art of Lebanese cooking. Although much of her life revolves around the church community, family ties, and Lebanese-American culture, Chris could not be described as necessarily "political." Although of purely Lebanese background, she does not fit the popular physical stereotype of the "dark-skinned Arab." She finds it particularly upsetting that, although her appearance raises no difficulty in airport security, her last name does. She is, for this reason, increasingly conscious of possibly being seen as an "Arab" and yet wishes to distance herself from the description, "Arab." "Arab" for her carries connotations of "Muslim," "terrorist," and "threat." "I wish to see myself and to be seen as an American, as Lebanese and as an Orthodox Christian, and nothing broader or more inclusive than that."

Even though Chris is deeply and directly connected to the original community from J'daidat Marj'ayoun—granddaughter of an immigrant priest, director of the choir in the same parish that her grandfather served, a participant in regional and national church conferences—she feels that to be involved in the church community is more to be Orthodox and less to be Lebanese. "It is not just a matter of the number of converts in the church, but also the large number of new immigrants from the Middle East. I don't look upon them as ... fellow Syrians or Arabs but as fellow Christians with accents.

The only thing left of being Lebanese is the annual Lebanese dinner. If that ends, what else is there? Oh, and I can still cuss in Arabic."[33]

Kayal writes that as a result of accepting non-Lebanese members and English-language services and the general westernizing of this primary cultural institution, "the churches of the Syrian-Lebanese Americans will die or become altered beyond recognition...signaling the end of the Syrian-Lebanese community as we know it."[34] Chris certainly does not lack pride in her heritage nor is she removed from tradition or institutions. Nevertheless, there is an acceptance of having "risen out of a certain national or ethnic past," and no apparent desire to take on a broader sense of ethnic identity.

Chris's husband, Warren Farha, is the grandson of Neman Saleem (N.S.) Farha of J'daidet Marj'ayoun. N.S. was the nephew of Nemtallah Farha, one of the earliest immigrants to establish a business in Wichita, Kansas, allowing his extended family to follow him from Marj'ayoun. Warren is also a member of the Cathedral choir and owns an independent bookstore that specializes in literature, philosophy, and theology, particularly Eastern Christian writings. He is also deeply involved in the Orthodox faith and community. He, too, avoids the "Arab" identifier. "When I was growing up, I remember my father brisling at the term, 'Arab.' It was always used as a term of derision, along with 'camel jockey,' 'sand nigger,' and 'West Side Indian.' He always insisted on being Lebanese. Arab meant Muslim. I guess that I still have those feelings." [35] He was told frequently as a child that the Lebanese were actually Phoenicians and not Arabs. Phoenician civilization predated the Arab invasion of the seventh century and the Hellenized Semitic people of the area were early converts to Christianity. "I was told that the Phoenicians were the great traders of the Mediterranean and that we were the descendents of that culture. I do not in anyway identify as an Arab. I am Lebanese and Orthodox. My earliest and most profound memories are of Sunday afternoons at the home of my *sitti* and *jhiddi*" (Arabic for "grandmother" and "grandfather"). The warmth of family and community is one of Warren's most formative memories. The connections to family and church are what it means to him to be Lebanese. Lebanese identity flows from those primary relationships. However, for him, the fact that the Church has become an inclusive institution, bringing those of all backgrounds to the faith, is very positive and rewarding.[36]

Steve Cohlmia is also the grandson of Fr. George Cohlmia and is Chris Farha's brother. Cohlmia is also a member of the Cathedral choir and an involved church member. His attitude is similar to those of his sister and her husband; he sees himself as American, as Lebanese, as Christian, but not necessarily as an Arab. "Maybe we are insulated here in Wichita. The Lebanese community is so well established, so successful, that we are known and respected. I have been subjected to some good-natured ribbing from friends, but I don't think that we any longer experience the kind of prejudice our ancestors had to deal with." Steve does acknowledge that, in the present climate, one does feel more conscious of ethnicity: "You don't want to draw attention to yourself under the circumstances." He feels that he is unfairly singled out by airport security officials. "I guess that it is the wavy hair, the dark eyes and skin. I am stopped multiple times in the course of moving from one location within an airport and another." He sees media coverage of the Middle East, particularly of the Israeli-Palestinian conflict and the war in Iraq, as very one–sided and acknowledges that the lack of a unified Arab American voice is, in part, responsible for this situation. Cohlmia, however, continues to see Lebanese heritage as something quite separate from Arab culture, which he associates with Islam.

Ken Kallail is the grandson of Joseph and Nora Salome and Joseph and Sophia Kallail, all originally from Ayn-Arab. A sub-deacon at St. Mary Syrian Orthodox Church, Ken feels that he grew up without a strong feeling of ethnicity or separateness. "I was the youngest child, and I seem to have arrived on the other scene after such things were settled and the community was assimilated. Ken feels that he has seen some additional pressure in airports since 9/11, but that this has not been nearly as pronounced as the pressure he felt during the Iran hostage crisis from late 1979 until early 1981. As far as feelings of being Lebanese or Arab, Ken feels that he has a lot of latitude when it comes to identity. "If I am in a circumstance in which it might seem interesting to be Arab, then I am Arab. If I feel less comfortable, I can downplay 'Arab' and be Lebanese. I enjoy this flexibility." He related one story in which he met an individual while traveling on the East Coast whom he believed to be of Middle Eastern origins. Having learned that this individual, who spoke with an Arabic accent, was Lebanese, Ken said that he too was Lebanese. "The guy listened to my accent and replied, "Oh, you're an American." In contrast, Ken's wife, Ro, originally a Maronite Catholic from Massachusetts who converted to Orthodoxy, said that his grandmother, an immigrant from Sarta in northern Lebanon, "made sure that we were Lebanese. There was no mention of being 'Arab,' ever." Her grandmother's family are the Franjiyas, an Arabic name meaning "French,"a powerful, politically important Maronite family in Lebanon. While Ro has also felt that they have received more scrutiny in airports since 9/11 ("The attention I receive seems to have more to do with my last name than my appearance"), she does not feel any additional personal sense of "Arabness," a concept foreign to her upbringing.[38]

In contrast to this perception, Eric Namee sees himself as Lebanese, Orthodox, and very much an Arab. Namee, an attorney, an active member of St. Mary's Orthodox Church, and the grandson of immigrants from Ayn-Arab, believes that people who trace their origins to Arabic-speaking communities in the Middle East, Christian or Muslim, are simply Arabs. "I am proud of my Lebanese heritage, but 'Lebanese' is a sub-category of 'Arab.' The language, customs, music, dance, and food are all Arabic. Whether or not we are aware of it, when we [Orthodox Lebanese in Wichita] refer to someone as 'bint-Arab' or 'ibn-Arab' [literally 'daughter of an Arab' and 'son of an Arab'] we are acknowledging that we are, literally, Arabs." Namee's parents spoke Arabic, something unusual for their generation, and closely followed Middle Eastern political events. Namee himself is politically active and aware and follows events, particularly in Israel/Palestine very closely. He believes, as does Cohlmia, media coverage of the Israeli-Palestinian conflict is very biased against the Palestinians, and again, that lack of a unified Arab American political voice is responsible.

As a teenager, he was acutely aware of his ethnicity. "My high school was about one-third white, one-third African American and one-third Hispanic. Because of my dark skin and hair, I always felt more comfortable with the Hispanic kids. I have raised my boys to be proud of their Arab heritage. They have been confronted in school, particularly after 9/11, with racial slurs—'towel heads,' 'sand niggers,' ' camel jockeys' and have even had teachers make negative comments about Arabs; comments that my sons have gotten in trouble for confronting." Namee relates these epithets to those confronted by his parents' generation. "That generation had to fight literally. They had to defend themselves against the slurs and attacks of their fellow students; attacks against the 'West Side Indians.'"

Namee does not want his sons to back down in the face of prejudice nor will he himself avoid confrontation. Following the Oklahoma City bombing, and before it was known that Timothy McVeigh was responsible, he was confronted with anti-Arab comments in a locker room at a local gym. He was, he says, very direct and honest in saying that he himself was an Arab and that he did not appreciate the use of these stereotypes. He is often, he believes "about 80% of the time," singled out in airport security for additional scrutiny based on his appearance or his last name. "It has become kind of a joke around the office that, if I am going to fly, I am going to be stopped by security." He and fellow Lebanese friends and family swap "war stories" about being profiled because of their ethnic appearance. "[A fellow St. Mary's member], I believe it was after the first World Trade Center bombing [1993], was pulled over by the [Wichita] police based entirely on his appearance. I believe that he had a beard at the time. My cousin was flying from El Paso to Chicago shortly after flights resumed after 9/11. A couple was fooling around in the aircraft's restroom, apparently trying to join the mile-high club before the plane had even taken off. When authorities identified them as of Middle Eastern origins, they identified Joe as being of Lebanese background. He was surrounded by authorities pointing guns and removed from the plane." Namee feels that once you have shared such experiences base on a common Arab ethnicity, it is difficult not to feel a common bond based on ethnicity. Namee believes that many of his parents' generation wished to distance themselves from their Arabic origins, becoming "Lebanese" or abandoning ethnicity altogether and that this has had an effect on his generation. "It was common for my parents' generation to refer to us as 'Phoenician' and to imply that 'Lebanese' was somehow not 'Arab.' "It is very difficult for Arab Americans to have the kind of political influence that we could have, simply because we are so divided into various religious and regional identities. But the American Arab Anti-Discrimination Committee [ADC] was formed by Jim Abourezk, a Lebanese Christian."[39] When I was in law school at the University of Kansas, we organized a campus Orthodox student group. The feeling of camaraderie between Lebanese, Palestinian, Syrian, and Egyptian was based on more than religious confession; it was also shared linguistic background, heritage, culture, and food."[40]

Similarly, Ted Farha grew up assuming that he was an Arab. Ted is the grandson of Nemtallah Farha, arguably the "patriarch" of the early Wichita, Kansas community from J'daitat. Ted's father always insisted on the family's Arab heritage, and Ted grew up believing that he was a Lebanese Christian and, as such, an Arab. "My father was very aware of the situation between the Jews and the Palestinians. Regardless of religion, we identified with the Palestinians fellow Arabs." Ted has not felt increased pressure or prejudice post–9/11 other than minor incidents with airport security. "Since my hair is not as dark as it once was and since I no longer wear a beard, I do not feel as noticed as I once did. Also, Lebanese seem to me to not have the same sharp, angular features as Arabs from further east and south in the Middle East." He is not, however, necessarily opposed to profiling. "We might as well acknowledge reality; America was attacked by young Arab males. When an elderly Anglo woman is patted down at the airport I just want to yell, Hey! Come and take a look at me. My last name is Farha!"

Farha believes that the Lebanese of Wichita, Kansas, are somewhat insulated by the success they have as the result of their parents' and grandparents' efforts. "Our grandparents saw economic success as the way to fight prejudice. If we worked hard and contributed, how could we be hated?" The key to that success, according to Farha, has been the sense of family and community. "That may be the one complaint I still hear about the Lebanese community: 'They all stick together.' However, there is a certain amount of envy involved in this prejudice. Non-Lebanese would like to have this secure sense of belonging. I try to explain that there are trade-offs; you have to check your ego and, in some ways your individualism, to be part of a tight-knit group."

Farha's attitude toward the Israeli–Palestinian conflict, toward U.S. policy in the Middle East, and toward media coverage of the same is that it is biased toward Israel. "Something has to change. I have not become more involved in Arab issues, but I do feel more strongly, especially in the last few years, that something needs to be done. We are all Arabs, and if becoming more unified in our efforts is what it takes to change things, then that is what we should do."[41]

Conclusion

The individuals who have herein expressed themselves represent the views of just that: a few individuals. Even so, one can detect in their responses many of the themes of "Arabness" in America: some embracing the identity of the non-Arab Lebanese, maybe even more tightly that under circumstances of threat and suspicion; some maintaining ethnic traditions of food, dance, religious practice, and yet opening those traditions to others, all the while avoiding the Arab origins of many of those traditions; others forcefully declaring their Arab identity and passing it on to their children in the face of misunderstanding and hostility. The responses, however, are highly individualized. The American Arab Anti-Discrimination Committee cites the population figure for

Arab Americans at 3 million, estimating the percentage of Christians in the group at 77%.[42] Yvonne Yazbeck Haddad has written, "The Arab-American community as a whole both Christian and Muslim, will continue to change both in Constituency and in its forms of self-identification in the years to come... affected by the level of U.S. tolerance or intolerance... and the necessary formulation of its own responses to those feeling"[43] However, writer Adele Younis asks, "What is an Arab American? As a concept, it includes both the life experience of assimilated Syrians and those of the Moslem Palestinian émigré all at the same time? Does this number... include fourth generation, English-speaking, disassociated, mixed-breed Americans with Arab last names? If so, is this legitimate?" Younis attributes this number to the Committee's political need for numbers to affect policy. "Arab American is a new creation, a summation, reflection, and reaction to present day Middle East and American political realities. It is too inclusive."[44]

The impression drawn from these individuals, the grandchildren of immigrants from the Ottoman Empire, is that both of these writers may be correct: "Arab–American" is too inclusive and too vague a construction to handle the varieties of experiences even within one generation of one community in the western United States. For that matter, so is the term "Hispanic." The very thing that makes the term too vague, however, is also the thing that makes it necessary: America's political and social requirement for rationalized categories. If the Arab American community, such as it is, sees the need to expand its constituency in the face of continued or increasing discrimination, they may eventually, in the manner described by Haddad, create an "Arab–American" identity out of the disparate elements of what is, as of now, an incoherent and conflicted entity. Lebanese Christians, those who see themselves quite consciously as Arabs, and those who do not, often expressed dismay at lack of political power that results from fragmented ethnicity and the bias in policy and media coverage that appears to result from that lack of power. The term "Arab–American" may be too inclusive. Even as pressures in this country created "Syrian Americans" out of divergent Christian villagers coming to America, a "Lebanese American" identity, if it develops, it will develop from pressures within the United States that result from events in the Middle East.

Notes

1. For a thorough history of the origins of this community, see Kelly Caswell, "Lebanese Immigration into Wichita Kansas 1890's to 1940" (master's thesis, Wichita State University, 1996).

2. William Cleveland, *A History of the Modern Middle East* (Boulder, CO: Westview Press, 2000), 81–83.

3. Bat Ye'or, *The Dhimmi: Jews and Christians Under Islam* (London: Associated University Presses, 1985), 86–87.

4. Yvonne Y. Haddad, *The Development of Arab-American Identity*, ed. Ernest N. Marcus (Ann Arbor: University of Michigan Press, 1997), 65.

5. Ye'or, 157.

6. The Maronites claim origins as a community back to the fourth-century Archbishop Maro, but who were more likely adherents to the Monothelete doctrine (belief in Christ's two natures but one divine will) excommunicated from Orthodox worship by the Council of Constantinople in 680. The community accepted the jurisdiction of Rome in 1182, and have ever since been under the jurisdiction of the Roman Catholic Church, although following an Eastern Rite liturgy, with strong ties to France. The Maronites of Lebanon have been the most powerful Christian sect of Lebanon, instrumental, along with their French allies, in establishing Lebanon's independent, Christian status. See, *The Oxford Dictionary of the Christian Church*, ed. F. L. Cross, 2nd ed. (Oxford: Oxford University Press, 1990), and Meir Zamir, *The Formation of Modern Lebanon* (Ithaca, NY: Cornell University Press, 1985).

7. Druze, as followers of the "vanished" Fatimid caliph, al-Hakim bi' Amr Allah, derive their history from Shi'ite Islam. Considered an heretical sect by later Muslim rulers of Egypt, the Druze settled in the remote areas around Mount Lebanon in the twelfth century. The history of modern Lebanon has involved tension between Maronite Catholic and Druze power centers. For a readable but detailed history of the Druze, their practices and beliefs, see Robert Benton Betts, *The Druze* (New Haven: Yale University Press, 1988).

8. Meir Zamir, *The Formation of Modern Lebanon* (Ithaca, NY: Cornell University Press, 1985), 9–10.

9. Charles P. Issawi, *The Lebanese in the World: A Century of Emigration.* eds. Albert Hourani and Nadeem Shehadi (London: I. B. Tauris and Co. Ltd., 1992), 21–22.

10. Zamir, 1 facing page.

11. Caswell, 27.

12. Alixa Naff, *The Development of Arab-American Identity*, ed. Ernest N. McCarus (Ann Arbor: University of Michigan Press, 1997), 24.

13. Phillip M. Kayal and Joseph M. Kayal, *The Syrian-Lebanese in America: A Study in Religion and Assimilation* (Boston: Twayne Publishers, 1975), 123.

14. Naff, 25.

15. *Oklahoma* is the 1943 stage play by Richard Rocers and Oscar Hammerstein II that was made into a motion picture. See Eddie Albert's performance as Ali Hakim, the "Persian" traveling dry good peddler in, *Oklahoma*, 20th-Century Fox, 1955.

16. Caswell, 45-50.
17. Caswell, 74-75.
18. Caswell, 94-96.
19. Kayal, 113.
20. Kayal, 125.
21. Michael Suleiman, ed., *Arabs in America: Building a New Future* (Philadelphia: Temple University Press, 1999), 7.
22. Kayal, 128.
23. Caswell, 99-103.
24. Ye'or, 117.
25. Kenneth Cragg, *The Arab Christian: A History of the Middle East* (Louisville: Westminster/John Knox Press, 1991), 26.
26. Cragg, 16.
27. Suleiman, 10.
28. Haddad, 79.
29. Nabeel Abraham, *The Development of Arab-American Identity*, ed. Ernest N. McCarus (Ann Arbor: The University of Michigan Press, 1997), 161-204.
30. Adele Younis, *The Coming of the Arabic-Speaking People to the United States*. Ed. Phillip Kayal (Staten Island, NY: The Center for Immigration Studies, 1995), 253.
31. Steven Salaita, "Ethnic Identity and Imperative Patriotism: Arab Americans Before and After 9/11," *College Literature*, 33 no. 2 (2005): 151.
32. Kayal, 235.
33. Chris Farha, personal interview, October 13, 2005.
34. Kayal, 235.
35. Early Lebanese settlement in Wichita took place in the Delano neighborhood referred to as "Little Lebanon," west of the Arkansas River, leading to the epithet "West Side Indian."
36. Warren Farha, personal interview, October 19, 2005.
37. Ken Kallail, personal interview, November 13, 2005.
38. Rosemary Kallail, personal interview, November 13, 2005.
39. James Abourezk, former Senator from South Dakota, founded the ADC in 1980. The organization's web site (www.adc.org) defines Arab as 'a cultural and linguistic term,' in much the same way Namee himself does. Dr. James Zogby, also a Christian, was the Executive Director of the organization and founded the Arab American Institute in 1985.
40. Eric Namee, telephone interview, October 20, 2005.
41. Ted Farha, telephone interview, October 24, 2005.
42. www.adc.org.
43. Haddad, 84.
44. Younis, 258-59.

Works Cited

Abraham, Nabeel. *The Development of Arab-American Identity*, ed. Ernest N.McCarus. Ann Arbor: University of Michigan Press, 1997.

Caswell, Kelly. "Lebanese Immigration into Wichita Kansas 1890s to 1940." Master's thesis, Wichita State University, 1996.

Cleveland, William. *A History of the Modern Middle East*. Boulder, CO: Westview Press, 2000.

Cohmia, Steve. Personal interview, October 20, 2005.

Cragg, Kenneth. *The Arab Christian: A History of the Middle East*. Louisville: Westminster/John Knox Press, 1991.

Farha, Chis. Personal interview, October 13, 2005.

Farha, Ted. Telephone interview, October 24, 2005.

Farha, Warren. Personal interview, October 19, 2005.

Haddad, Yvonne T. *The Development of Arab-American Identity*, ed. Ernest N. McCarus. Ann Arbor: The University of Michigan Press, 1997.

Issawi, Charles P. *The Lebanese in the World: A Century of Emigration*, ed. Albert Hourani and Nadeem Shehadi. London: I.B. Tauris and Co. Ltd., 1992.

Kallail, Rosemary. Personal interview, November 13, 2005.

Kayal, Phillip M., and Joseph M. Kayal. *The Syrian-Lebanese in America: A Study in Religion and Assimilation*. Boston: Twayne Publishers, 1997.

Ken, Rosemary. Personal interview, November 13, 2005.

Namee, Eric. Telephone interview, October 20, 2005.

Salaita, Steven. "Ethnic Identity and Imperative Patriotism: Arab Americans Before and After 9/11." *College Literature*, 33 no. 2 (2005): 146-68.

Suleiman, Michael, ed. *Arabs in America: Building a New Future*. Philadelphia: Temple University Press, 1999.

Ye'or, Bat. *The Dhimmi: Jew and Christians under Islam*. London: Associated University Presses, 1985.

Younis, Adele. *The Coming of the Arabic-Speaking People to the United States*, ed. Phillip Kayal. Staten Island, NY: The Center for Immigration Studies, 1995.

Zamir, Meir. *The Formation of Modern Lebanon*, Ithaca, NY: Cornell University Press, 1985.

5

Stereotypes, Popular Culture, and School Curricula: How Arab American Muslim High School Students Perceive and Cope with Being the "Other"

Nader Ayish

Arab American Muslims are one of the least understood ethnic and religious groups in the United States.[1] To many Americans, Arabs and Islam seem alien and shrouded in mystery. Similar to other minority groups in America, Arab American Muslims are frequent targets of negative stereotypes and discrimination. In contrast to many other minority groups, though, the stereotypical image of Arabs and Muslims remains overtly negative and pervasive throughout society. Few positive images counter these negative stereotypes.

In 2003, I conducted a study on Arab American Muslim high school students and how they perceive and cope with stereotypes in order to provide educators, researchers, policy makers, and society with insight into how best to meet the needs of these students. The study consisted of three groups of participants; first, five Arab American Muslim high school students; second, one parent for each student; and third, one teacher for each student. The five students selected to participate were chosen because they were second-generation Americans (i.e., born and raised in the United States); they self-identified as Arab Muslim or Arab American Muslim; they had intact families in which both parents were from the same Arab country (i.e., Egypt, Iraq, Lebanon, Palestine, or Saudi Arabia); and they were either in eleventh or twelfth grade at the time of the study. Because of the way their cultures and religion are portrayed in popular culture and in school curricula, these Arab American Muslim high school students report feeling disconnected from school, peers, and society.

Statement of the Problem

The effect stereotypes have on individuals is well documented (e.g., lower self-esteem, self-concept, self-perception, and academic performance).[2] Over the past few decades, scholarship on this topic has expanded to include not only concern with African American student achievement, but a greater recognition of other ethnic groups in the United States.[3] However, despite the attention now given to the growing ethnic diversity in the United States, some populations, such as Arab Americans Muslim students, remain insufficiently researched.

As a relatively new immigrant group, the education and social adjustments of Arab Americans has received less scholarly attention than other ethnic groups.[4] This oversight is striking because Arab Americans today are one of the fastest-growing ethnic groups in major metropolitan areas, and distinct immigration patterns have produced an internally diverse community whose attitudes and behaviors vary by nativity, social class, religion, and culture. For example, Arab Americans are comprised of both Christians and Muslims, approximately two-thirds were born in the United States, and 36% (almost double the national average) hold a bachelor's degree or higher.[5]

Arab American Muslim students, unlike many other minorities, have not been studied as a group with historic ties to the United States. In fact, in research studies, Arab American Muslim students are almost always treated as foreign students wherein these studies typically focus on adjustment problems.[6] Consequently, their educational needs and social experiences are less known and less understood. This reality has placed an unnecessary burden on schools to adequately meet the needs of this group and on Arab American Muslim parents to ameliorate this lack of research and understanding.

Background of the Problem

Arabs, like other ethnically, racially, and socially stigmatized groups in America, are frequent targets of negative stereotypes and discrimination.[7] However, in contrast to many other ethnic and racial groups, the stereotypical image of Arabs remains overtly negative and pervasive throughout society. Few positive images counter these negative stereotypes.[8] Indeed, according to numerous researchers, Arabs remain the only ethnic group routinely vilified, caricatured, and disparaged in film, the media, and popular culture.[9] While Hollywood's portrayal of women and select ethnic and racial groups has evolved, e.g., *Norma Rae* (1979) and *Dances with Wolves* (1990), its portrayal of

Arabs remains the notorious "other."[10]   Ironically, in an age of political correctness, it is still acceptable to malign Arabs, as evidenced by any number of recent Hollywood films, e.g., *The Siege* (1998) and *Rules of Engagement* (2000). Indeed, according to Alvarez, "the culture for which Hollywood has shown its greatest contempt has been the [Arab or] Middle East culture."[11]

There are many reasons why Arab and Muslim stereotypes remain pervasive in contemporary American society. Although some of the circumstances that have contributed to these stereotypes will be provided, this chapter focuses instead on how five Arab American Muslim high school students perceive and cope with such stereotypes. Here it is important to note, for the purposes of this discussion, that the terms *Arab American* and *Arab American Muslim* are used interchangeably. This reflects the inaccurate but popular perception among many typical Americans (and perpetuated in popular culture) that Arab Americans—irrespective of their religious affiliation—are the same.

Unfortunately, despite finding numerous studies on stereotypes, little has been written about the effect stereotypes have on Arab Americans in general or, in particular, the problems confronting Arab American Muslim children while attending school. In fact, I discovered little research in my search for literature about Arab American Muslim children in K–12 education. A few studies have examined the general school experience of Arab American children, but I found no studies that explicitly investigated the effect stereotypes have on these children or how Arab American Muslim children cope with stereotypes. [12] What I find most disconcerting about the paucity of research on Arab Americans, however, is that at a time when historically disenfranchised groups are demanding fair and accurate representation and inclusion of their culture in society and in school curricula, the voices of Arab Americans remain unheard. Even multicultural education, which has elevated the voices of many marginalized groups, has not managed to overcome the negative consequences of exclusion and isolation experienced by Arab Americans. Consequently, the perception that Arab Americans are somehow different from other Americans continues to be inevitably nurtured and reinforced.

Furthermore, given how much negative attention Arabs receive in popular culture it is ironic that society in general—and researchers in particular—seem to have little interest in better understanding this group. Even in school curricula, it has been shown that information about Arabs, if mentioned at all, is likely to be negative and stereotypical.[13] More often than not, accurate information about the rich cultural traditions and important historical contributions (e.g., numerals, mathematics, medicine, architecture, and astrology) Arabs and Muslims made to civilization is excluded from curricula. For example, history and geography textbooks typically represent the Middle East in terms of deserts, camels, and nomads.[14] Indeed, as Shaheen noted, Arabs are "hardly ever seen as ordinary people, practicing law, driving taxis, singing lullabies or healing the sick."[15] Unfortunately, the cumulative effect of such omissions on the academic experience, academic performance, and self-perception of Arab American students is not known.

However, it is known that recognizing and incorporating students' culture, history, and heritage into education is important to students' academic and social success and social identity.[16] As Rich asserted, when "someone with the authority of a teacher" compels a student to conclude that the society in which he or she lives has no public presence, such an experience can generate "a moment of psychic disequilibrium, as if you looked into a mirror and saw nothing."[17] The fact that we do not know how Arab American Muslim children are affected by a lack of inclusion or accurate representation of their culture, history, and religion in education reflects a serious gap in the research on this group. It is also known that certain attitudes individuals holds toward their own ethnicity may affect their degree and quality of involvement with their culture, religion, and heritage.[18] This degree of involvement in one's own ethnicity is seen to be strongly influenced by the view the dominant culture has of one's ethnic group.[19] Erikson and Tajfel point out that individuals from a minority group may internalize the negative views of the dominant society, thereby developing a negative self-perception and identity. [20] These researchers offer insight into the importance of understanding how individuals are affected by the way they perceive themselves represented in society. In the case of Arab American Muslim high school students, the acceptance or rejection of their culture by the larger society and the wide cultural gap between many Arab American Muslims and other Americans affects how these students form their identity and relate to their Arab cultural heritage.[21]

Stereotyping, Teachers, Arabs, and Muslims

A "stereotype" is a duplicate metal printing plate cast from a mold from which the printed image is repeatedly reproduced.[22] As a concept, the term *stereotype* was first used by Lippmann (1922) to refer to beliefs about groups. He defined stereotypes as generalizations about social groups that are rigidly held, illogically derived, and negative. He also described stereotypes as "pictures in our heads," which constituted "erroneous representations acquired other than through direct experience of the reality they claim to represent."[23] Despite Lippmann's research, it has only recently been established that most devaluing group stereotypes are known throughout society.[24] Many researchers, however, now agree with Devine (1989) that because communicative processes (such as public discourse, popular culture, and school curricula) play such a central role in the acquisition of stereotypes, knowledge of cultural stereotypes is shared by people regardless of one's level of prejudice—including those being stereotyped.[25] Therefore, it is worth noting that all three groups of participants in this study (students, parents, and teachers) are likely to be aware of the same stereotypes about Arabs and Muslims that are generally known throughout society.

It is also worth noting that teachers, while not necessarily prejudiced against Arabs and Muslims, are nevertheless aware of and affected by the kinds of stereotypes that exist about this group. However, while the field of social psychology, in particular, has surveyed the content of stereotypes, examined their effect on social perception and behavior, examined motivational bases of prejudice, and, along with personality psychologists, examined the origins of prejudice, surprisingly little research has been conducted on discrimination on the part of individual teachers.[26] In light of the fact that stereotyping is often described as one of the most fundamental psychological processes that determine the course of social relations, and, considering the inherently personal and intimate nature of teaching, the fact that we do not know how stereotyping by teachers of various ethnic and religious groups affects these groups (such as Arab American Muslim students) suggests a serious gap in our understanding of stereotypes.[27]

Although stereotype research during the 1920s, 1930s, and 1940s did not include Arabs or Muslims, the image of an Arab or Muslim can nevertheless be gleaned from news accounts and film images from that time. For example, according to several researchers, the image of the Arab during the early part of the twentieth century was that embodied by Rudolph Valentino as he appeared in the movie *The Sheikh* (1921).[28]   Arabs were seen as "exotic desert dwellers," "brute savages," and "lecherous sheikhs" out to harm the dashing Western hero and to seduce the fair Western heroine, while all but ignoring—

or worse, enslaving—the hoards of nameless, faceless, and oppressed Arab women.[29] This "picture in our heads" remained intact throughout the 1920s and 1930s and shaped an entire generation's image of Arabs and Muslims.

Importantly, as Shaheen revealed, unlike stereotypes for some ethnic groups, this stereotype has neither been eliminated nor replaced.[30] Instead, it has been altered—with varying modification—only to be recycled and resurrected in countless other films.[31] As one movie producer recently explained, the image of the Arab is a "ready-made stereotype" just waiting to be tapped.[32] Thus, Arab and Muslim stereotypes serve a dual purpose—they are easily recognized by viewers with little or no prompting, and they are ready-made, not requiring much thought on the part of scriptwriters and producers.[33]

Given the nature of stereotype research in the early 1900s and considering that the Arab and Muslim American population at the time was relatively small, it is not surprising that Arabs and Muslims were overlooked. After all, immigration officials were just beginning to recognize Arabs as citizens of distinct nations. What is revealing, however, is that despite the increased number and visibility of Arab and Muslim Americans today, despite the growth of stereotype research into virtually every aspect of human interaction, and despite the September 11, 2001, tragedy, Arabs and Muslims remain relatively excluded from such research.[34]

Persistence of Stereotypes

Allport was aware of one process that could account for the persistence of stereotypes. He used the term *refencing* to describe the strong tendency displayed by people to appraise disconfirming behavior as being performed by exceptions in the group.[35] He also suggested that judging individuals to be atypical and not representative members of a group offers an effective strategy to maintain preexisting beliefs. Other researchers have since confirmed his findings.[36]

This notion of refencing offers insight into why certain stereotypes about Arabs and Muslims persist despite efforts to alter them. Indeed, attempts to mitigate Arab and Muslim stereotypes by providing Americans with opportunities to interact with Arabs and Muslims have been met with little success.[37] Research conducted by Naber and Shaheen suggests that until a fundamental shift occurs in the environment in which such stereotypes are created, nurtured, and sustained (i.e., in popular culture and school curricula), overcoming the effects of refencing by simply increasing contact between Arab and Muslim Americans and other Americans will not be sufficient to alter negative Arab and Muslim stereotypes.[38]

Unfortunately, although researchers have investigated the effect of disconfirming evidence relative to a number of groups (e.g., African Americans, Hispanics, and women) no such comparable research exists for Arab and Muslim Americans.[39] This lack of research suggests once again that important researchers like such as Allport did not think that Arab and Muslim Americans were important enough to single out as victims of stereotypes.[40] Despite this lack of research, however, it is apparent that in the face of Allport's notion of disconfirming evidence, Arab and Muslim stereotypes have remained fundamentally the same.[41] Although Arab and Muslim stereotypes have taken on a variety of forms over the years, there is no research evidence to indicate that these stereotypes have either changed in the sense that a particular stereotype has evolved from negative to positive—as in the case of German and Japanese stereotypes before and after World War II—or that they have been eliminated altogether—as in the case of African Americans and the common perception during the 1930s that they were superstitious.[42]

Recent research offers an explanation as to why certain stereotyped groups (e.g., African Americans, Jews, Arabs, and Muslims) seem to persist and resist change over time. According to Schaller and Schaller and Conway, some ethnic groups are more likely to be talked about than others.[43] While there are many reasons why these ethnic groups figure more prominently in conversations (e.g., visual appearance and dress, religious differences, and population size), it has been determined that the way people talk about others has a causal effect on stereotyping.[44] In other words, the more traits are discussed, the more likely they are to be stereotypical. Furthermore, those traits that are most discussed are also most likely to become and remain part of the popular stereotypes of ethnic groups.[45]

In the case of Arabs and Muslims, Hollywood's reliance on the traditional Arab kafeeya (checkered headdress) as an instantly recognizable symbol to identify an Arab character (despite the fact that the vast majority of Arabs do not wear kafeeyas) is an example of a visual appearance and dress that contributes to the maintenance of a stereotype that has become indelibly linked to Arabs. Not surprisingly, it has been shown that unfavorable traits are more likely than favorable traits to emerge in the stereotypes of ethnic minorities—especially in groups that are less populous and that seem more foreign.[46]

Thus, traits that are identified as being stereotypical are likely to remain stereotypical for an extended period, especially if the traits are part of an ongoing conversation about an ethnic group. Arabs and Muslims and their images and stereotypes have been an integral part of Hollywood, popular culture, and even school curricula for decades. Therefore, given that people regularly think or talk about Arabs and Muslims and their accompanying traits and stereotypes, it makes sense that Arab and Muslim stereotypes remain alive more than the stereotypes for other groups that receive less attention.

For example, one common stereotype about Arabs and Muslims that has existed for the last 100 years in film is that of the oppressed Arab and Muslim women.[47] This stereotype has been perpetuated in film, popular culture, and even school curricula to such an extent that many Americans are convinced that the stereotype is accurate. It slips into conversation as a fact known to all rather than as a practice limited to certain cultures and traditions.

The hijjab or headscarf is the most visible manifestation of this stereotype. While many Americans may identify with the stereotypical view that the hijjab is oppressive to women, the fact that most Arab and Muslim women perceive the hijjab as a cultural, religious, and even liberating garment is lost.[48] The point is that many Americans speak about the hijjab as an example of Arab and Muslim female oppression. That the hijjab is talked about at all by individuals with otherwise little accurate knowledge of Arabs and Islam illustrates the notion that the more stereotypes are communicated, the more likely they are to remain intact.

Given the lack of inclusion of Arabs and Muslims in stereotype research, it is necessary to look elsewhere for evidence of such stereotypes. In this regard, examining once again how Arabs and Muslims have been depicted in film over the years can be illuminating. Indeed, it was recognized early on that film was the most powerful tool to shape people's understanding of others. Following World War I and the lessons learned from producing war propaganda, for example, the head of Paramount Pictures claimed that "as an avenue of propaganda, as a channel for conveying thought and opinion, the movies are unequaled by any form of communication."[49]

Three phases of Arab and Muslim stereotypes in film have developed over the years.[50] While each phase is distinct in many ways, all three share much in common. The Arab and Muslim male stereotype emanating from Hollywood early in the twentieth century was that of "stooges-in-sheets, slovenly, hook-nosed potentates intent on capturing pale-faced blondes for their harems."[51] Women were portrayed as "bosomy belly dancers leering out from diaphanous veils" or as "scantly clad harem maidens with bare midriffs, closeted in the palace's women's quarters."[52] Movies such as *The Sheikh* (1921) and *The Arab* (1924), are representative of the type of genre that emanated from Hollywood at the time. Although it is worth acknowledging that Hollywood did not necessarily create these stereotypes, but rather inherited them from British and French colonial literature and propaganda, film is nevertheless responsible for making these stereotypes more widely known to American audiences.[53]

The second phase of Arab stereotypes took shape after the Arab–Israeli war of 1948. It incorporated many of the stereotypes from the first phase, but it developed its own characteristics. Arabs and Muslims came to be seen as terrorists out to kill Americans, Europeans, Israelis, and even other Arabs.[54] The 1967 Arab–Israeli war contributed to the widespread image of this genre in films produced to this day.

The third phase of Arab and Muslim stereotypes in film came about after the 1973 Arab oil embargo. This phase incorporated a familiar image but with new, more sinister overtones in which oily-sheikh billionaires, invariably sporting sunglasses and goatees, were out to buy up America.[55] During this phase, this stereotype evolved further by incorporating elements from earlier phases. Arabs and Muslims came to be seen as fundamentalist terrorists, identifiable by particular garb (i.e., kafeeyas), still coveting the blond Western heroine, but now seeking to dominate all that is valued in Western civilization or destroy all that cannot be dominated.[56] Thus, all of the original stereotypes of Arabs and Muslims remain, albeit, in some cases in slightly different form, ready to be resurrected whenever they are needed. As United States foreign policy tilted even more in favor of Israel, the stereotypes of Arabs and Muslims, with few exceptions, evolved into that of fundamentalist terrorists.[57]

It cannot be denied, though, that some Arabs and Muslims have committed horrible acts of terrorism. The problem, however, is that the "picture in our heads" of these small groups or organizations have come to represent 300 million Arabs and 1.3 billion Muslims.[58] Discourse among Arab and Muslim Americans and other Americans is dominated by the images and the acts of these few Arabs and Muslims, complicating the ability of Arab and Muslim Americans to be understood and accurately portrayed. This attitude has been reinforced since September 11, 2001.

Fein and Spencer argued that because stereotypes are likely to be a salient and particularly effective means for people to restore a threatened self-image, stereotyping others might be a common way for people to maintain a positive image of themselves. In the context of America's relationship with Arabs and Islam, this could partly explain why Arabs and Muslims continue to be so heavily stereotyped despite the trend toward more accurate and sympathetic portrayals of ethnic, racial, and religious groups in popular culture and school curricula. Given the historic tension between Arabs/Muslims and the West (especially since the 1940s), stereotypes of Arabs and Muslims serve to enhance the West's perception of cultural, political, and economic superiority over Arabs and Muslims.[59]

With regard to the subject of this study, because Arab American Muslim students are likely to be aware of the same stereotypes about Arabs and Muslims that are prevalent in society, an added layer of burden is often placed on them to cope with these stereotypes. While we do not know what effect such knowledge has on Arab American Muslim students, we do know how other groups are affected by being aware of stereotypes.

For example, significant research has been done on African American students, girls, and gender differences. It has been shown that because of stereotype threat, African American students perform worse on exams when they are made aware of a stereotype about their academic ability.[60] It has also been shown that some girls in middle and high school perform worse in math and science when they experience stereotype threat. If our understanding of the effects of stereotype threat on African American students and on girls is any indication, the effect of stereotypes on Arab American Muslim students will also be detrimental.

For the purposes of this discussion, therefore, a stereotype will be regarded as "a representation of a culture which teaches that the people of that culture are by nature inferior."[61] This definition best reflects the type of stereotype confronting Arabs and Muslims in America and also echoes Allport's notion of refencing.[62] After all, the most prevalent type of stereotype confronting Arabs and Muslims is one that contends that Arabs and Muslims possess inherently flawed characteristics (e.g., fundamentalist, oppressive, womanizer, greedy, unsophisticated, and violent) and that nothing on their part can be done to alter this condition.[63]

The consequences of such false conclusions can be detrimental for both individuals and groups. For instance, while it is true that a small number of

Arabs are fabulously wealthy and derive their wealth from oil, the truth is that most Arabs are, in fact, relatively poor. Over time, the effect of such an erroneous stereotype can adversely affect people's understanding of Arabs and Muslims and negatively influence American domestic, economic, and foreign policies.[64]

In the Students' Own Words: Emergent Themes

Two broad themes emerged as I analyzed the data.[65] The first theme, context, includes three sub-themes that describe the environment in which students perceive and cope with stereotypes:

> 1. Curricula: How the students perceive and cope with stereotypes associated with the inclusion or exclusion of Arabs, Islam, and Arab Americans in the curricula.
> 2. Accommodations: How the students react to the types of accommodations made (or not made) by teachers and administrators to meet their cultural and religious needs.
> 3. Post-September 11: How the students address stereotypes associated with the events of September 11 and its aftermath, thereby asserting their pride as Arab American Muslims.

The second theme, coping, includes two sub-themes that reveal the way in which students cope with stereotypes:

> 1. Joke: How the students turn stereotypes into jokes or perceive them as jokes in order to defuse tense or uncomfortable situations. Incidents of stereotyping are often euphemistically labeled as *jokes*.
> 2. Educate: How the students try to educate the stereotyper (when possible) about Arabs, Islam, and Arab Americans in order to bring about a change in the source.

These broad themes and sub-themes are shared by all student participants and presented through their words, perspectives, and experiences. Due to space limitations, however, only a limited number of student quotes are included here.

Context

The way student participants perceive and cope with stereotypes varies according to the circumstances—or context—in which the incident occurred. For instance, the way Arab ethnicity, culture, and Islam are portrayed in school, the school curricula, and the larger society (through popular culture) have a profound influence on the way students perceive and cope with stereotypes. While commonalties exist among all five of these students, there have been particular incidents in which they behaved in a unique fashion.

Nevertheless, although these student participants perceive and cope with stereotypes in a variety of ways, one essential factor affects them: the perceived intent of the stereotyper. According to these students, a stereotyper can be either a friend, an acquaintance, or a stranger. While each type of stereotyper possesses numerous characteristics, the most critical factor is the stereotyper's intent.

For example, only when a friend stereotypes does a student participant seem to automatically perceive the stereotype as nothing more than "just a joke" or "just an ignorant comment," to take no offense, and to respond in kind by "giving it back," all the while trying to educate and inform the stereotyper. Generally, it appears that the student seems to assume no malicious intent on the part of friends who stereotype.

Where the intent of a stereotyper (either an acquaintance or a stranger) is perceived to be innocent and harmless, the student participant typically considers the stereotyper to be simply "uninformed," "ignorant," and/or in need of "enlightenment." Instead of taking offense, the student tends to see such incidents of stereotyping as opportunities to "represent Arabs and Islam" in the best possible light. In these situations, the student usually attempts to educate and inform the stereotyper by explaining how he or she is misguided, misinformed, or just "clueless."

An experience encountered by Nabil, one of the student participants, exemplifies such situations. Recalling comments made by classmates about his religious obligation to fast during the holy month of Ramadan, Nabil said:

> They always make the same ignorant comments every year—like, "That's crazy that you starve yourself" and "If you eat lunch, nobody's going to find out." They just don't get why we're supposed to fast and pray, so I have to explain over and over to them. I mean, I get tired of explaining all the time, but I guess it's okay as long as they listen. It's important to show them what we believe.

If, however, the student participant perceives any malice on the part of the stereotyper (either an acquaintance or a stranger), the student often takes offense at the stereotype, reacts in a way that confronts the offending stereotyper, and asserts his or her pride in Islam, Arab culture, or both. In this situation, the desire to educate the stereotyper takes on less immediate importance as the student is forced to defend himself or herself in the face of what is perceived to be an unacceptable attack.

Maya's experience shows one example of how these students cope with situations in which stereotypers are perceived to harbor malicious intent. During a class debate she feels compelled to confront her classmates:

> They were insulting my religion and my background, so I answered back. And I did what I didn't mean to do, which is I insulted them. Like, when I talk back and answer, I try not to be disrespectful to that person. And, you know, I was disappointed in myself because I got so mad that I insulted them and their religion. Which is not what I was aiming to do.

Maya reveals part of the dilemma these student participants face. On the one hand, they feel compelled to defend their culture and religion when confronted by their peers' intent on stereotyping them and causing them harm. On the other hand, standing up to their peers can cause student participants to feel bad about themselves because they end up treating others in the same way they were treated. As Maya's example illustrates, this reaction is a potential burden that can weigh heavily on these students because a student may inadvertently compound the negative consequences of the very stereotype he or she is trying to address.

What is particularly noteworthy about this incident is that, in the end, Maya attempts to educate and inform these individuals about Arabs and Islam—despite her strong feelings about the stereotypers and their intent. This is a consistent reaction among student participants, and it suggests that they understand that unless they act to correct or change such beliefs, stereotypes about Arabs, Muslims, and Arab Americans will persist.

Student participants also perceive stereotypes coming from the larger society (e.g., popular culture), and in these cases, they often cope differently. Here, they may not only perceive stereotypes as being directed at Arabs or Muslims generally, but may also feel less capable to deal with such stereotypes because they cannot readily confront the stereotyper.

Indeed, while these student participants cited numerous instances when they perceived Arabs and Muslims being stereotyped—in film, for instance, only Basil and Lina reacted (and only on two occasions) by writing letters of protest to the directors of these films. Unfortunately, neither Basil nor Lina received replies to their letters, leading them to conclude that there "isn't much you can do" to change "these kinds of stereotypes." In such instances, students tend to simply acknowledge the hurtfulness of these hackneyed images, but then dismiss them as "unfair" and "not true"—a quick and efficient way of coping with stereotypes that are perceived to be difficult to address directly.

Curricula

Student participants must contend with curricula that they perceive neither adequately includes nor properly reflects their culture or religion. These students perceive the lack of inclusion of their culture and of their religion in the curricula as an indication that their school neither recognizes nor respects an important part of their identity. This affects their sense of place in school and adds an undue burden with which they must contend as they attempt to balance the social and academic demands of growing up Arab American and Muslim in the United States.

What students perceive to be a lack of inclusion of their culture and religion is, in fact, an absence of their culture and religion in textbooks and other curricula.[66]   What is significant about this finding is not the fact that these five Arab American Muslim high school students generally do not see themselves in the curricula. Rather, it is the fact that research reveals that when students do not see themselves reflected in the curricula, numerous negative consequences may result—including lower self-esteem, lower self-perception, and decreased academic achievement.[67] It is unfortunate, therefore, that teachers, administrators, and policy makers have not adequately addressed the lack of Arab and Muslim material in school curricula.

The fact that Arab culture and Islam is not adequately incorporated into the curricula has several important implications for students, parents, and teachers. Three specific steps are required to overcome the challenges posed by this finding. The first two steps, while "commonsensical," are necessary to establish a solid foundation upon which the third step can be implemented.

The first step requires that the frequency with which Arabs, Arab Americans, and Islam appear in textbooks and other curricular material should be substantially increased. After all, many Americans neither accurately nor adequately know about Arabs, Arab Americans, or Islam. In addition, textbooks and other curricular material should be rewritten and updated to reflect more accurately and more fully information about Arabs, Arab Americans, and Islam.[68] Excellent curricular and supplementary material has been produced recently that could greatly enhance the relevancy and effectiveness of material used in schools.[69]

Second, Arab Americans and Muslims should be integrated in the study of American history. Like other ethnic and religious groups that contributed to America's "salad bowl," Arab and Muslim Americans are an integral part of the American experience—and that experience should be reflected in the study of American history.[70] Countless opportunities to include the contributions of Arab and Muslim Americans in the curricula exist—from science and education to politics and entertainment. The continued exclusion of Arab and Muslim Americans from the study of American history only contributes to the perception that these groups are not part of what it means to be an American.[71] This exclusion is just one more layer of burden with which Arab American Muslim children must cope as they go through school.

Third, a shift should occur from an emphasis on understanding the Islamic faith (e.g., the five pillars of Islam) to understanding Arab society (e.g., the people, culture, and history). As all five student participants noted, they have repeatedly studied the five pillars of Islam. However, they have not studied the people who actually practice Islam or the customs, traditions, or history that stem from that practice. Studying the rich mosaic that makes up Arab society and history—which includes Islam—would enhance student understanding of not only Islam but also the millions of people who practice it.[72]

Finally and most importantly, in order to ensure that all of the new material produced and provided to schools is integrated fully into the overall curricula, state standardized tests (such as Virginia's Standards of Learning [SOL]) and county curricula guides must increase the number of questions dealing with Arabs, Arab Americans, and Islam. Given that high-profile and high-stakes standardized tests often drive what is actually taught in schools (irrespective of what some school systems claim they teach), including more questions about these groups and Islam will greatly enhance the likelihood that teachers actually expose students to more meaningful information about Arabs, Arab Americans, and Islam.

The potential benefits to students, parents, and teachers of implementing these three steps are tremendous. For instance, the general student population would become better informed about this important area of the world; students and, eventually, the general United States public would hopefully become more tolerant and open-minded. In addition, student participants would finally see themselves more fully and accurately represented in curricula. This would certainly contribute to a more welcoming school environment and would likely increase the feelings of inclusion and connection among Arab American Muslim students.

For parents, shifting the burden of having to constantly overcome the lack of accurate information about Arabs, Arab Americans, and Islam in curricula could free them to focus on other aspects of their children's academic experience. Like their children, these parents are tired of the constant need to address incidents of stereotyping. The issue for parents, essentially, is a matter of opportunity cost. As Basil's father explained, he would prefer to dedicate his time and energy to building up his children, rather than spending what little time and energy he has in "deflecting the punches and blows" that inevitably come his children's way due to prejudice and stereotyping.

For teachers, not only would they have access to more accurate and comprehensive material dealing with Arabs, Arab Americans, and Islam, but incorporating this material into their lesson plans would mean that an otherwise marginalized group of students would feel included and valued. This could contribute to an increase in Arab American Muslim student involvement in school and could even lead to higher academic achievement.

Finally, misunderstanding and tension among some Christians, Muslims, and Jews could potentially be reduced.[73] A more informed and educated student population could eventually lead to a more informed and enlightened adult population in which historic and religious differences among Christians, Muslims, and Jews are addressed with mutual respect and understanding.

Accommodations

Student participants frequently cope with a lack of adequate accommodations in their schools. Existing accommodations are perceived as inadequate and reluctantly implemented. This situation, perceived or real, only contributes to the sense that the students' culture and religion is not respected, understood, or recognized. Indeed, participants gave numerous examples that depicted the few accommodations made by teachers and administrators as "too little, too late." This belief weighs heavily on these students and is reflected in the words they use to describe their experiences in school.

Accommodating the needs of Arab American Muslim students remains an ongoing process. Basil, however, illustrates that schools can successfully reform both formal and informal curricula in order to meet at least some of the needs of Arab American Muslim students. For instance, he provided several examples where Madison High School creatively accommodated the needs of Muslim students—to the apparent satisfaction of these students, their parents, and Muslim community members. Thus, Basil's experience with accommodations indicates that meeting at least some of the needs of Arab American Muslim students is possible under the right circumstances, and, therefore, several steps should be taken. Ideally these steps should occur concurrently, however, because of the lack of accommodations currently, it might be more effective and practical to introduce them gradually.

Ultimately, the key to successfully implementing these steps is to use as a model—and as a justification—the efforts of other ethnic and religious groups who have managed to bring about appropriate accommodations for their own needs in school. In particular, examining how the Jewish community has successfully managed to incorporate their religious and cultural traditions and practices in the schools would serve Arab American Muslims well.

Muslims and Jews share many of the same beliefs and practices and similar historic school experiences. Indeed, Jews in the past experienced, like many Arab American Muslims today, some of the same challenges posed by a lack of inclusion and proper accommodations of their cultural and religious needs. What is most important is that the religious and cultural traditions of both groups tend to occur outside of the times set aside to celebrate Christian religious and cultural traditions. The fact that many Jewish religious and cultural needs have been accommodated in school with little apparent disruption to the functioning of the school suggests that the same could be done for Muslim religious and cultural needs and practices.

For example, including the dates of major Islamic holidays and celebrations, such as Ramadan, Eid al Adha, and Eid al Fitr, on school calendars could easily be accomplished. Indeed, this has already been done in some school districts across the country. Incorporating these dates in the planning of major tests and school activities could contribute to a sense among Arab American Muslim students that their celebrations, similar to those for Christians and Jews, are recognized and valued. At a minimum, Arab American Muslim students who wish to celebrate their holidays should have their absences from school excused without penalty. This could reduce the kind of tension that often arises when Arab American Muslim students perceive a lack of sensitivity to their needs.

Finally, integrating the recognition of these holidays and traditions across the curricula as they occur throughout the year would be more relevant and meaningful than designating a distinct month (such as Hispanic or African American Awareness Month) for that purpose. Doing so would remind students that Arab and Muslim religious and cultural practices are an integral part of society rather than a distinct phenomenon to be thought of only at certain times of the year.

In terms of prayer accommodations, teachers and administrators could follow the example set at one high school—with one important caveat. The school could provide time on Friday for a meditation or reflection session, not a prayer session, to accommodate all religions, as well as students who do not belong to an organized religion. So long as meditation or reflection sessions are led by students, concerns regarding the separation of church and state will have been appropriately addressed. Designating a room for such purposes could go a long way in helping religiously observant Muslims feel that their needs are being appropriately met.

Such an accommodation would take approximately twenty minutes out of a Muslim student's schedule. To minimize classroom disruptions, those students wishing to meditate or reflect could do so during their designated lunchtime. However, given that there are typically several lunch periods in a large high school, more than one session would likely need to be held in order to accommodate all of the students wishing to participate.

Implementing these accommodations would contribute greatly to the perceptions among Arab American Muslim students that genuine efforts by teachers and administrators are being made to meet the students' reasonable cultural and religious needs. This would have the added benefit of making these students feel more valued and included in the school. Parents would also find that many of their concerns would be alleviated regarding the lack of cultural and religious recognition and the lack of accommodations made by the school.

The Effects of September 11, 2001, on Arab American Muslim High School Students

The period after September 11, 2001, has created an additional context within which students perceive and cope with stereotypes. Although the aftermath of this tragic event has been difficult on these students, they see September 11 as just one disastrous incident (albeit the most harmful) among many with which

Arab American Muslims have had to contend. Ironically, students did not report personally experiencing any new discrimination in the aftermath of September 11. Instead, the kinds of stereotypes (and the students' feelings associated with those stereotypes) that existed before September 11 were simply magnified and compounded.

One surprising finding is that after September 11, these students have come to identify more strongly with being Arab American Muslim. Before September 11, they were as likely to identify with their national origin (i.e., Egyptian, Iraqi, Lebanese, Palestinian, or Saudi Arabian) as they were with the more generic term *Arab American*. Unfortunately, due to the way the media, the government, and others have portrayed those responsible for the September 11 attacks (i.e., referring to them simply as "Arab" and "Muslim" instead of making it clear that they constitute a small radical fringe group with profoundly little support throughout the Arab and Muslim world [despite what we constantly hear in the media] and not as nationals from particular countries) students feel that they too have been transformed from being perceived as Egyptian, Iraqi, Lebanese, Palestinian, or Saudi Arabian Americans in the eyes of many Americans to collectively and generically being labeled "Arab" and "Muslim." Thus, any distinctions that may have existed among these nationalities prior to September 11 have been subsumed by the desire of some people to reduce them all to being just "Arab" or "Muslim." Ironically, this has made these students feel the need to identify even more strongly with each other as Arab American Muslims.

The consequences of this perception for students are many. In particular, they now feel the sting of stereotypes more broadly. Now, when an Arab or Muslim is stereotyped, these students, irrespective of their national origin, feel that they personally are being stereotyped. This treatment has added to their level of anxiety about domestic and international events—events over which they feel they have no control as Arab American Muslims. Furthermore, they also now feel generally less accepted in school and in society. Thus, students are confronted by an additional burden—coping with perceived discrimination and stereotypes that might have nothing to do with them per se, but that nevertheless affects them personally. Therefore, in order to address the fallout from September 11, several steps should be taken.

First, educators must recognize that, while September 11 affected all students, Arab American Muslim students in particular experienced certain challenges unique to their circumstances. Second, educators must understand that when domestic or international events (large or small) involve Arabs or Muslims, Arab American Muslim students feel singled out because of the negative way the media tend to portray these events. Therefore, schools must do a better job of teaching about the media and how the media and film influence student thinking. Finally, Arab American Muslim students must be made to feel welcome and safe at school. A zero tolerance policy should be instituted that penalizes students and staff who blame Arab American Muslim students for events unrelated to them personally or who exhibit discriminatory positions against Arabs or Muslims. Zero tolerance, along with integrating lessons that explore the importance of not attributing outside events to individuals, such as Arab American Muslims, would go a long way in addressing the fallout from September 11.

The way students cope with stereotypes is by either joking about the incident, educating the stereotyper, or both. What follows is a description of these two approaches under the theme of coping.

Coping

The theme of coping with stereotypes—both in and out of school—is a major area of concern for student, parent, and teacher participants. Although stereotypes manifest themselves in many ways and students offered numerous examples of encountering stereotypes in their daily lives, it is important to note that they gave few examples of feeling singled out for attack personally. This is not surprising. As was noted earlier, the type of stereotypes plaguing Arab American Muslims tend not to manifest themselves as images directed at individuals. Rather, student, parent, and teacher participants spoke about the collective stereotyping of Arabs and Muslims.

Indeed, more common were the general feelings of being part of a group that is stereotyped, misrepresented, ridiculed, and at times demonized. As Amira's teacher so aptly put it, Arab American Muslim children experience "shame by association." That is, when an individual who happens to be an Arab or a Muslim commits an act of violence, much of the media invariably portray the incident as an act committed not by an individual, but by an Arab or Muslim. While the casual observer may find such a characterization to be benign, student, parent, and many teacher participants find them to be unfair, demeaning, and harmful.

These participants pointed to the 1995 bombing of the Murrah Federal Building in Oklahoma City and to September 11 as the most obvious manifestation of this perception. In the case of the Oklahoma City bombing, many in the media and politics were quick to blame Arabs and Muslims for the terrorist attack. As a result, the Arab and Muslim American community experienced a dramatic increase in hate crimes, discrimination, and isolation. The fact that the individuals responsible for the bombing were radical White Christian Americans and that the media did not impugn those affiliations only reinforced the perception held by these participants that the media is biased against Arabs and Muslims.

In many ways, coping with stereotypes that are attributed generally to Arabs and Muslims may be more difficult for these students to contend with than those stereotypes in which a student feels personally singled out. In the former, student participants must carry the burden of correcting a stereotype that is broad and all encompassing. This scenario is especially difficult to resolve because the stereotype often originates from an unknown and inaccessible source (such as a movie producer). In the latter case, the source of the offending stereotype is usually known and accessible and is, therefore, easier to confront.

Because these student participants are exposed to the same stereotypical images of Arabs and Islam outside of school— what Cortes called the societal curricula— their thoughts and their feelings about how they perceive themselves and how they cope with stereotypes are remarkably similar.[74] What is telling is how similar these students perceive and cope with stereotypes both in school and in the larger society despite their different national origins, school contexts, home environments, and socioeconomic backgrounds.

The "Joke" Strategy

The way student participants perceive stereotypes as jokes or the way they turn stereotypes into jokes in order to cope with them reveals a strong desire to minimize the negative effects stereotypes have on friendships and peer relationships. There are several reasons why these students perceive stereotypes as jokes or turn them into jokes.

First, it is a way for student participants to cope with difficult and awkward situations—situations that often involve friends and peers with whom they feel comfortable and with whom they wish to maintain positive relationships. Perceiving a stereotype as a joke reduces the tension a stereotype causes; this is important because it allows these students more control over their emotions and increases the opportunity to engage the stereotyper in a meaningful way. As Lina said, "It reduces the tension." Thus, students are acutely aware that the tension caused by stereotypes is detrimental to their ability to cope with uncomfortable situations. Reducing the tension is important because it allows students more control over their own feelings and emotions and it increases the opportunity to engage the stereotyper in a meaningful way.

Next, because these students regularly encounter incidents of stereotyping, they often choose to perceive stereotypes as jokes in order to minimize the number of incidents with which they must contend. This reaction enhances their ability to manage awkward and uncomfortable situations and feelings; it also allows them to minimize the need to confront friends and other peers and risk causing a rift in their relationship.

Finally, because these students identify with Arabs and Muslims more broadly today than they did before September 11, the number of incidents they are likely to encounter has increased greatly. Therefore, perceiving stereotypes as jokes reduces the threat they pose and the need to actively confront such hackneyed images directly.

Another implication of the "joke" strategy is that it might cause student participants to assume that their status among friends or in society is better than it really is. Over time, however, this attitude can unravel as these students become increasingly conflicted. They know that they are stereotyped. However, by denying that their friends are the cause, for instance, they suppress their true feelings. This attitude can lead to frustration and anger about the way they are perceived and treated.

Overall, however, the "joke" strategy appears to be mostly effective. After years of being confronted by stereotypes, these students have come to recognize that not all stereotypes and stereotypers are the same. Indeed, there is a lesson in this for Arab American Muslim students of all ages who may not be coping with stereotypes as well as these particular student participants.

If Arab American Muslim students can be trained to identify the intent of the stereotyper, then it will be easier to cope with the types of stereotypes typically encountered by these student participants in and out of school. Such training could be facilitated through small group sessions and be led by school counselors who could be trained through sensitivity workshops. Until the environment changes that fosters the stereotyping of Arabs and Islam, helping Arab American Muslim students to better cope with stereotypes is a worthwhile goal.

Other ethnic groups have had experience using joking as a coping strategy. Indeed, studies of joking relations in different cultural contexts have been of interest in psychology and anthropology for at least a half century. However, the literature is incomplete as it relates to the use of joking as a coping strategy against stereotypes.[75] Nevertheless, that these student participants use joking as a coping strategy to deal with stereotypes reflects what some members of other ethnic groups likely do to cope as well.

Educate

Another issue related to how these student participants perceive and cope with stereotypes has to do with the need to constantly educate stereotypers and others about Arab culture and Islam. It is worth noting that these students feel compelled to educate others—and not rely on their parents to do the educating—because they typically encounter stereotypes when parents are not present (i.e., in school, at the movies, or simply going about their daily routines). Such encounters with stereotypes often require an immediate response. Therefore, these students have come to rely on themselves to cope with such incidents and use the coping mechanism "educate" as one effective strategy.

According to these students, they always try to show people that they are decent, responsible, and good individuals—images they believe most people rarely associate with Arabs and Muslims. While there are several reasons why they do this, these students seem to intuitively understand that in order to eliminate a stereotype and maintain the relationship they must not simply confront the stereotyper, but they must also show that the stereotype is false and replace it with something more positive.

Unfortunately, these students face an additional problem. Even after demonstrating that the stereotype is inaccurate and does not apply to that particular student, the stereotyper may nevertheless continue to assume that the stereotype does apply to other Arabs and Muslims.[76] This is a dilemma for these students who wish to eliminate the stereotype all together. Indeed, as Basil noted, the image of Arabs and Muslims took a giant step backward after September 11: "Now, they think we're all terrorists. But I guess I can't blame them, because that's all they see on TV."

The implications of Basil's feelings for these student participants are noteworthy. Because they feel uneasy with the consequences of uncontrollable events (e.g., they feel like hostages to the fallout from such events as

September 11), they are never certain about their place in society or among peers. This uncertainty may lead them to partially disconnect from school, stifling their involvement in academic and extracurricular activities. Over time, the consequences of not being fully engaged academically or in extracurricular activities can prevent students from meeting their full potential.

In addition, the burden of constantly educating and informing others about their culture and religion is tiring and frustrating. Although students recognize the importance and the potential benefit of educating and informing others, constantly doing so takes a great deal of time and energy—time and energy that could be used for other purposes. What students find most disappointing, however, is the need to educate friends, peers, and even some teachers about basic aspects of their culture and religion. The need to do this is a constant reminder that their culture and religion are not adequately included in the curricula, and it is a reflection of the low status of their group in society. This lack of knowledge adds to the students' perception that schools fail to offer the kind of environment they need (and want) in order to see themselves reflected positively and fully.

The need to constantly educate others about their heritage can be diminished by increasing the quality and quantity of curricula that include education on Arabs and Islam. Although state standardized tests and county curricular guides tend to drive what is taught in schools, teachers and administrators can take steps on an individual school level to ensure that more information about Arabs and Islam is included in their particular schools. This additional information can come from various sources, including many recent educational publications produced by universities and by prominent Arab and Muslim organizations. In addition, tapping into local Arab and Muslim communities can be rich sources of information. Little evidence exists that indicates that schools have made any effort to reach out to this segment of our society. Indeed, like many other minorities, this group has historically been ignored and underutilized. The problem, as discussed above, is that, in the absence of accurate information in the curricula, lack of active involvement of Arab American Muslims only adds to the difficulty of meeting the needs of children from this background.

If schools can develop outreach programs to specifically target the active involvement of the Arab American Muslim community, as has already been attempted with other minority groups (albeit not always successfully), the potential benefits are tremendous. Certainly, such efforts are only stopgap measures. However, until more substantive changes occur in the development of curricula and in the school environment, these measures can serve a useful purpose.

Conclusion

Given that the estimated 3.5 million Arab Americans and the 9 million Muslims living in the United States are an integral part of American society, it is imperative that researchers, educators, policy makers, and society in general better understand this diverse ethnic, religious, and cultural group.

Unfortunately, the scope of this initial study did not allow for an exploration of the deeper psychological effect stereotypes have on these Arab American Muslim high school students. However, just as Arab American Muslim students are essentially absent from most research studies related to education, so too are they absent from research studies in the area of psychology. Therefore, researching the psychological effect stereotypes have on Arab American Muslim students—beginning in elementary school—would contribute greatly to our understanding of this important topic.

Also, exploring the role Islam plays in the lives of Arab American Muslim students (whether or not they are practicing Muslims) could contribute to a better understanding of the importance of integrating Islamic culture and traditions into both the curricula and the school environment (i.e., school calendar, holiday celebrations, and so on). In addition, the effect the societal curricula has on Arab American Muslim students should be better understood. [77] Considering that the typical American student spends more time watching television than sitting in a classroom and that the image of Arabs and Muslims in this medium is overwhelmingly stereotypical and negative, teaching children how to interpret and manage this powerful source of information is critical. Although a societal shift is needed in the way Arabs and Islam are portrayed in popular culture, so too is the need to educate children about an aspect of society—media literacy—that arguably has more of a long-term effect on child development than what is taught in school.

While this chapter has included the perceptions of teachers, the primary focus has been on students. Therefore, researching more thoroughly the beliefs and experiences of teachers in their dealings with Arab American Muslim students could contribute worthwhile information and insight for public policy makers and teacher education programs. Knowing what teachers believe about Arab American Muslim students and determining what resources they need to better understand this population would go a long way in helping teachers to better meet the needs of these (and all) children.

Finally, this essay reveals the critical role these Arab American Muslim parents play in ensuring that their children are knowledgeable and proud of their heritage. The importance student participants place on parents to supplement what they do not learn about their culture and religion should be explored further. It is especially important to understand more fully the burden these parents endure in order to protect their children from stereotypes and from the fallout from national and international events, such as September 11. Such understanding will assist Arab American Muslim parents in dealing with the challenges confronting them in their efforts to raise well-adjusted and academically successful children.

Notes

1. Nadine C. Naber, "Ambiguous Insiders: An Investigation of Arab American Invisibility," *Ethnic and Racial Studies* 23, no. 1 (2000): 37–61; Sonia Nieto, *Affirming Diversity: The Sociopolitical Context of Multicultural Education* (New York: Longman, 2000); Jack Shaheen, *The TV Arab* (Bowling Green State University: Bowling Green Popular Press, 1984); Jack Shaheen, *Reel Bad Arabs: How Hollywood Vilifies a People* (New York: Olive Branch Press, 2001); Ronald Stockton, "Ethnic Archetypes and the Arab Image," in *The Development of Arab American Identity*, ed. Ernest McCarus, 182–214 (Ann Arbor: University of Michigan Press, 1994); Michael F. Suleiman, *Educating the Arab American Child: Implications for Teachers* 1996 (ERIC Document Reproduction Service No. ED 392864); James Zogby, "The Politics of Exclusion," *Civil Rights Journal* 3, no. 1 (1998): 42–48.

2. Gordon W. Allport, *The Nature of Prejudice* (Cambridge, MA: Addison Wesley, 1954); Yehuda Amir, "Contact Hypothesis in Ethnic Relations," *Psychological Bulletin* 71 (1969): 319–42; Geoffrey V. Bodenhausen and Robert S. Wyer, "Effect of Stereotypes on Decision Making and Information-Processing Strategies," *Journal of Experimental Social Psychology* 48 (1985): 267–82; Joshua A. Fishman, "An Examination of the Process and Function of Social Stereotyping," *Journal of Social Psychology* 43: 27–64; Susan T. Fiske, "Controlling Other People: The Impact of Power on Stereotyping," *American Psychologist* 48 (1993): 621–38; David L. Hamilton and Jeff W. Sherman, "Stereotypes," in *Handbook of Social Cognition*, ed. Robert S. Wyer, and Thomas. K. Srull, 1, 1–68 (Hillsdale, NJ: Erlbaum, 1994); Larry Lepore and Robert Brown, "Category and Stereotype Activation: Is Prejudice Inevitable," *Journal of Personality and Social Psychology*, 72 (1997): 275–87; Penny Oakes, Alex Haslam and John C. Turner, *Stereotyping and Social Reality* (Cambridge, MA: Blackwell, 1994); John U. Ogbu, "Minority Coping Responses and School Experiences," *The Journal of Psychohistory*, 18 (1991): 433–56.

3. Miles Hewstone, "Revision and Change of Stereotypic Beliefs: In Search of the Elusive Subtyping Model," in *European Review of Social Psychology*, ed. Wolfgang Stroebe and Miles Hewstone, 5 (1994): 69-109; Yueh-Ting Lee, L. Jussim, and Clark McCauley, *Stereotype Accuracy: Toward Appreciating Group Differences* (Washington, DC: American Psychological Association, 1995); Nieto, *Affirming Diversity*; Mark Schaller and Lucian G. Conway III, "From Cognition to Culture: The Origins of Stereotypes That Really Matter," in *Cognitive Social Psychology: The Princeton Symposium on the Legacy and Future of Social Cognition*, ed. Gordon B. Moskowitz, 163-76. (Mahwah, NJ: Erlbaum, 2001); Michael F. Suleiman, *Educating the Arab American Child: Implications for Teachers*, 1996 (ERIC Document Reproduction Service No. ED 392864); Christine J. Yeh and Yu-Wei Wang. "Asian American Coping Attitudes, Sources, and Practices: Implications for Indigenous Counseling Strategies," *Journal of College Student Development*, 41, no. 1 (2000): 94-103.

4. K. N. Ahmed, "Voices from within the Invisible Minority: A Phenomenological Study of School and Social Experiences of Arab American Students" (Ph.D. diss., State University of New York at Buffalo, 1998); Nieto, *Affirming Diversity*; Theodore Pulcini, "Trends in Research on Arab Americans," *Journal of American Ethnic History*, 12, no. 4 (1993): 28-43; Jack Shaheen, *Reel Bad Arabs: How Hollywood Vilifies a People* (New York: Olive Branch Press, 2001); Michael F. Suleiman, *Educating the Arab American Child: Implications for Teachers*, 1996 (ERIC Document Reproduction Service No. ED 392864); Michael F. Suleiman, *Image Making of Arab Americans: Implications for Teachers in Diverse Settings*, 2001. (ERIC Document Reproduction Service No. ED 452310); Marvin Wingfield and Bushra Karaman, "Arab Stereotypes and American Educators," *Social Studies and the Young Learner*, 6, no. 7 (1995): 7-10.

5. Nabil Abraham, "Arab Americans," in *Gale Encyclopedia of Multicultural America*, ed. Rudolph J. Veroli, Judy Gallens, Anna Sheets, and Robyn V. Young, 1, 84-98 (Farmington Hills, MI: Gale, 1995); Alixa Naff, "Arabs," in *Harvard Encyclopedia of American Ethnic Groups*, ed. Stephan Thernstrom, 12–136 (Cambridge, MA: Harvard University Press, 1980); U.S. Bureau of the Census. *Statistical Abstract of the U.S. 1990*, 110th ed. (Washington, DC: U. S. Government Printing Office, 1990a); U.S. Bureau of the Census. *Social and Economic Characteristics, 1990*, Census of Population and Housing, CP-2-1 (Washington, DC: U.S. Government Printing Office, 1990b); U.S. Bureau of the Census, *Ancestry of the Population of the United States, 1990*, Census of Population and Housing, CP-3-2 (Washington, DC: U. S. Government Printing Office, 1990c).

6. Ahmed, "Voices From Within the Invisible Minority"; B. E. Alatom, "Orientalist Stereotyping in Modern American Popular Culture" (Ph.D. diss., The University of Texas, Arlington, 1997); Yvonne Y. Haddad and Jane I. Smith, ed., *Muslim Minorities in the West: Visible and Invisible* (Walnut Creek, CA: AltaMira Press, 2002); Ernest McCarus, ed., *The Development of Arab-American Identity* (Ann Arbor: University of Michigan Press, 1994).

7. Nathan Hernandez, "The Chicano/Hispanic Image in American Film," *Harvard Educational Review*, 66, no. 2 (1996): 58-82; Nadine C. Naber, "Ambiguous Insiders: An Investigation of Arab American Invisibility," *Ethnic and Racial Studies*, 23, no. 1 (2000): 37-61; John U. Ogbu, "Origins of Human Competence: A Cultural

Ecological Approach," *Child Development*, 51 (1981): 413-29; Nieto, *Affirming Diversity: The Sociopolitical Context of Multicultural Education* (New York: Longman, 2000); Jack Shaheen, *Reel Bad Arabs: How Hollywood Vilifies a People* (New York: Olive Branch Press, 2001).

8. Nieto, *Affirming Diversity*; Jack Shaheen, *The TV Arab* (Bowling Green State University: Bowling Green Popular Press, 1984); Jack Shaheen, "The Persian Gulf Crisis Gives Scholars a Chance to Encourage More Accurate Depictions of Arabs," *The Chronicle of Higher Education*, 36, no. 28, (1990): B1; Jack Shaheen, "Arab Images in American Comic Books," *Journal of Popular Culture*, 28 (1994): 123-34; Suleiman, *Educating the Arab American Child: Implications for Teachers*.

9. Alatom, "Orientalist Stereotyping in Modern American Popular Culture"; Naber, "Ambiguous Insiders: An Investigation of Arab American Invisibility"; Shaheen, *Reel Bad Arabs*.

10. David Atkin, "An Analysis of Television Series with Minority-Lead Characters" *Critical Studies in Mass Communication*, 9 (1992): 337-49; Melbourne Cummings, "The Changing Image of the Black Family on Television," *Journal of Popular Culture*, 22 (1988): 75-86; Bradley S. Greenberg and J. Brand, "Minorities and the Mass Media: 1970s to 1990s," in *Media Effects: Advances in Theory and Research*, ed. Jennings Bryant and Dolf Zillmann (Hillsdale, NJ: Earlbaum, 1994): 273-314; Bradley S. Greenberg and Larry Collette, "The Changing Faces on TV: A Demographic Analysis of Network Television's New Seasons, 1966-1992," *Journal of Broadcasting and Electronic Media*, 41 (1997): 1-13; Shaheen, *Reel Bad Arabs*.

11. Cited in Shaheen, *Reel Bad Arabs*, 1.

12. Ahmed, "Voices from within the Invisible Minority"; Molly Farquharson, "Ideas for Teaching Arabs in a Multicultural Setting," paper presented at the Annual Meeting of the Teachers of English to Speakers of Other Languages, Chicago, IL, 1988 (ERIC Document Reproduction Service No. ED 296575); Nieto, *Affirming Diversity*; Loukia K. Sarroub, "The Sojourner Experience of Yemeni American High School Students: An Ethnographic Portrait," *Harvard Educational Review*, 71 (2001): 37-49.

13. Barlow, *Evaluation of Secondary Level Textbooks for Coverage of the Middle East*; Jacqueline Jordan, "Demanding a Multicultural Curriculum," in *Ethnic Conflict*, ed. Charles Cozic (San Diego, CA: Greenhaven Press, Inc., 1995); Glenn Perry, "Treatment of the Middle East in American High Schools," *Journal of Palestine Studies*, 14, no. 3 (1975): 46-58; Suleiman, *Image Making of Arab Americans*.

14. Barlow, *Evaluation of Secondary Level Textbooks for Coverage of the Middle East*; M. G. Nabti, "Coverage of the Arab World in American Secondary School World Studies Textbooks: A Content Analysis" (Ph.D. diss., Stanford University, 1981); Glenn Perry, "Treatment of the Middle East in American High Schools," *Journal of Palestine Studies*, 14, no. 3 (1975): 46-58; Suleiman, *Image Making of Arab Americans*; Janice J. Terry, "Arab Stereotypes in Popular Fiction," *Indiana Social Studies Quarterly*, 36, no. 1 (1983): 24-27.

15. Jack Shaheen, "The Media Image of Arabs," *Newsweek*, November 10, 1988, 1.

16. Andrew M. Mecca, *The Social Importance of Self-Esteem* (Los Angeles, CA: University of California Press, 1989); Jay Nel, "Preventing School Failure: The Native American Child," *The Clearinghouse* 67 (1994): 169–74; Nieto, *Affirming Diversity*.

17. Ronald Takaki, *A Different Mirror: A History of Multicultural America* (Boston: Little, Brown and Company, 1993), 16.

18. Jean S. Phinney, "Ethnic Identity in Adolescents and Adults: A Review of Research," *Psychological Bulletin*, 108 (1990): 499–514; Henri Tajfel, *Human Groups and Social Categories* (Cambridge, UK: Cambridge University Press, 1981); John C. Turner, *Rediscovering the Group* (Oxford: Blackwell, 1987).

19. John U. Ogbu, "Origins of Human Competence: A Cultural Ecological Approach," *Child Development*, 51 (1981): 413–29; Jean S. Phinney, "Ethnic Identity in Adolescents and Adults."

20. Erik Erikson, *Identity: Youth and Crisis* (New York: Norton, 1968); Henri Tajfel, *The Social Psychology of Minorities* (New York: Minority Rights Group, 1978).

21. Patricia Arredondo, "Multicultural Counseling Competencies as Tools to Address Oppression and Racism," *Journal of Counseling and Development*, 77 (1999): 102–8; Michael F. Suleiman, "Early Arab-Americans: The Search for Identity," in *Crossing the Waters: Arabic Speaking Immigrants to the United States Before 1940*, ed. Eric Hooglund, 37–55 (Washington, DC: Smithsonian Institution Press, 1987); Henri Tajfel, *Human Groups and Social Categories* (Cambridge, UK: Cambridge University Press, 1981).

22. Arthur Miller, *In the Eye of the Beholder* (New York: Praeger, 1982).

23. Walter Lippmann, *Public Opinion* (New York: Harcourt, Brace, and Co., 1922), 12.

24. Martha Augustinos, Cheryl Ahrens, and Michael J. Innes, "Stereotypes and Prejudice: The Australian Experience," *British Journal of Social Psychology*, 33 (1994): 124–41; Patricia Devine, "Stereotypes and Prejudice: Their Automatic and Controlled Components," *Journal of Personality and Social Psychology*, 56 (1989): 5–18; Lepore and Brown, "Category and Stereotype Activation."

25. See Daniel Katz and Kenneth Braly, "Racial Stereotypes of One Hundred College Students," *Journal of Abnormal and Social Psychology*, 28 (1933): 280–90.

26. Frances Aboud, *Children and Prejudice* (Oxford, England: Basil Blackwell, 1988); Richard D. Ashmore and Frances K. Del Boca, "Conceptual Approaches to Stereotypes and Stereotyping," in *Cognitive Process in Stereotyping and Intergroup Behavior*, ed. Devine C. Hamilton, 1–35 (Hillsdale, NJ: Erlbaum, 1981); Marilynn B. Brewer, "In-Group Bias in The Minimal Intergroup Situation: A Cognitive-Motivational Analysis," *Psychological Bulletin*, 86 (1979): 307–24; Patricia Devine, "Stereotypes and Prejudice: Their Automatic and Controlled Components," *Journal of Personality and Social Psychology*, 56 (1989): 5–18; Michael Diehl and Klaus Jonas, "Measures of National Stereotypes as Predictors of the Latencies of Inductive Versus Deductive Stereotypic Judgments," *European Journal of Social Psychology*, 2 (1991): 202–4; Samuel Fein and Janet T. Spencer, "Prejudice as Self-Image Maintenance: Affirming the Self through Negative Evaluations of Others," *Journal of Personality and Social Psychology*, 73 (1997): 31–44; Henri Tajfel, *The Social Psychology of Minorities* (New York: Minority Rights Group, 1978); James J. Hilton and William von Hippel, "Stereotypes," *Annual Review of Psychology*, ed. Janet T. Spencer, John. M. Darley, and D. J. Foss, 237–71 (Palo Alto,

CA: Annual Reviews, 1996); James J. Hilton and William von Hippel, "The Role of Consistency in the Judgment of Stereotype-Relevant Behaviors," *Personality and Social Psychology Bulletin*, 16 (1990): 430–48; Joshua A. Fishman, "An Examination of the Process and Function of Social Stereotyping," *Journal of Social Psychology*, 43 (1956): 27–64.

27. David L. Hamilton and Jeff W. Sherman, "Stereotypes," in *Handbook of Social Cognition*, ed. Robert S. Wyer, and Thomas K. Srull, 1, 1–68 (Hillsdale, NJ: Erlbaum, 1994); James J. Hilton and William von Hippel, "Stereotypes," in *Annual Review of Psychology*, ed. Janet T. Spencer, John. M. Darley, and D. J. Foss, 237–71 (Palo Alto, CA: Annual Reviews, 1996).

28. Alatom, "Orientalist Stereotyping in Modern American Popular Culture"; Naff, "The Early Arab Immigration Experience"; Ernest McCarus *The Development of the Arab-American Identity* (Ann Arbor: University of Michigan Press, 1994); Gregory Orfalea, *Before the Flames: A Quest for the History of Arab Americans* (Austin: University of Texas Press, 1988); Shaheen, "Arabs and Muslim Stereotyping in American Popular Culture."

29. Jack Shaheen, *Reel Bad Arabs*.

30. Shaheen, *The TV Arab*; Shaheen, *Reel Bad Arabs*.

31. B. E. Alatom, "Orientalist Stereotyping in Modern American Popular Culture"; Bradley S. Greenberg and J. Brand, "Minorities and the Mass Media: 1970s to 1990s," in *Media Effects: Advances in Theory and Research*, ed. Jennings Bryant and Dolf Zillmann (Hillsdale, NJ: Lawrence Erlbaum Associates, 1994), 273–314; Bradley S. Greenberg and Larry Collette, "The Changing Faces on TV: A Demographic Analysis of Network Television's New Seasons, 1966–1992," *Journal of Broadcasting and Electronic Media*, 41 (1997): 1–13; Shaheen, "Arabs and Muslim Stereotyping in American Popular Culture."

32. Shaheen, *Reel Bad Arabs*.

33. Shaheen, *Reel Bad Arabs*.

34. Sameer Y. Abraham and Nabil Abraham, *The Arab World and Arab-Americans: Understanding a Neglected Minority* (Detroit: Wayne State University Center for Urban Studies, 1981); Alixa Naff, "Arabs" in *Harvard Encyclopedia of American Ethnic Groups*, ed. Stephan Thernstrom, 12–136 (Cambridge, MA: Harvard University Press, 1980); Pulcini, "Trends in Research on Arab Americans."

35. Gordon W. Allport, *The Nature of Prejudice* (Cambridge, MA: Addison Wesley, 1954).

36. See Geoffrey V. Bodenhausen and Robert S. Wyer, "Effect of Stereotypes on Decision Making and Information-Processing Strategies," *Journal of Experimental Social Psychology* 48 (1985): 267–82; David L. Hamilton and Jeff W. Sherman, "Stereotypes," in *Handbook of Social Cognition*, ed. Robert S. Wyer, and Thomas. K. Srull, 1, 1–68 (Hillsdale, NJ: Erlbaum, 1994); Jacques-Philippe Leyens, Vincent Y. Yzerbyt, and George Schadron, *Stereotypes and Social Cognition* (London: Sage, 1994).

37. Karima Alavi, "At Risk of Prejudice: Teaching Tolerance about Muslim Americans," *Social Education*, 63, no. 2 (2001): 67–81; Suleiman, *Image Making of Arab Americans*; Marvin Wingfield and Bushra Karaman, "Arab Stereotypes and American Educators," *Social Studies and the Young Learner*, 6, no. 7 (1995): 7–10.

38. Nadine C. Naber, "Ambiguous Insiders: An Investigation of Arab American Invisibility" *Ethnic and Racial Studies*, 23, no. 1 (2000): 37-61; Shaheen, "Arabs and Muslim Stereotyping in American Popular Culture"; Shaheen, "Hollywood's Muslim Arabs," *The Muslim World*, 90, no. 1 (1997): 22-38.

39. Thomas F. Pettigrew, "The Intergroup Contact Hypothesis Reconsidered," in *Contact and Conflict in Intergroup Encounters*, ed. Miles Hewstone and Rupert Brown, 169-95 (Oxford, England: Basil Blackwell, 1986); Mark Schaller, "Unintended Influence: Social-Evolutionary Processes in the Construction and Change of Culturally-Shared Beliefs," in *Social Influence: Direct and Indirect Processes*, ed. Jeff P. Forgas and K. D. Williams, 77-94 (Philadelphia: Psychology Press, 2001).

40. Allport, *The Nature of Prejudice*.

41. Allport, *The Nature of Prejudice*.

42. Marvin Karlins, Thomas L. Coffman, and Gary Walters, "On the Fading of Stereotype Consensus," in *The Social Psychology of Stereotyping and Group Life*, ed. Russel Spears, Penelope J. Oakes, Naomi Ellemers, and S. Alexander Haslam, 119-43 (Oxford, England: Blackwell, 1969).

43. Mark Schaller, "Unintended Influence: Social-Evolutionary Processes in the Construction and Change of Culturally-Shared Beliefs," in *Social Influence: Direct and Indirect Processes*, ed. Joseph P. Forgas and Kipling D. Williams, 77-94 (Philadelphia: Psychology Press, 2001); Mark Schaller and Lucian G. Conway III, "Influence of Impression-management Goals on the Emerging Contents of Group Stereotypes: Support for a Social-Evolutionary Process," *Personality and Social Psychology Bulletin*, 25 (1999): 81-33; Mark Schaller and Lucian G. Conway III, "From Cognition to Culture: The Origins of Stereotypes that Really Matter," in *Cognitive Social Psychology: The Princeton Symposium on the Legacy and Future of Social Cognition*, ed. Gordon B. Moskowitz, 163-76. (Mahwah, NJ: Erlbaum, 2001).

44. Mark Schaller, "Unintended Influence: Social-Evolutionary Processes in the Construction and Change of Culturally-Shared Beliefs," in *Social Influence: Direct and Indirect Processes*, ed. Joseph P. Forgas and Kipling D. Williams, 77-94 (Philadelphia: Psychology Press, 2001); Mark Schaller and Lucian G. Conway III, "Influence of Impression-Management Goals on the Emerging Contents of Group Stereotypes: Support for a Social-Evolutionary Process," *Personality and Social Psychology Bulletin*, 25 (1999); Mark Schaller and Lucian G. Conway III, "From Cognition to Culture."

45. Schaller, "Unintended Influence"; Schaller and Conway III, "From Cognition to Culture"; Schaller and Conway, "Influence of Impression-Management Goals."

46. Brian Mullen, Drew Rozell, and Craig Johnson, "Ethnophaulisms for Ethnic Immigrant Groups: Cognitive Representation of 'the Minority' and 'the Foreigner,' *Group Process and Intergroup Relations*, 3 (2000): 5-24.

47. Alatom, "Orientalist Stereotyping in Modern American Popular Culture"; Yvonne Y. Haddad, *The Muslims of America* (New York: Oxford University Press, 1991); Shaheen, "Arabs and Muslim Stereotyping in American Popular Culture"; Shaheen, *Reel Bad Arabs*.

48. Alatom, "Orientalist Stereotyping in Modern American Popular Culture"; Richard Antoun, "Sojourners Abroad: Migration for Higher Education in a Post-Peasant Muslim

Society," in *Islam, Globalization and Postmodernity*, ed. Akbar S. Ahmed and Haslam Donna, 161-89 (New York: Routledge, 1994); Loukia K. Sarroub, "The Sojourner Experience of Yemeni American High School Students: An Ethnographic Portrait" *Harvard Educational Review*, 71 (2001): 37-49; Shaheen, *Reel Bad Arabs*.

49. Adolph Zukor, as cited by Shaheen, *Reel Bad Arabs*, 30.

50. Shaheen, *Reel Bad Arabs*, 19.

51. Shaheen, "Hollywood's Muslim Arabs"; Shaheen, *Reel Bad Arabs*.

52. Shaheen, *Reel Bad Arabs*, 22.

53. Shaheen, *Reel Bad Arabs*.

54. Yvonne Y. Haddad and Jane I. Smith, ed., "Muslim Minorities in the West: Visible and Invisible," (Walnut Creek, CA: AltaMira Press, 2002); Shaheen, "Hollywood's Muslim Arabs"; Shaheen, *Reel Bad Arabs*.

55. Alatom, "Orientalist Stereotyping in Modern American Popular Culture"; Shaheen, "Hollywood's Muslim Arabs"; Shaheen, *Reel Bad Arabs*.

56. Shaheen, "Hollywood's Muslim Arabs"; Shaheen, *Reel Bad Arabs*.

57. Alatom, "Orientalist Stereotyping in Modern American Popular Culture"; Shaheen, *Arabs and Muslim Stereotyping in American Popular Culture*. Shaheen, "Hollywood's Muslim Arabs"; Shaheen, *Reel Bad Arabs*.

58. Haddad, "Muslim Minorities in the West"; Shaheen, "Hollywood's Muslim Arabs." 59. Alatom, "Orientalist Stereotyping in Modern American Popular Culture"; Haddad, "American Foreign Policy in the Middle East and Its Impact on the Identity of Arab Muslims in the United States."

60. Claude M. Steele, "A Threat in the Air: How Stereotypes Shape Intellectual and Identity Performance," *American Psychologist*, 52 (1997): 613-29; Claude M. Steele and Joshua Aronson, "Stereotype Threat and the Intellectual Test Performance of African Americans," *Journal of Personality and Social Psychology*, 69 (1995): 797-811.

61. Alatom, "Orientalist Stereotyping in Modern American Popular Culture."

62. Gordon W. Allport, *The Nature of Prejudice* (Cambridge, MA: Addison Wesley, 1954).

63. Haddad and Jane I. Smith, eds., "Muslim Minorities in the West: Visible and Invisible"; Shaheen, *The TV Arab*; Shaheen, "Arabs and Muslim Stereotyping in American Popular Culture"; Ronald Stockton, "Ethnic Archetypes and the Arab Image," in *The Development of Arab American Identity*, ed. Ernest McCarus, 182-14 (Ann Arbor: University of Michigan Press, 1994).

64. John L. Esposito, "American Perceptions of Islam and Arabs," *TheDiplomat*, 1 (1996): 10-11; Haddad, "American Foreign Policy in the Middle East and its Impact on the Identity of Arab Muslims in the United States"; Shaheen, *The TV Arab*; Shaheen, *Reel Bad Arabs*.

65. Nader Ayish, "Stereotypes and Arab American Muslim High School Students: A Misunderstood Group" (Ph.D. diss., George Mason University, 2003).

66. Elizabeth Barlow, ed., *Evaluation of Secondary Level Textbooks for Coverage of the Middle East* (Ann Arbor: Middle East Studies Association/Middle East Outreach Council, 1994); Jacqueline Jordan, "Demanding a Multicultural Curriculum," in *Ethnic Conflict*, ed. Charles Cozic (San Diego, CA: Greenhaven Press, Inc., 1995); Glenn Perry, "Treatment of the Middle East in American High Schools" *Journal of Palestine Studies*,

14, no. 3 (1975): 46-58; Suleiman, *Educating the Arab American Child*; Suleiman, "Image Making of Arab Americans"; Marvin Wingfield and Bushra Karaman, "Working with School Systems: Educational Outreach and Action Guide."

67. Patricia Arredondo, "Multicultural Counseling Competencies as Tools to Address Oppression and Racism," *Journal of Counseling and Development*, 77 (1999): 102-8; Jacqueline Jordan, "Demanding a Multicultural Curriculum," in *Ethnic Conflict*, ed. Charles Cozic (San Diego, CA: Greenhaven Press, Inc., 1995); Jay Nel, "Preventing School Failure: The Native American Child," *The Clearinghouse* 67 (1994): 169-74; Michael F. Suleiman, *Image Making of Arab Americans: Implications for Teachers in Diverse Settings* (ERIC Document Reproduction Service No. ED 452310).

68. Barlow, ed., *Evaluation of Secondary Level Textbooks for Coverage of the Middle East*; Nabti, "Coverage of the Arab World in American Secondary School World Studies Textbooks: A Content Analysis"; Glenn Perry, "Treatment of the Middle East in American High Schools," *Journal of Palestine Studies*, 14, no. 3 (1975): 46-58; Wingfield and Karaman, "Arab Stereotypes and American Educators."

69. Ahmed, "Voices from within the Invisible Minority: A Phenomenological Study of School and Social Experiences of Arab American Students"; Zeina A. Seikaly, "At Risk of Prejudice: The Arab American Community," *Social Education*, 65, no. 6 (2001): 301-306; Wingfield and Karaman, "Arab Stereotypes and American Educators"; Wingfield and Salam, "*Working with School Systems: Educational Outreach and Action Guide*," American-Arab Anti-Discrimination Committee.

70. Haddad, "Muslim Minorities in the West: Visible and Invisible"; Orfalea, *Before the Flames*. Shaheen, *Reel Bad Arabs*; Ronald Takaki, *A Different Mirror: A History of Multicultural America*. (Boston: Little, Brown and Company, 1993).

71. Ahmed, "Voices From Within the Invisible Minority: A Phenomenological Study of School and Social Experiences of Arab American Students" (PhD diss., State University of New York at Buffalo, 1998); Seikaly, "At Risk of Prejudice; Shaheen, *Reel Bad Arab*; Wingfield and Karaman, "Arab Stereotypes and American Educators," *Social Studies and the Young Learner*, 6, no. 7 (1995): 7-10.

72. Ahmed, "Voices From Within the Invisible Minority: A Phenomenological Study of School and Social Experiences of Arab American Students"; Haddad, "American Foreign Policy in the Middle East"; Wingfield and Karaman, "Arab Stereotypes and American Educators."

73. Ahmed, "Voices From Within the Invisible Minority: A Phenomenological Study of School and Social Experiences of Arab American Students"; Haddad, "American Foreign Policy in the Middle East"; Wingfield and Karaman, "Arab Stereotypes and American Educators."

74. Carlos E. Cortes, *The Children are Watching: How the Media Teach about Diversity* (New York: Teachers College Press, 2000).

75. Jei Jung, "Ethnic Group and Gender Differences in the Relationship Between Personality and Coping," *Anxiety, Stress, and Coping*, 8 (1995): 113-26; Valerie O. Pang and Li-Rong Lilly Cheng, ed. *Struggling to be Heard: The Unmet Needs of Asian Pacific American Children* (Albany: State University of New York Press, 1998); Jean S. Phinney, Cindy Lou Cantu, and Dawn A. Kurtz, "Ethnic and American Identity as Predictors of Self-

Esteem Among African American, Latino, and White Adolescents," *Journal of Youth and Adolescence*, no. 26 (1997): 165–85; Christine J. Yeh and Yu-Wei Wang, "Asian American Coping Attitudes, Sources, and Practices: Implications for Indigenous Counseling Strategies," *Journal of College Student Development*, 41, no.1 (2000): 94–103.

76. Allport, *The Nature of Prejudice*.
77. Cortes, *The Children Are Watching*.

Works Cited

Aboud, Frances. *Children and Prejudice*: Oxford, England: Basil Blackwell, 1988.

Abraham, Nabil. "Arab Americans." In *Gale Encyclopedia of Multicultural America*, ed. Rudolph J. Veroli, Judy Gallens, Anna Sheets, and Robyn V. Young. Farmington Hills, MI: Gale, 1995.

Abraham, Samier. Y., and Nabil Abraham. *The Arab World and Arab-Americans: Understanding a Neglected Minority*. Detroit: Wayne State University Center for Urban Studies, 1981.

Ahmed, K. N. "Voices From Within the Invisible Minority: A Phenomenological Study of School and Social Experiences of Arab American Students." Ph.D. diss., State University of New York at Buffalo, 1998.

Alatom, B. E. "Orientalist Stereotyping in Modern American Popular Culture." Ph.D. diss., The University of Texas, Arlington, 1997.

Alavi, Karima, "At Risk of Prejudice: Teaching Tolerance About Muslim Americans." *Social Education*, 63, no. 2 (2001): 67–81.

Allport, Gordon W. *The Nature of Prejudice*: Cambridge, MA: Addison Wesley, 1954.

Amir, Yehuda. "Contact Hypothesis in Ethnic Relations." *Psychological Bulletin*, 71 (1969): 319–42.

Antoun, Richard. "Sojourners Abroad: Migration for Higher Education in a Post-Peasant Muslim Society." In *Islam, Globalization and Postmodernity*, ed. Akbar S. Ahmed and Haslam   Donna, 161–89. New York: Routledge, 1994.

Arredondo, Patricia. "Multicultural Counseling Competencies as Tools to Address Oppression and Racism." *Journal of Counseling and Development*, 77 (1999): 102–8.

Ashmore, Richard D., and Frances K. Del Boca. "Conceptual Approaches to Stereotypes   and Stereotyping." In *Cognitive Process in Stereotyping and Intergroup Behavior*, ed. Devine C. Hamilton, 1–35. Hillsdale, NJ: Erlbaum, 1981.

Atkin, David. "An Analysis of Television Series with Minority-Lead Characters." *Critical Studies in Mass Communication*, 9 (1992): 337–49.

Augustinos, M., C. Ahrens, and M. J. Innes. "Stereotypes and Prejudice: The Australian Experience." *British Journal of Social Psychology*, 33 (1994): 125–41.

Ayish, Nader. "Stereotypes and Arab American Muslim High School Students: A Misunderstood Group." Ph.D. diss., George Mason University, 2003.

Barlow, Elizabeth, ed. *Evaluation of Secondary Level Textbooks for Coverage of the Middle East*. Ann Arbor: Middle East Studies Association/Middle East Outreach Council, 1994.

Bodenhausen, Geoffrey V., and Robert S. Wyer. "Effect of Stereotypes on Decision Making and Information-Processing Strategies." *Journal of Experimental Social Psychology*, 48 (1985): 267–82.

Brewer, Marilynn B. "In-Group Bias in the Minimal Intergroup Situation: A Cognitive-Motivational Analysis." *Psychological Bulletin*, 86 (1979): 307–24.

Cortes, Carlos E. *The Children Are Watching: How the Media Teach about Diversity*. New York: Teachers College Press, 2000.

Cummings, Melbourne. "The Changing Image of the Black Family on Television." *Journal of Popular Culture*, 22 (1988): 75–86.

Devine, Patricia. "Stereotypes and Prejudice: Their Automatic and Controlled Components."*Journal of Personality and Social Psychology*, 56 (1989): 5–18.

Diehl, Michael, and Klaus Jonas. "Measures of National Stereotypes as Predictors of the Latencies of Inductive versus Deductive Stereotypic Judgments." *European Journal of Social Psychology*, 2 (1991): 202–4.

Erikson, Erik. *Identity: Youth and Crisis*: New York: Norton, 1968.

Esposito, John L. "American Perceptions of Islam and Arabs." *The Diplomat*, 1 (1996): 10–11.

Farquharson, Molly. "Ideas for Teaching Arabs in a Multicultural Setting." Paper Presented at the Annual Meeting of the Teachers of English to Speakers of Other Languages, Chicago, IL, 1988 (ERIC Document Reproduction Service No. ED 296575).

Fein, S., and J. T. Spencer. "Prejudice as Self-Image Maintenance: Affirming the Self Through Negative Evaluations of Others." *Journal of Personality and Social Psychology*, 73 (1997): 31–44.

Fishman, Joshua A. "An Examination of the Process and Function of Social Stereotyping." *Journal of Social Psychology*, 43 (1956): 27–64.

Fiske, Susan T. "Controlling Other People: The Impact of Power on Stereotyping," *American Psychologist* 48 (1993): 621–38.

Greenberg, Bradley S., and J. Brand. "Minorities and the Mass Media: 1970s to 1990s." In *Media Effects: Advances in Theory and Research*, ed. Jennings Bryant and Dolf Zillmann. Hillsdale, NJ: Earlbaum, 1994.

Greenberg, B. S., and L. Collette. "The Changing Faces on TV: A Demographic Analysis of Network Television's New Seasons, 1966–1992." *Journal of Broadcasting and Electronic Media*, 41 (1997): 1–13.

Haddad, Yvonne Y. "American Foreign Policy in the Middle East and Its Impact on the Identity of Arab Muslims in the United States" In *The Muslims of America*, ed. Yvonne Y. Haddad, 217–35. New York: Oxford University Press, 1991.

———. *Muslim Minorities in the West: Visible and Invisible*, ed. Yvonne Y. Haddad and Jane I. Smith. Walnut Creek, CA: AltaMira Press, 2002.

———. *The Muslims of America*. New York: Oxford University Press, 1991.

Hamilton, David L., and Sherman, Jeff W. "Stereotypes." In *Handbook of Social Cognition*, ed. Robert S. Wyer and Thomas. K. Srull, 1–68: Hillsdale, NJ: Erlbaum, 1994.

Hernandez, Nathan. "The Chicano/Hispanic Image in American Film." *Harvard Educational Review*, 66, no. 2 (1996): 58–82.

Hewstone, Miles. "Revision and Change of Stereotypic Beliefs: In Search of the Elusive Subtyping Model." *European Review of Social Psychology*, no. 5 (1994): 69–109.

Hilton, James J., and William Von Hippel. "Stereotypes." In *Annual Review of Psychology*, ed.Janet T. Spencer, John. M. Darley, and D. J. Foss, 237–71.Palo Alto, CA: Annual Reviews, 1996.

———."The Role of Consistency in the Judgment of Stereotype-Relevant Behaviors." *Personality and Social Psychology Bulletin*, 16 (1990): 430–48.

Jordan, Jacqueline. "Demanding a Multicultural Curriculum" In *Ethnic Conflict*, ed. Charles Cozic. San Diego, CA: Greenhaven Press, 1995.

Jung, Jei. "Ethnic Group and Gender Differences in the Relationship between Personality and Coping." *Anxiety, Stress, and Coping*, 8 (1995): 113–26.

Karlins, Marvin, Thomas L. Coffman, and G. Walters. "On the Fading of Stereotype Consensus." In *The Social Psychology of Stereotyping and Group Life*, ed. Russel Spears, Penelope J. Oakes, Naomi Ellemers, and S. Alexander Haslam, 119–43. Oxford, England: Blackwell, 1969.

Katz, D., and K. Braly. "Racial Stereotypes of One Hundred College Students." *Journal of Abnormal and Social Psychology*, 28 (1933): 280–90.

Lee, Yueh-Ting T., L. Jussim, and Clark McCauley. *Stereotype Accuracy: Toward Appreciating Group Differences*: Washington, DC: American Psychological Association, 1995.

Lepore, Larry, and R. Brown. "Category and Stereotype Activation: Is Prejudice Inevitable." *Journal of Personality and Social Psychology*, 72 (1997): 275–87.

Leyens, Jacques-Philippe, Vincent Y. Yzerbyt, and George Schadron. *Stereotypes and Social Cognition.* London: Sage, 1994.

Lippmann, Walter. *Public Opinion.* New York: Harcourt, Brace, and Co., 1922.

McCarus, Ernest, ed. *The Development of Arab-American Identity*: Ann Arbor: University of Michigan Press, 1994.

Mecca, Andrew M. *The Social Importance of Self-esteem*: Los Angeles: University of California Press, 1989.

Miller, Arthur. *In the Eye of the Beholder*. New York: Praeger Publishers, 1982.

Mullen, Brian, Drew Rozell, and Craig Johnson. "Ethnophaulisms for Ethnic Immigrant Groups: Cognitive Representation of 'the Minority' and 'the Foreigner.' *Group Process and Intergroup Relations*, 3 (2000): 5–24.

Naber, Nadine C. "Ambiguous Insiders: An Investigation of Arab American Invisibility." *Ethnic and Racial Studies*, 23, no. 1 (2000): 37–61.

Nabti, M. G. "Coverage of the Arab World in American Secondary School World Studies Textbooks: A Content Analysis." Ph.D. diss., Stanford University, 1981.

Naff, Alixa. "Arabs." In *Harvard Encyclopedia of American Ethnic Groups*, ed. Stephan Thernstrom, 12–136. Cambridge, MA: Harvard University Press, 1980. Cambridge, MA: Harvard University Press.

———. "The Early Arab Immigration Experience." In *The Development of the Arab-American Identity*, ed. Ernest McCarus. Ann Arbor: The University of Michigan Press, 1994.

Nel, Jay. "Preventing School Failure: The Native American Child." *The Clearinghouse* 67 (1994): 169–74.

Nieto, Sonia. *Affirming Diversity: The Sociopolitical Context of Multicultural Education*. New York: Longman, 2000.

Oakes, P., A. Haslam, and John C. Turner. *Stereotyping and Social Reality*: Cambridge, MA: Blackwell Publishers, 1994.

Ogbu, John, U. "Minority Coping Responses and School Experiences." *The Journal of Psychohistory*, no. 18 (1991): 433–56.

———. "Origins of Human Competence: A Cultural Ecological Approach." *Child Development*, 51 (1981): 413–29.

Orfalea, Gregory. *Before the Flames: A Quest for the History of Arab Americans*. Austin: University of Texas Press, 1988.

Pang, Valerie O., and Li-Rong Lilly Cheng, ed., *Struggling to Be Heard: The Unmet Needs of Asian Pacific American Children*. Albany: State University of New York Press, 1998.

Perry, Glenn. "Treatment of the Middle East in American High Schools." *Journal of Palestine Studies*, 14, no. 3 (1975): 46–58.

Pettigrew, Thomas F. "The Intergroup Contact Hypothesis Reconsidered." In *Contact and Conflict in Intergroup Encounters*, ed. Miles Hewstone and Rupert Brown, 169–95. Oxford, England: Hasil Blackwell, 1986.

Phinney, Jean S. "Ethnic Identity in Adolescents and Adults: A Review of Research." *Psychological Bulletin*, 108 (1990): 499–514.

Phinney, Jean S., C. L. Cantu, and D. A. Kurtz. "Ethnic and American Identity as Predictors of Self-Esteem among African American, Latino, and White Adolescents." *Journal of Youth and Adolescence*, no. 26 (1997): 165–18.

Pulcini, Theodore. "Trends in Research on Arab Americans." *Journal of American Ethnic History*, 12, no. 4 (1993): 28–43.

Sarroub, Loukia K. "The Sojourner Experience of Yemeni American High School Students: An Ethnographic Portrait." *Harvard Educational Review*, 71 (2001): 37–49.

Schaller, Mark. "Unintended Influence: Social-Evolutionary Processes in the Construction and Change of Culturally-Shared Beliefs." In *Social Influence: Direct and Indirect Processes*, ed. Jeff P. Forgas and K. D. Williams, 77–94. Philadelphia: Psychology Press, 2001.

Schaller, Mark, and Lucian Conway III. "From Cognition to Culture: The Origins of Stereotypes That Really Matter." In *Cognitive Social Psychology: The Princeton Symposium on the Legacy and Future of Social Cognition*, ed. Gordon B. Moskowitz, 163–76. Mahwah, NJ: Erlbaum, 2001.

———. "Influence of Impression-Management Goals on the Emerging Contents of Group Stereotypes: Support for a Social-evolutionary Process." *Personality and Social Psychology Bulletin*, 25 (1999): 819–33.

Seikaly, Zeina A. "At Risk of Prejudice: The Arab American Community." *Social Education*, 65, no. 6 (2001): 301–306.

Shaheen, Jack. "Arabs and Muslim Stereotyping in American Popular Culture." Washington, DC: Georgetown University, Center for Muslim-Christian Understanding. Occasional Paper Service, 1997.

———. "Arab Images in American Comic Books." *Journal of Popular Culture*, 28 (1994): 123–34.

———. "Hollywood's Muslim Arabs." *The Muslim World*, 90, no. 1 (1997): 22–38.

———. *Reel Bad Arabs: How Hollywood Vilifies a People*. New York: Olive Branch Press, 2001.

———. "The Media Image of Arabs." *Newsweek*, November 10, 1988, p. 1.

———. "The Persian Gulf Crisis Gives Scholars a Chance to Encourage More Accurate Depictions of Arabs." *The Chronicle of Higher Education*, 36, no. 28 (1990): B1.

———. *The TV Arab*. Bowling Green State University: Bowling Green Popular Press, 1984.

Steele, Claude M. "A Threat in the Air: How Stereotypes Shape Intellectual and Identity Performance." *American Psychologist*, 52 (1997): 613–29.

Steele, Claude M., and Joshua Aronson. "Stereotype Threat and the Intellectual Test Performance of African Americans." *Journal of Personality and Social Psychology*, 69 (1995): 797–811.

Stockton, Ronald. "Ethnic Archetypes and the Arab Image." In *The Development of Arab American Identity*, ed. Ernest McCarus, 182–214. Ann Arbor: University of Michigan Press, 1994.

Suleiman, Michael F. "Early Arab-Americans: The Search for Identity." In *Crossing the Waters: Arabic Speaking Immigrants to the United States Before 1940*, ed. Eric Hooglund, 37–55. Washington, DC: Smithsonian Institution Press, 1987.

———. *Educating the Arab American Child: Implications for Teachers*. (ERIC Document Reproduction Service No. ED 392864, 1996).

———. *Image Making of Arab Americans: Implications for Teachers in Diverse Settings* (ERIC Document Reproduction Service No. ED 452310, 2001).

Tajfel, Henri. *Human Groups and Social Categories*: Cambridge, UK: Cambridge University Press, 1981.

———. *The Social Psychology of Minorities*. New York: Minority Rights Group, 1978.

Takaki, Ronald. *A Different Mirror: A History of Multicultural America*. Canada: Little, Brown and Company LTD, 1993.

Terry, Janice J. "Arab Stereotypes in Popular Fiction." *Indiana Social Studies Quarterly*, 36, no. 1 (1983): 24–27.

Turner, John C. *Rediscovering the Group*: Oxford: Blackwell, 1987. U. S. Bureau of the Census. *Ancestry of the Population of the United States, 1990*. Census of Population and Housing, CP-3-2. Washington, DC: U.S. Government Printing Office, 1990c.

———. *Statistical Abstract of the U.S. 1990*, 110th ed. Washington, DC: U.S. Government Printing Office, 1990a.

———. *Social and Economic Characteristics, 1990*. Census of Population and Housing, CP-2-1, Washington, DC: U.S. Government Printing Office 1990b.

Wingfield, Marvin, and Bushra Karaman. "Arab Stereotypes and American Educators." *Social Studies and the Young Learner*, 6, no. 7, (1995): 7–10.

———. *Working with School Systems: Educational Outreach and Action Guide*. American-Arab Anti-Discrimination Committee, 1995 (ERIC Document Reproduction Service No. ED 433 400).

Yeh, Christine J., and Yu-Wei Wang. "Asian American Coping Attitudes, Sources, and Practices: Implications for Indigenous Counseling Strategies." *Journal of College Student Development*, 4, no. 1 (2000): 94–103.

Zogby, James. "The Politics of Exclusion." *Civil Rights Journal*, 3, no. 1 (1998): 42–48.

6

Arabs in Honduras: Immigration, Integration, and the Palestinian Presence

Sharon Lopez and Katharine S. Speer

Visitors to the northwestern area of Honduras are probably surprised to discover a region that offers even more diversity than the typical Latin American mélange of European, African, and Native peoples. San Pedro Sula and numerous surrounding towns[1] can offer the tourist a unique opportunity to explore Middle Eastern culture, for with the exception of Chile, Honduras has the highest number of immigrants from the Middle East of any Latin American country.[2] While it is difficult to ascertain the exact number of Hondurans who are descendents of Arabic immigrants, it is estimated that three percent or 150,000–200,000 of Honduras' population of nearly seven million can trace their ancestry to the Middle East.[3] The majority, or 99% of these citizens who trace their roots to the Middle East, are Christian Palestinians.[4] They arrived in Central America at different times for assorted reasons. More than a century of Palestinian presence in Honduras has created a prosperous community influenced by the intermingling of diverse cultures. As a result, both the immigrants and Hondurans of other ethnic backgrounds have been forever changed and enriched.

This chapter will examine the experience of Arab immigrants to Honduras, with a special emphasis on the Palestinian population from Bethlehem, Beit Sahur, and Beit Jala. Much of the current scholarship on Arabs in Honduras is focused on the city of San Pedro Sula, due to its long history of Arab immigration and the large Palestinian population currently living there. Consequently, much of the information in this chapter is drawn from studies based in this industrial city in northern Honduras, near the border with Guatemala. What follows is a discussion of migrants' motivations, both push and pull factors, as well as an overview of early immigrants' experiences in Honduras. The second half of the article will focus on processes that have played out largely since the end of World War II and the creation of

Israel in 1948. It will discuss Palestinians' integration into Honduran society by looking at language, marriage patterns, business success, involvement in politics, and social roles.

Immigration Patterns

Migration Motivations

The earliest Palestinian immigrants to Central America left the Middle East for many reasons. They departed in search of better economic conditions, freedom from religious persecution, and to escape the draft. Deteriorating conditions in the Ottoman Empire, which ruled the Holy Land for some four hundred years, prompted further emigration during the second half of the nineteenth century. Nancie L. Gonzalez, author of *Dollar, Dove, and Eagle: 100 Years of Palestinian Migration to Honduras*, reports that while there was some clandestine migration in the last decade of the nineteenth century, Christians could not legally leave the Empire until 1896.[5] In 1909, Christians became eligible for the draft, and in 1914, the Ottoman Empire entered World War I.[6] This combination of events most surely encouraged many Palestinian Christians to leave home. Christians had been fleeing the West Bank since the middle of the nineteenth century, when the weakening of the Ottoman Empire subjected them to various types of discrimination, including labor levies and protection-style demands for money and goods to ensure their safety.[7] According to Gonzalez, though the Ottoman Empire attempted to "modernize" after the Crimean War (1853–1856), "local conditions continued to worsen" and hence provided further incentive for Palestinian Christians to emigrate.[8]

Elias Larach, descendent of a circa World War I immigrant, retells the experiences of the Palestinian community's "fathers and grandfathers" in an interview with writer and photographer Larry Luxner: "The Arab people were obliged by the Ottoman Empire to fight against the Allies. Often they did not come back. So our grandmothers tried to help us leave the country for a while."[9] Others made the decision to migrate as a result of the hard economic times following World War I. Years later, the creation of Israel prompted further migration, and the recent escalation of violence in the Middle East has led to increased emigration of Christian and Muslim Palestinians. The economy, especially the tourist industry has been hit hard by this most recent violence, which provoked the emigration of an estimated 3,000 Bethlehem-area Christians between 2000 and 2005.[10] Following a typical chain migration pattern, many migrants who have family or business ties in Honduras choose this small Central American country as their final destination.

Accidental Destination

Not all Arab immigrants to Honduras were following a family member, however. Somehow, the first immigrants had to arrive in Honduras, and there was quite a bit of chance involved in that first journey. Getting to Honduras, or anywhere in America, was no easy task during the late eighteenth and early nineteenth centuries. Immigrants scraped together their savings, says Honduran-born Antonio Jacobo Saybe,[11] and "bought third class tickets, the most they could afford." Many migrants who set out for the United States were obstructed either by U.S. immigration authorities or by their lack of understanding of American geography. They bought tickets to America, intending to travel to the United States, but due to unscrupulous travel brokers or honest misunderstanding, some ended up in Honduras. Others only cared about landing somewhere in America. José Segebre, from Beit Jala, remembers traveling through Marseilles, "where we'd see a ship in the harbor, ask where it was going and be told it was going to America. That was enough for us. We hurried to get on, and get off wherever it went."[12]

Fortune Seekers

Before 1948, many immigrants did not intend to permanently relocate to Honduras. In fact Gonzalez points out that the "tradition of traveling to obtain one's fortune" is at least 200 years old, as demonstrated by the *Tales of the Arabian Nights*.[13] Interestingly, Gonzalez reports that many Christian Palestinians, "perhaps the majority," left the farm behind and undertook solely commercial activities from approximately "the last quarter of the eighteenth century."[14] These peddlers could have spent months or years traveling throughout the Middle East and Europe before returning home. Indeed, some traveled as far as Honduras in search of their fortune. Considering the cultural template for travel–and–return fortune-seeking, newcomers to Honduras may not have worried too much if they did not feel fully accepted in this new land. Their point of reference was always the Holy Land.

Furthermore, in the early days many Arab immigrants probably considered the standard of living in Honduras to be somewhat primitive compared to what they were accustomed to. This situation may have reinforced their intention to capitalize on the developing country's demand for trade goods and then travel home again to marry and settle. All this changed, however, with the creation of Israel in 1948. Adams affirms that with "the partition of Palestine...the motive for migration shifted."[15] The possibility of not being able to return home made it very important for Palestinian Christians not only to succeed economically but also to establish a place within Honduran society. Gonzalez describes this as the turning point when Palestinians developed "a new commitment to the New World, a new culture, and a new nation."[16]

Los Turcos

Hondurans referred to the first Arabic immigrants as *turcos*.[17] The Turkish passports issued to emigrants by the Ottoman Empire prompted this label, and the appellation stuck. Interestingly, many immigrants who arrived around 1900 carried no documents, let alone a Turkish passport; "they came without any papers, and without a penny in their pockets," says Saybe.[18] After 1952, when Jordan took control of the West Bank, people from Bethlehem, the ancestral home of many Honduran Palestinians, were granted Jordanian citizenship, and may have carried a Jordanian passport.[19] Most immigrants arrived in Honduras after passing through several ports, so their travel documents likely did not mention Palestine or the Ottoman Empire.[20] For Hondurans to apply the name *turco* to all Middle Eastern (non-Jewish) immigrants, there must have been characteristic factors that united the group. Examination of the Arab experience in Honduras reveals a tightly knit community that relies on family connections in business and preserves ethnic traditions in the home. Paradoxically, the Palestinian population is also famous for its success adapting to life in Honduras.

The Immigrant Experience

Late in the nineteenth century, Christian Palestinians began to flee persecution and economic difficulty under the Ottoman Empire for the prospect of freedom and prosperity in America.[21] Gonzalez describes the early Palestinian arrivals to Honduras as traveling merchants who sold a variety of products such as brooms and dry goods over a wide area of the country. These industrious men carried their merchandise by canoe and railway, and they took orders for household necessities in numerous small towns throughout the region. According to Darío A. Euraque's work, "The Arab-Jewish

Economic Presence in San Pedro Sula, the Industrial Capital of Honduras: Formative Years, 1880s–1930s," the first documented Arab in Honduras was Constantino Nini, who "arrived in La Ceiba in 1893."[22] Arab peddlers worked hard and thrived, and the word spread quickly that someone with limited capital and a strong work ethic could find good business opportunities in Honduras. By 1930 there were around 24,500 Arabs living in San Pedro Sula; by 1940, that number had jumped to around 40,500.[23]

Based on the success stories of early immigrants, friends and family members decided to join these early entrepreneurs. Over time, families would amass enough capital to establish a small store that in some instances evolved into a factory, a number of which are still in operation. As a result of her investigations, Gonzalez remarks, "Middle Easterners were notoriously innovative in the new world, providing goods and services previously unavailable."[24] According to Gonzalez, Arab men established the first cigarette factory in San Pedro Sula in 1914. She also credits Arabs with being the first to sell "ground coffee in the streets from two-wheeled carts."[25] Luxner states that by 1918, forty-two percent of the businesses in San Pedro, the industrial capital of Honduras, were owned by Arab immigrants.[26]

Several factors helped the first Arab peddlers to achieve success. The custom among Middle Eastern farmers to sell produce, crafts, and other merchandise on the side and the developing tradition of Christian Palestinians' involvement in ambulatory trade gave immigrants a strong practical background in commerce. Moreover, according to Gonzalez's research, the majority of the Palestinians who moved to Honduras came from Bethlehem and the nearby villages of Beit Sahur and Beit Jala.[27] The comfort that immigrants from this region felt with each other meant that they could easily depend on one another, which led to mutually beneficial business relationships. Third, Bethlehem was home to high-quality educational opportunities, especially for Christians, at schools founded by various European groups.[28] The farmer-peddlers who eventually migrated to Honduras were probably reasonably well educated; it was likely that they spoke English or French, and they had considerable skills in running a small business. These skills plus Palestinian immigrants' tendency to stick together and support each other in business and social matters was an excellent formula for economic success on the North coast of Honduras.

Familiarity with English was especially advantageous in northern Honduras because of the proximity and influence of Belize, formerly known as

British Honduras. In addition, English-speaking Arab immigrants were able to capitalize on well-established links between northern Honduras and centers of commerce in the United States, notably New Orleans and Mobile and participate in the lucrative banana and tobacco industries.[29]

Despite their growing commercial success, Arab merchants on the north coast of Honduras in the 1920s felt significant economic pressure from the company store, and it seems some individuals took action to try to put an end to the competition. According to Euraque, a 1924 U.S. Consul report of banana worker strikes near La Ceiba and Puerto Castilla "blamed...non-Honduran 'agitators,' some of whom included Syrians, Armenians and Palestinians who objected to the banana companies' commercial monopoly."[30]

Accounts like this, or that of a 1929 law requiring Arabs to deposit $2,500 upon entering the country clearly illustrate the obstacles Arab immigrants encountered in their struggle to establish and maintain a place in Honduran society.[31] Until recently though, accounts of the first Arab immigrants to Latin America, in particular to Honduras, have been based on local legends and family stories, which tend to romanticize immigrants' experiences and gloss over the difficulties they faced. Researchers and historians are beginning to develop a more sophisticated understanding of the chronicle of Arabs in Honduras and other Latin American countries, but there is still considerable room for further investigation.

Integration into Honduran Society

Arabic and Discrimination

Upon arrival in Central America, and during the early period of their residence in Honduras, Arabic speaking immigrants undoubtedly experienced some discrimination and problems with acculturation. Some local people may have been suspicious of the Arab salesman's imperfect Spanish, and they might have been reluctant to do business with him, for fear they would be over–charged. Honduran–Arab business partnerships, where clear communication was so important, would have experienced difficulties as well. The language difference, therefore, was one factor that encouraged Arabs to group together and to rely on one another for business assistance. New immigrants often received help from sympathetic friends, relatives, or people from their hometown. José Segebre[32] reveals, "A friend gave me yam[s] and clothes, and I opened a tienda in downtown San Pedro Sula, though I had no experience."

Changing Marriage Patterns

Gonzalez reports that, although some early immigrants had children with Hondurans and some married local women, the majority returned to the Middle East to bring back a spouse.[33] They also traveled to the Holy Land to participate in important religious rituals, such as baptisms and marriages. It was not just sentiment that called these individuals home. There was an important legal aspect to consider as well, because marriages conducted in Honduras were not legally recognized by Ottoman or British authorities in the Holy Land.[34] Once larger communities of Palestinians were established in the New World, more men found their wives in Honduras. Interestingly, Gonzalez reports that Arabs' choice of wives sometimes led to misunderstanding with the local population because they "tended to marry women Hondurans would have considered kin."[35] She explains that Middle Easterners often married their cousins,[36] which Catholic Hondurans did not view positively.

A Visible Presence in Honduras

Over time, marriages between Arabs and Hondurans became more common. As evidence of this phenomenon, Gonzalez estimates that 25 percent of the population of San Pedro Sula has Palestinian roots.[37] Today, visitors to San Pedro will easily notice the contributions and influence of these Palestinian Hondurans. According to Gonzalez, a 1979 survey conducted by cultural geographer William K. Crowley revealed that 75 percent of the stores in the busiest section of downtown San Pedro were Palestinian owned.[38] The shining star of the Arab scholastic realm is the Escuela Trilingüe San Juan Bautista,[39] where the children learn Spanish, English, and Arabic, perform Arab dances, and learn about their Middle Eastern heritage. The school, with well over 100 students, is the only trilingual school of its type in Central America. Nearby is the Orthodox Christian Church of San Juan Bautista. Founded in 1963, the church is the only Orthodox Church in Central America.[40] Some 220 families reportedly belong to the church.[41]

Luxner reports finding only one Middle Eastern restaurant in San Pedro Sula,[42] but a wide range of Middle Eastern foods can be enjoyed at the Central Social Hondureño-Árabe.[43] The latter is an elegant country club that started out as a small social center in the suburbs of San Pedro in 1968.[44] Interestingly, Euraque reports that in the year the club was built, Arab employers oversaw "36 per cent and 45 per cent of the manufacturing labour force in Tegucigalpa [the capital] and San Pedro Sula, respectively."[45] Luxner reports that today the Central Social Hondureño-Árabe consists of an impressive array of buildings worth more than $15 million dollars.[46]

Not Fully Honduran?

In her research on the economic impact of Christian Palestinians in Honduras, Gonzalez confirms that owing to a long history of economic success, the descendants of Arab immigrants perform an important leadership role in the commercial and industrial sectors of San Pedro Sula.[47] At the same time, she notes, "they are less than fully accepted by the larger Honduran society."[48] Gonzalez ties this lack of recognition of Arab Hondurans as fully Honduran to the migration and settlement pattern of the first immigrants. Early immigrants followed family members and neighbors to Honduras and relied heavily on these relationships for support while they established themselves. This strategy has led to the endurance of Arab ethnic identification and slowed the integration into Honduran society. Gonzalez also refers to the "protracted conflict in their original homeland," as a possible basis for lack of acceptance.[49]

Political Roles

Counterevidence to the claim that Arabs are not well accepted by Hondurans is the fact that Christian Palestinians in Honduras have begun to play an important role in the politics of the country. The mother of Carlos Roberto Flores Facusse, president from 1998 to 2002, was from Bethlehem,[50] and the former minister of industry and commerce and ambassador, Oscar Kafati, traces his roots to the town of Beit Jala, on the West Bank.

Kafati expresses the view that "Twenty or thirty years ago, there was a lot of discrimination. They didn't accept immigrants of Arab origin as elected officials."[51] As a matter of fact, between 1900 and 1936, no Arab names appear on San Pedro Sula's records of municipal committees.[52] The doors seem to have opened, however, since the last decade of the twentieth century. Since then, Honduras has seen political figures of Arabic origin such as William Handal, former vice-president; Juan Bendeck, minister at large; Victoria Asfoura, president of the Central Bank, and several deputies in the House of Parliament assume office.[53] Influential Arab Hondurans can also be found in the ranks of all three major political parties in the country.

Social Roles and Charity

During President Flores Facusse's term in office, Hurricane Mitch devastated Tegucigalpa and other parts of Honduras. In response to this massive disaster, Luxner reports that "two women's organizations—the Association of Arab Orthodox Women and the Honduran Arab Ladies' Association" assisted in relief efforts.[54] Years before Mitch hit, Arab business owners participated in a social outreach project through the chamber of commerce of San Pedro Sula. According to an article published on the Honduran presidential Web site, the Fundación Mhotivo, "Más Hondureños Teniendo Identidad, Valores y Orgullo," was founded in 1992 with the goal of providing quality education in the arts, sciences, and languages, to less-fortunate students.[55] In December of 2004, the school served 771 boys and girls from kindergarten through fourth grade.[56] While both Arab and non-Arab members of the chamber maintain the foundation, Luxner reports that "most of the names on the plaque at the school's entrance—names like Emilio Hawit Lara, Jacobo Faraj, and George Chair—have a distinctively Arab flavor."[57]

Conclusion

Although Palestinians make up the largest and best-studied group of Arabs living in Honduras, there are Syrians, Armenians, and Lebanese populations as well. Sizeable populations of Arabs have settled throughout Latin America, and though they have some characteristics in common with Honduran Palestinians, there are many variables and unique circumstances that distinguish each population. The body of research on the Arab diaspora to Latin America is growing, but there is much yet to be investigated.

This article has briefly examined migrants' motivations for leaving Palestine after the Crimean War, during both World Wars and upon the creation of Israel, while also addressing the difficulties faced and successes achieved by these immigrants. In some ways, Palestinians have integrated very well into Honduran society. They are important business and political figures who have also contributed to the growth of the nation through charity and service. Nevertheless, Palestinians and other Arabs still face obstacles to full inclusion in Honduran society. Family cohesion and adherence to tradition have helped Arabs accomplish much in Honduras, but they may also contribute to the community's lingering disconnection from Honduran society. Is this scenario repeated in other parts of Latin America, or have other communities of Arab immigrants been able to achieve a balance between maintaining cultural traditions and integrating into Latin American society?

With regard to Palestinian immigration to Honduras and other areas of Latin America, further research could explore the historical influence of Palestinian–Israeli relations on the type and level of migration. With the possibility of a peace agreement between Palestine and Israel in the future, do Palestinians in Latin America feel strongly about the creation of a Palestinian state? Do they travel home to encourage this cause, and do they support Palestinian political organizations? Finally, how do contemporary Palestinian migrants to Honduras view their immigration status in light of a possible future Palestinian state? Do young Palestinian immigrants plan to establish a permanent home in Honduras, as has been the trend since 1948, or are they, like their late nineteenth and early twentieth century counterparts, traveling to Honduras in search of economic opportunities with the ultimate intention of returning to the Holy Land?

Notes

1. Nancie L. Gonzalez, *Dollar, Dove, and Eagle: One Hundred Years of Palestinian Migration to Honduras* (Ann Arbor: University of Michigan Press, 1992), 63. Other cities in Honduras with sizeable Palestinian communities are San Lorenzo, Comayagua, Puerto Comes, El Progreso, and the capital Tegucigalpa.
2. Larry Luxner, "Arab Pride of Honduras," *Americas*, 54. 2 (2002): par. 8.
3. Luxner, par. 8.
4. Luxner, par. 53.
5. Gonzalez, *Dollar, Dove, and Eagle: One Hundred Years of Palestinian Migration to Honduras*, 88.
6. Gonzalez, *Dollar, Dove, and Eagle: One Hundred Years of Palestinian Migration to Honduras*, 28.
7. See note 5 above.
8. See note 5 above.
9. Luxner, par. 24.
10. Ken Ellingwood, "Strife Spurs Slow Exodus of West Bank Christians," *Los Angeles Times*, April 14, 2005, par. 3.
11. Saybe is the son of Palestinian immigrant Jacobo Saybe. The 69-year-old Saybe owns Fundidora del Norte S.A., a factory that produces agricultural equipment in San Pedro Sula, Honduras. See Luxner, par. 23.
12. Luxner, par. 30.
13. Gonzalez, *Dollar, Dove, and Eagle: One Hundred Years of Palestinian Migration to Honduras*, 26.
14. Gonzalez, *Dollar, Dove, and Eagle: One Hundred Years of Palestinian Migration to Honduras*, 81.

15. David Adams, "You See How Many We Are," *St. Petersburg Times*, January 2, 2001, par. 17.

16. Gonzalez, *Dollar, Dove, and Eagle: One Hundred Years of Palestinian Migration to Honduras*, 67–68.

17. The term *turco* is sometimes used disparagingly, as this Honduran teenager did in 1984, "We work, but a Turco is like an octopus. All they think about is money." See Thomas E. Ricks, "Palestinians Prospering in Honduras Find Themselves in an Uneasy Position," *Wall Street Journal* (Eastern Edition), May 2, 1984, available from Proquest Online database at Friends University, http://www.library.friends.edu. *Turco* can also be used without the negative connotation, to describe an Arab person, though the term *árabe* is a more polite option.

18. Luxner, par. 23.

19. Gonzalez, *Dollar, Dove, and Eagle: One Hundred Years of Palestinian Migration to Honduras*, 184.

20. For a list of Caribbean and Central American countries used as stop-off points before immigrants arrived in Honduras, see Luxner, par. 23. For a discussion of the Arab communities in the port cities of Colombia, see Adams, par. 16.

21. Luxner, par. 24–25.

22. Gonzalez, *Dollar, Dove, and Eagle: One Hundred Years of Palestinian Migration to Honduras*, 107.

23. Euraque bases these figures on San Pedro Sula municipal records of the 1940s. These data also show that Arabs did not account for more than 0.7 percent of San Pedro's population during these years, and that 95 percent of the Arab residents of San Pedro were Palestinian. See Darío A. Euraque, "The Arab-Jewish Economic Presence in San Pedro Sula, the Industrial Capital of Honduras: Formative Years, 1880s–1930s," *Arab and Jewish Immigrants in Latin America: Images and Realities*, ed. Ignacio Klitch and Jeffrey Lesser (London: Frank Cass, 1998), 107.

24. Gonzalez, *Dollar, Dove, and Eagle: One Hundred Years of Palestinian Migration to Honduras*, 93.

25. See note 24 above.

26. Luxner, par. 24.

27. Gonzalez, *Dollar, Dove, and Eagle: One Hundred Years of Palestinian Migration to Honduras*, 61.

28. Gonzalez states that "from the time of Constantine," European relations with the Christians of Bethlehem were strong and fruitful (*Dollar, Dove, and Eagle: One Hundred Years of Palestinian Migration to Honduras*, 83). The Franciscans, as well as "Italian, French, German, English and American religious groups" established schools of all types in and around Bethlehem. "Even today," she says, "Muslim Palestinians flock to Christian schools" (*Dollar, Dove, and Eagle: One Hundred Years of Palestinian Migration to Honduras*, 184–85).

29. Some Southerners, discontented with the outcome of the Civil War, moved to Honduras to escape the "foreign invaders" from the North (Gonzalez, *Dollar, Dove, and Eagle: One Hundred Years of Palestinian Migration to Honduras*, 68).

30. Euraque, 111.

31. Euraque quotes the 1929 law in which "immigrant *Arabs, Turcos, Sirios, Armenios, Negros,* and 'Coolies'" were strictly limited in their access to Honduras. The laws instituted in 1934 were even stricter, and Arabs were required to "give guarantee which proves...that they come exclusively to devote themselves to agriculture or the

introduction or improvement of new industries." The "Law of Foreigners," which applied only to undesirable immigrants, stated that anyone who had not begun their agricultural or industrial work within six months would be deported (105).

32. Luxner interviewed Segebre, a Palestinian immigrant from Beit Jala near Bethlehem, who was the first member of his family to migrate to Honduras. According to the interview, once Segebre had established his business, he sent for his parents to join him. When he left Marseilles, Segebre did not know to which part of America he was traveling. "We'd see a ship in the harbor," he says, "ask where it was going and be told it was going to America. That was enough for us. We hurried to get on, and get off wherever it went" (par. 30).

33. Gonzalez, *Dollar, Dove, and Eagle: One Hundred Years of Palestinian Migration to Honduras*, 189.

34. Gonzalez, *Dollar, Dove, and Eagle: One Hundred Years of Palestinian Migration to Honduras*, 188–89.

35. Gonzalez, *Dollar, Dove, and Eagle: One Hundred Years of Palestinian Migration to Honduras*, 88.

36. Gonzalez explains the traditional expectation that a young woman should be betrothed to a "real or classificatory father's brother's son" (*Dollar, Dove, and Eagle: One Hundred Years of Palestinian Migration to Honduras*, 113).

37. Gonzalez, *Dollar, Dove, and Eagle: One Hundred Years of Palestinian Migration to Honduras*, 10.

38. Gonzalez, *Dollar, Dove, and Eagle: One Hundred Years of Palestinian Migration to Honduras*, 99.

39. Luxner cites school rector George Faraj as the source for all statistics on the Escuela Trilingüe (par. 4).

40. Wendy Griffin, "Christian Arabs Come of Age in Honduras," *Honduras This Week*, March 13, 2000, Online edition 14, par. 3.

41.An interview with Father Boulos E. Moussa, or "Padre Pablo" provided Luxner's information on the Orthodox Church (par. 5-6).

42. Luxner, par. 42.

43. The kitchens at the Centro Social Hondureño Árabe serve "felafel, kibbe, and babaganush, or typical Honduran dishes like fajitas or a plato tipico" (Luxner, par. 37). According to Luxner's report, there is also a sushi bar (par. 36).

44. According to Luxner, eight Honduran Arabs started the club in 1968 by building a swimming pool. Today 1,600 families, including a few Jewish families, are members of the club (par. 35-36).

45. Luxner, par. 95.

46. Luxner, par. 35.

47. Several of Luxner's informants are important San Pedro Sula businessmen: Juan Canahuati, textiles; George Elias Mitri, mattresses; Roberto Handal, shoes; Elias S. Larach, hardware store; Gabriel Kafati, coffee; Antonio Jacobo Saybe, farm equipment; Nawal Canahuati, Comisariato Los Andes (one of the largest supermarkets in the country).

48.Nancie L. Gonzalez, "The Christian Palestinians of Honduras: An Uneasy Accommodation," in *Conflict, Migration and the Expression of Ethnicity*, ed. Nancie L. Gonzalez and Carolyn S. McCommon (Boulder: Westview Press, 1989) , 75-90.

49. Gonzalez, "The Christian Palestinians of Honduras: An Uneasy Accommodation," 75.

50. Luxner, par. 9.

51. Luxner, par. 15.

52. The lack of Arab representation in politics before 1950 may have been partly due to the fact that most Arabs living in Honduras at that time were not Honduran citizens (Euraque, 95).

53. In addition to these specific officials, Luxner claims that about 5% of the Honduran parliament, "at least half a dozen of the 120 deputies," is of Palestinian descent (par. 16).

54. Luxner, par. 48.

55. Presidency of the Republic of Honduras, par. 15.

56. Presidency of the Republic of Honduras, par. 19.

57. Luxner, par. 49–50.

Works Cited

Adams, David. "You See How Many We Are." *St. Petersburg Times.* January 2, 2001.

Ellingwood, Ken. "Strife Spurs Slow Exodus of West Bank Christians." *Los Angeles Times.* April 14, 2005.

Euraque, Darío A. "The Arab-Jewish Economic Presence in San Pedro Sula, the Industrial Capital of Honduras: Formative Years, 1880s–1930s." In *Arab and Jewish Immigrants in Latin America: Images and Realities,* eds. Ignacio Klitch and Jeffrey Lesser, 94–124. London: Frank Cass, 1998.

Gonzalez, Nancie L. *Dollar, Dove, and Eagle: One Hundred Years of Palestinian Migration to Honduras.* Ann Arbor: University of Michigan Press, 1992.

———. "The Christian Palestinians of Honduras: An Uneasy Accommodation." In *Conflict, Migration and the Expression of Ethnicity,* edited by Nancie L. Gonzalez and Carolyn S. McCommon, 75–90. Boulder: Westview Press, 1989.

Griffin, Wendy. "Christian Arabs Come of Age in Honduras." *Honduras This Week.* Online edition 14. March 13, 2000.

Presidency of the Republic of Honduras. "Fundación Mhotivo ofrece concierto de gala en homenaje a la Primera Dama." Presidencia de la República de Honduras, http://www.casapresidencial.hn/2004/12/08_3.php.

Luxner, Larry. "Arab Pride of Honduras." *Americas* 54, no.2 (2002): 46–51.

Ricks, Thomas E. "Palestinians Prospering in Honduras Find Themselves in an Uneasy Position." *Wall Street Journal* (Eastern edition). May 2, 1984, available from Proquest Online Database at Friends University, http://www.library.friends.edu.

Part 3

Assessing the Americas

7

Gazing East from the Americas: Assessing the Cultural Significance of Modern Arab American Literature

Steven Salaita

"The gaze" is probably approaching the status of cliché these days in literary study. The term gained currency with the advent and evolution of feminist, postmodernist, and postcolonial theories, from which arose such familiar phrases such as the "male gaze," the "Western gaze," the "colonial gaze," and so forth, each of which denotes a form of oppression symbolized by an invented reality that supplements the respective oppressor's interests or that satisfies his needs. Today, though, it is possible to liberate "the gaze" from this traditional usage and speak of it in the context of migratory communities that reflect through various media on their places of origin. This essay will examine how modern Arab American writers illuminate moral and philosophical spaces in North America by invoking themes drawn from and relevant to the Arab World, thus engaging in an inverted form of the traditional gaze. This sort of geographical interplay, though, has helped undermine the unilateral production of knowledge about Arabs in North America, in the United States particularly, and has influenced the development of American literature generally by introducing new thematic elements, cultural manifestations, and political imperatives.

The fact that people other than professional commentators and affiliated politicos use the setting of North America to reflect on life and culture in the Arab World is a positive development, especially as it affects literary criticism. Indeed, a brief overview of modern Arab American literature, which appears to be entering into a prolific era, indicates that it is of great significance to contemporary literary culture in the United States. The most conspicuous feature of its significance has been the ability of Arab American authors to explore the landscape of North America in the framework of political, aesthetic, and cultural peculiarities common to the Arab World. Arab American authors thus reinvent the Western gaze by reconfiguring what it means to illuminate the Arab World from the United States. In so doing, they have altered the commonplaces of American literary production.

It is important to note that "Arab American literature," like other ethnic or national literary traditions, is not a singular or even unified entity. What might strike a critic most immediately about Arab American fiction, for instance, is its thematic diversity and the way this diversity has fallen into certain patterns that lend themselves to subcategorization. While it might have been difficult twenty or even ten years ago to teach an entire course on Arab American fiction, it is not only possible to teach one now, but possible to teach many based on various overarching themes. One could construct a course focused on the Israel–Palestine conflict using Miriam Cooke, Shaw Dallal, Ibrahim Fawal, and Kathryn K. Abdul-Baki.[1] One also could interrogate the American social landscape and examine issues such as immigration, acculturation, xenophobia, gender, and ethnic identity by assigning Diana Abu-Jaber, Laila Lalami, Joseph Geha, and Laila Halaby.[2] Alternatively, one could develop a curriculum based on fictive explorations of the Lebanese Civil War using Etel Adnan, Patricia Sarrafian Ward, and Rabih Alameddine.[3] One could, of course, teach all of these subcategories as different units in the same course.

The same, I might add, is true of the genres of poetry, drama, and nonfiction. Poetry is without question the most sophisticated genre in the Arab American literary tradition, owing partly, no doubt, to the importance of poetry in the Arab World dating to the pre-Islamic period. (The Arabic novel was largely inherited from Europe.) The complexity of this poetry, both traditionally and at present, speaks to the multiple spaces that Arab Americans inhabit culturally and politically and choose to explore when producing art. The complexity also belies widespread notions in the United States of Arab American homogeneity, a notion that certainly might be countered through political discourse but might just as well be challenged by the dissemination of reading lists. Arab American poets such as Khaled Mattawa, Naomi Shihab Nye, Lawrence Joseph, Lisa Suhair Majaj, Mohja Kahf, Nathalie Handal, David Williams, D. H. Melhem, and Samuel Hazo have achieved success extending well beyond the Arab American community; each poet employs an assortment of themes and poetic devices, none quite like any of the others.[4] Similarly, playwrights such as Betty Shamieh, Elmaz Abinader, Kathryn

Haddad, Amani Elkassabani, and Annemarie Jacir have extended both generic and thematic possibilities, as have various nonfiction writers engaged in both life narrative and politics.

Of what relevance are these observations? First of all, they connote a maturation of Arab American literature that demands acknowledgment in critical and pedagogical conversations. Second, they indicate that the diversities inherent in the Arab American community—diversities that generally are unacknowledged in popular discussion of Arabs and Islam—are being articulated in Arab American literature, in both its themes and structures. Third, although I believe it is necessary in critical approaches to literature to favor poetic analysis over political commentary, it is evident that these diversities help challenge the homogenized stereotypes of Arab Americans circulating widely in American society. Finally, these diversities ensure that the task of the literary critic, and in turn the instructor, will become more complex, with presumably a positive and productive effect. In short, then, the maturation of Arab American literature has conferred to its critics exciting and rewarding possibilities—analysis of Eastward gazes, for instance. Even though it is often considered naïve or passé in critical circles today to surmise that literature affects material issues, it seems that Arab American literature has real transformative power and that one of the tasks of the critic and instructor of this literature is to explore its transformative power and tap into it morally and philosophically.

Let us extend this discussion to include specific thematic phenomena. It can be said that all ethnic literary traditions are discrete, although the extent of their discreteness is indeterminate. Whatever discreteness exists among those traditions can be illuminated not through discussion of style or structure, devices that transcend group and nation, but through identification of thematic particularities. African American literature, for instance, has focused on issues of slavery and segregation more consistently than, say, Asian American literature, even though both African American and Asian American writers have this century employed postmodern and modernist poetics with roughly the same consistency. The themes of slavery and segregation, then, help render African American literature discrete, although this literature is by no means focused exclusively on those themes, just as those themes are not exclusive to African American literature. Conversely, Native American authors have explored colonial dynamics in their work with great passion, an understandable focus given the historical conditions that influence their

cultural practices. Without the existence of detectable thematic patterns we
have little to rely on in identifying discrete literary traditions other than
authorial ethnicity, a highly problematic criterion. Arab American literature,
in all its genres, has recently developed thematic patterns that are most
detectable by virtue of their geographic—and, in turn, cultural—emphasis. (All
of these categories, it should be mentioned, are quite amorphous, for any
literary categorization ultimately is a slippery enterprise.)

Arab American writers explore in their art Middle Eastern cultures and
politics more frequently than do authors from other ethnic minority
communities. To be sure, issues in the Arab World do not constitute the
totality of authorial explorations—or even a majority of them—but the
landscape of West Asia and North Africa and the various political and ethnic
cultures in existence in those regions are invoked frequently enough to
constitute something of a discrete literary tradition. The focus here is on the
Eastward gaze as the primary device that allows critics to identify a proper
tradition because no other device affords us such a possibility. The point, in
any event, is not to seek a proper tradition, which many would rightly consider
a fool's mission; rather, we are better served by detecting thematic patterns
that bespeak a traditional literary cohesiveness worth critical attention.
Immigration, a crucial and long-standing theme in Arab American literature,
is unavailable in such a critical framework because it has been explored with
equal or greater frequency in other literary traditions—in Chicano/a and Asian
American writing, for instance. The same is true of thematic patterns such as
migration, transnationalism, gender, class, and cultural multiplicity. Authors
writing, consciously or not, from within any literary category will approach any
or all of these thematic patterns uniquely, but even if those patterns are
grouped according to their usage in specific ethnic categories they will be
heterogeneous to the point of polyglot and thus will be unable to highlight the
attributes of a tradition.

Of course, it is no revelation that Arab American writers explore West
Asian and North African themes more frequently and consistently than
writers from other ethnic literary traditions. Given the physical, cultural, and
geographical origins of Arab Americans, it would be shocking if Arab
American authors didn't explore the Arab World frequently and consistently
in their art. The obvious, however, is never a very interesting basis for a literary
inquiry. Understanding why a phenomenon becomes obvious in a specific
point in time and to a particular audience, though, is one of the most

interesting forms of inquiry available. A number of Arab American literary critics have observed that the Arab World is invoked in Arab American literature, but little has been said about the intents and effects of such invocations. In this instance, the phenomena allowing for the obvious existence of ethnic and transnational affinity happen also to frame morally and philosophically the sort of questions that might facilitate sophisticated inquiry into Arab American literature. The most relevant question follows: Why is there transnational and ethnic affinity between Arab America and the Arab World, and to what end, and using which means, do Arab American writers maintain that affinity?

It might be too causal to conflate one's origin with his or her worldview, but among Arab American authors of all genres a thematic affinity in the form of an Eastern gaze is evident. This affinity is far from universal, and it is not articulated uniformly; it is merely common—common enough, in any event, to deduce that it is not a cultural or historical accident. Furthermore, it is not causal to speculate that an Eastern gaze has allowed Arab American literature to obtain a discrete category in the critical and literary marketplaces. Conversely, the Eastern gaze of the Arab American author has affected the cultural and moral commonplaces of North America, most explicitly by reinventing the philosophical apparatus that traditionally has influenced American perceptions of Eastern cultures—and by exposing the problematic assumptions underlying many of those perceptions. If Arab American writers have created for themselves a perceptible cultural significance in the United States, then, it usually has been the result of gazing East from the Americas, or has arisen somehow in that context.

Naomi Shihab Nye, for example, has long employed themes related to Palestine and the Palestinians, most conspicuously in her pieces "Shrines," "Blood," and "My Father and the Fig Tree."[5] These themes have been cultural and political, and they have drawn aesthetic inspiration from the profound tradition of verse in the Arab World. In fact, if one reads enough modern Arab American poetry and fiction, one will surely notice that Palestine arises recurrently, in both major and minor ways. The same is true, as noted above, of the Lebanese Civil War and a number of other geopolitical issues in places such as Egypt, Morocco, and Iraq. (Laila Lalami's new book, to provide one example, offers an interesting, and heretofore unexplored, illustration of migration from the Southern Hemisphere to the Northern.) The novel *The Bullet Collection* is a noteworthy case of an author gazing Eastward in the framework of the Lebanese Civil War. By incorporating the war and its surrounding landscape into the moral groundwork of the novel, its author, Patricia Sarrafian Ward, managed to transcend mere hybridity or mediation and created instead a text in which North America is given definition as the object functioning as counterpart to the Eastern subject.

Laila Halaby's *West of the Jordan* also explores the many schisms and unities between Near East and North America. Its title suggests that Halaby will be concerned somehow with geographical and geopolitical spaces, a suggestion that Halaby fulfills by conceptualizing the West as a heterogeneous entity with a connection physically and spiritually to its Eastern counterpart. A comparable geopolitical dialectic can be found in Diana Abu-Jaber's *Arabian Jazz*, Kathryn K. Abdul-Baki's *Ghost Songs*, and Samia Serageldin's *The Cairo House*.[6] The same dialectic exists—with, of course, the appropriate generic variations—in a broad range of Arab American verse published during the past five years. Even the political nonfiction composed recently by Arab Americans—a process in which, I add humbly, I have played a small role—has been attuned quite explicitly to the influences of the Arab World on the coalescence of an identifiable Arab American community. All of these examples supplement the more critical point that Arab American literature has played a role in altering traditional conceptions of American literature, not always directly, although this does happen, but more often merely by existing.

This argument is tricky by virtue of its seemingly prescriptive outlook. Certainly it might be rejected on the grounds that the appearance of any published text in the United States necessarily alters the tone and tenor of American literature. The better texts manage to go further and alter traditional conceptions of American literature. Even so, what I have in mind is quite less complex than epistemological transmutations. I would like instead to offer a far more basic point that itself raises numerous questions: "American literature" is today a meaningless category. The category is not meaningless because the literature of the United States has no inherent value or because it is ineffectual as a cultural phenomenon. Rather, the category is meaningless because it has no meaning outside of a highly limited notion of "America" and "Americanness." Either the category of American literature is meaningless or its most meaningful contribution to its own survival will continue to be its exclusivity. However, there is no need to become pessimistic: The same features that render American literature meaningless as a category render it meaningful as a literary tradition.

Arab American literature has played a role—lately, a substantial role—in this formation of meaning. By entering into a literary productivity in the United States, Arab American writers have amended what it means to be an American producer and consumer of textual matter and in turn have displaced the venerable (sometimes racist) subject-positioning of the White Christian as characteristically American. If we can argue, as countless others before us have, that the American heartland provided an inspired dynamic through which Wallace Stegner created meaning in supposedly a quintessentially American manner, then I see no reason beyond perhaps anachronistic exclusivity or subtle racism why Palestine cannot provide the same impetus for, say, Naomi Shihab Nye's quintessentially American poetry. Indeed, that Nye and many others can utilize Palestine to create various sets of meanings in a specifically American framework indicates that American literature's best attribute may be its flexibility, the same attribute that renders it categorically ambiguous. American literature is best identified by this prominent irony. Arab American literature is best identified by its contributions to the irony's prominence.

This is all to say that modern Arab American writing has been in a productive dialogue with what traditionally has been known as American literature for some time, to the benefit of both categories and to the ultimate evolution into a much-needed heterogeneity of the latter. It would be foolish to attribute that evolution solely or even largely to the contribution of Arab American writers; long before Rabih Alameddine created his fictive pastiche and Gregory Orfalea explored his family's passage from Near East to New World writers of color were changing what it means to be American and thus to produce the sort of text that becomes "American literature."[7] Arab American writers, though, have participated in this process. Trying to determine the extent of this participation is unnecessary (and in any case impossible); the existence of the participation historically and at present is more apropos of illuminating the cultural significance of Arab American literature. The greatest case that can be made for its significance is that it has not merely existed and informed and, in some cases, provided comfort and pleasure, and in other cases trepidation and introspection, but that it also has played a transformative role in the development of its own community and the many other communities, both minority and mainstream, with whom Arab

Americans have long been in dialogue. If readers are uncomfortable attributing to a literary tradition such extensive influence, then I am happy to resign myself to the more humble argument that Arab American literature is significant culturally because it is produced, marketed, packaged, and, on frequent occasions, read, analyzed, repackaged, and discussed formally in book chapters and monographs. It would have been ludicrous to present the previous sentence to readers fifty or even twenty years ago. There is much significance in the fact that I offer the sentence at this point in time with unrelenting confidence.

I hope not to have insinuated that Arab American literature came into existence only recently. In fact, Arab Americans have been producing literature in the United States for over a century. *Al-Muhjar*, for instance, were a loosely organized group of immigrant writers from the Near East, Greater Syria primarily, and included among its participants well-known figures such as Ameen Rihani and Kahlil Gibran. It is thus inaccurate to conceptualize writing by Americans of Arab origin as a newfangled enterprise. Arab American literature, in other words, is not new; the category of "Arab American literature" is. The same, with some temporal differences, is true of African American literature and other ethnic minority traditions. Black folk have been producing literature in North America for centuries—good, insightful, enduring literature, as that, e.g., of *al-Muhjar*. Even so, the category of "African American literature" entered common parlance in the late 1960s and did not really gain a meaningful foothold in English departments until the 1980s (though many universities still cling stubbornly to their Eurocentrism). These categories are really little more than byproducts of modernity and often do not have much to do with organic realities. Therefore, while it is quite significant—and, in my mind, desirable—that a category of "Arab American literature" has recently come into existence and has entered into the parlance of literary studies, it might not be wise to allow the existence of the category to determine the boundaries of the textual material from which it is organized.

As I noted at the start of this essay, Arab American literature has grown substantially in the past few years; Arab American authors, who become more numerous each month, show little sign of slowing down or developing an unoriginal aesthetic. Certain themes and patterns have become detectable within, and sometimes throughout, generic components, but in general the published authors writing somehow under the guise of an "Arab American" identification have attempted, using their unique voices, to alter longstanding commonplaces about Arabs, Islam, the East, and Arab Americans. It would be inappropriate to speculate whether these attempts have been fully or partially successful, if at all, but this is a rare case in which intention is more important than result. That Arab American authors often gaze Eastward to generate meaning is a phenomenon worth attention on its own merit. The fact that, in so doing, they have appended to American literary studies and its poetic tradition an innovative and important dialectic is even more significant.

The Eastern gaze undertaken by many Arab American writers, it should be mentioned, has not generally been idealized or romanticized. Indeed, one of its primary effects has been to ameliorate stereotypes about the Arab World in addition to demystifying nostalgic longings for an invented past or foolish conceptions of a benign social order. Both of these effects are evident most conspicuously in the fiction of Rabih Alameddine, a Lebanese American with an extraordinary talent for the demystification of anything sacred or hegemonic. In his first novel, *KOOLAIDS: The Art of War*, Alameddine does not invoke Lebanon as the idealized alternative to the failures of Americana, but instead positions it as an entity sanctified in nationalist discourses but that in reality is an alternative to Americana only in the sense that it offers a different set of problems and failures. This particular Eastward gaze privileges neither the Arab World nor the United States but rather locks them into a dialectic in which both can be defined only in relation to one another. Such a dialectic exemplifies how transnational interplay has come to be utilized in a good amount of modern Arab American literature.

This argument functions essentially as an accounting of what Arab American literature, broadly conceived, is doing these days and what issues comprise its primary emphases. The literature is diverse enough to make this sort of accounting difficult to accomplish. Invocation in many different forms of the Arab World by Arab American writers, however, is common enough to constitute a pattern worth critical appraisal. This thematic pattern represents a new type of poetics in the modern American literary tradition, one in which cultural epistemologies are formed not by exploring native soil, but by incorporating foreign locales into discussion of familiar landscapes. Almost everything about modern American literature, it can be said, is foreign to the United States. In analyzing such a category we are dealing no longer with a national literature, but with an international tradition.

This development, I hasten to add, is positive in numerous ways, primary among them its potential to eliminate whatever provincial tendencies linger in American literature and the critical apparatuses surrounding it. The most significant cultural achievement of Arab American literature, then, may be more qualitative than quantifiable. In fact, its many positive qualities can be discerned not by scouring an invented American nationhood but by gazing East in its profoundly imagined mobility.

Notes

1. For representative texts about the Israel-Palestine conflict written by these authors, please see Miriam Cooke's *Hayati* (Syracuse: Syracuse University Press, 2000), Shaw Dallal's *Scattered Like Seeds* (Syracuse: Syracuse University Press, 1998), Ibrahim Fawal's *On the Hills of God* (Montgomery, AL: Black Belt, 1998) , or Kathryn Abdul-Baki's *Ghost Songs* (Pueblo, CO: Passeggiata, 2000).

2. Diana Abu-Jaber's novel *Arabian Jazz* (New York: Harvest, 1993) discusses issues of migration, acculturation, and assimilation, as does Laila Lalami's *Hope and Other Dangerous Pursuits* (Chapel Hill, NC: Algonquin, 2005) which has a transnational setting. Joseph Geha's *Through and Through* (St. Paul, MN: Graywolf, 1990) and Laila Halaby's *West of the Jordan* (Boston: Bluestreak, 2003) both invite readers to explore the issues of ethnic identity and Americanization.

3. Specifically, please see Etel Adnan's *Sitt Marie Rose* (Sausalito, CA: Post-Apollo Press, 1982), Patricia Sarrafian Ward's *The Bullet Collection* (St. Paul, MN: Graywolf, 2003), and Rabih Alameddine's *KOOLAIDS: The Art of War* (New York: Picador, 1998).

4. For example, see Samuel Hazo's *Just Once: New and Previous Poems* (Pittsburgh: Autumn House, 2002), Naomi Shihab Nye's *19 Varieties of Gazelle* (New York: Harper Tempest, 2005),   Khaled Mattawa's *Zodiac of Echoes* (Keene, NY: Ausable, 2003), Lawrence Joseph's *Codes, Precepts, Biases, and Taboos* (New York: Farrar, Straus, and Giroux, 2005), Nathalie Handal's *The Neverfield* (New York: Interlink, 2005), Mohja Kahf's *E-Mails from Scheherazad* (Gainesville: University Press of Florida, 2003), and D. H. Melhem's *New York Poems* (Syracuse: Syracuse University Press, 2005).

5. These poems are all anthologized in Salma Khadra Jayyusi's edited collection, *Anthology of Modern Palestinian Literature* (New York: Columbia University Press, 1992).

6. Kathryn Abdul-Baki's *Crescent* (New York: W. W. Norton, 2003), like *Arabian Jazz*, explores the multiethnic realities of American landscapes. Samia Serageldin's *The Cairo House* (Syracuse, NY: Syracuse University Press) is an example of Arab American fiction that takes place largely in the Arab World, and is also noteworthy because Serageldin shifts emphasis from West Asia and focuses on North African settings in Egypt.

7. These explorations occur in Orfalea's *Before the Flames: A Quest for the History of Arab Americans* (Austin: University of Texas Press, 1988). His latest book, *The Arab Americans: A History* (New York: Olive Branch Press, 2005), also explores Orfalea's Middle Eastern background in the broader context of an Arab American community.

Works Cited

Abdul-Baki, Kathryn. *Ghost Songs*. Pueblo, CO: Passeggiata, 2000.

———. *Tower of Dreams*. Colorado Springs, CO: Three Continents, 1995.

Abu-Jaber, Diana. *Arabian Jazz*. New York: Harvest, 1993.

———. *Crescent*. New York: W. W. Norton, 2003.

Adnan, Etel. *Sitt Marie Rose*. Trans. Georgina Kleege. Sausalito, CA: Post-Apollo Press, 1982.

Alameddine, Rabih. *I, The Divine*. New York: W. W. Norton, 2001.

———. *KOOLAIDS: The Art of War*. New York: Picador, 1998.

Cooke, Miriam. *Hayati*. Syracuse: Syracuse University Press, 2000.

Dallal, Shaw. *Scattered Like Seeds*. Syracuse: Syracuse University Press, 1998.

Fawal, Ibrahim. *On the Hills of God*. Montgomery, AL: Black Belt, 1998.

Geha, Joseph. *Through and Through: Toledo Stories*. St. Paul, MN: Graywolf, 1990.

Halaby, Laila. *West of the Jordan*. Boston: Bluestreak, 2003.

Handal, Nathalie. *The Neverfield*. New York: Interlink, 2005.

Hazo, Samuel. *Just Once: New and Previous Poems*. Pittsburgh: Autumn House, 2002.

Jayyusi, Salma Khadra ed. *Anthology of Modern Palestinian Literature*. New York: Columbia University Press, 1992.

Joseph, Lawrence. *Codes, Precepts, Biases, and Taboos: Poems 1973–1993*. New York: Farrar, Straus, and Giroux, 2005.

Kahf, Mohja. *E-Mails from Scheherazad*. Gainesville: University Press of Florida, 2003.

Lalami, Laila. *Hope and Other Dangerous Pursuits*. Chapel Hill, NC: Algonquin, 2005.

Mattawa, Khaled. *Zodiac of Echoes*. Keene, NY: Ausable, 2003.

Melhem, D. H. *New York Poems*. Syracuse: Syracuse University Press, 2005.

Nye, Naomi Shihab. "Blood." *Anthology of Modern Palestinian Literature*. Ed. Salma Khadra Jayyusi. New York: Columbia University Press, 1992.

———. "My Father and the Fig Tree." In *Anthology of Modern Palestinian Literature*, ed. Salma Khadra Jayyusi. New York: Columbia University Press, 1992.

———. *19 Varieties of Gazelle*. New York: HarperTempest, 2005.

———. "Shrines." In *Anthology of Modern Palestinian Literature*, ed. Salma Khadra Jayyusi. New York: Columbia University Press, 1992.

Orfalea, Gregory. *The Arab Americans: A History*. New York: Olive Branch Press, 2005.

———. *Before the Flames: A Quest for the History of Arab Americans*. Austin: University of Texas Press, 1988.

Serageldin, Samia. *The Cairo House*. Syracuse: Syracuse University Press, 2000.

Ward, Patricia Sarrafian. *The Bullet Collection*. St. Paul, MN: Graywolf, 2003.

8

Belly Dancing for Liberation:
A Critical Interpretation of Reclamation Rhetoric in the American Belly Dance Community

Amira Jarmakani

"I saw my belly dancing as an important step toward reclaiming our family's status as not just Lebanese Americans, but as prominent, visible members of the local Lebanese community," writes Anne Thomas Soffee, author of *Snake Hips: Belly Dancing and How I Found True Love.*[1] In so doing, she foregrounds the preservation of her cultural and ethnic roots as an important project for herself and her family, and she identifies an aspect of her cultural heritage—belly dancing—as the means to do so. Moreover, belly dancing becomes a tool for Soffee's self-affirmation, as a Lebanese American and also as a sexy woman in a culture that demonizes any amount of fat on a female body.

Her memoir credits belly dancing not only with helping her through a hard breakup with her boyfriend, but also with bringing her back to a love of self, which, the reader comes to realize, is the "true love" she was looking for all along. The role that belly dancing comes to play in Soffee's odyssey toward self-love, which seems to be associated with liberal feminist notions of self-esteem and empowerment, is as a tool of reclamation. Because the abrupt ending of her relationship ultimately leaves her feeling as if she has lost herself, the narrative goes, she seeks a way to reconnect with her own identity, history, and "Lebanese heritage." Belly dancing proves to be the perfect vehicle for her project of reclamation not only because it cites her ethnic roots, but also because it offers her a tangible means of revaluing her voluptuous and fleshy female body, which she also seeks to reclaim in the wake of her breakup. In this way, her optimistic memoir gives readers a sense of how a historically eroticized dance, which has been a major part of Orientalist discourse about the Middle East, can finally be understood for the powerful potential it has always offered women.

Even so, however laudable Soffee's goals are, the premise of her project sits on unstable ground. She frames her discovery of belly dancing in terms of reclaiming her ethnic roots. Indeed, Soffee's claim that belly dancing is an important and crucial link to her Lebanese heritage serves as a telling example of the way in which American belly dancing is tied to notions of authenticity. Despite her association of belly dancing with ethnic Arab roots, however, given the history of American belly dance, she is actually reclaiming a performance of authenticity. Soffee would, no doubt, refer to me as the "ethnic police" for being so picky about the ways in which the authentic claim further eclipses the cultural realities she seeks to recapture for herself and her family. I am aware that my argument will potentially feel policing to her as well as to the larger American belly dance community; however, it is not my intention to scold or judge, but rather to ask probing questions about the gap between good intentions and enacted realities. In its many incarnations in the U.S. context, belly dancing has almost always been marketed as a pure representation of Middle Eastern culture, unmediated by the U.S. cultural context. However, its positioning as exotic spectacle in the 1893 Chicago World's Fair, amusement parks, cabaret shows, and, I would argue, exercise videos, demands a performance that enacts authenticity, rather than demonstrating an authentic form in and of itself.

What, then, is at stake in the authentic claim? To take Soffee as a case study, it seems that there are two major strands to her project: She is invested in a search for authentic origins and she is interested in reclaiming her ethnic heritage (and, ultimately, her sense of self) through the belly dance form. These strands are woven together with the thread of authenticity, however fabricated, because it is the authentic claim that serves to legitimize both Soffee's intentions to recover her sense of self in ethnic expression and her argument that belly dancing leads her to a kind of liberation (from a bad relationship and negative body image). Soffee is certainly neither alone in her desire to reclaim belly dancing as a tool for women's empowerment nor are Arab Americans the only group to appropriate the belly dance in this way. In fact, the majority of American belly dance communities since the 1970s have consisted of white American women.[2] These communities have committed themselves to a lively and vibrant appreciation for American belly dance that categorically rejects associations of the dance with striptease or erotic dancing (for men's viewing pleasure) and celebrates the dance form as ancient, enduring proof of the power of female sexuality. Like Soffee, these dancers see themselves as preservers of culture, in that they seek to restore the art form to its original, or authentic, roots. However, the well-intentioned insistence on a return to ancient origins is problematic in the respect that it conveniently elides the performative aspect of a cultural form that is largely understood as spectacle in the United States. While I use the case study of Soffee's memoir to frame my argument here, I am actually interested in exploring the way in which an almost exclusively white female belly dance community has interpreted and deployed belly dancing as a tool for self-empowerment.

Because recent (in the past few decades) and contemporary belly dance movements are interested in appropriating the dance as a means of speaking back to a U.S. patriarchal discourse, which has devalued the voluptuous female body and dismissed or harnessed the power of female sexuality, this essay explores the viability of using the belly dance to interrupt such interpretations of femininity and female sexuality. Can the reclamation of belly dancing as a woman-centered activity help to revalue and reframe female sexuality as generative and powerful? Though the contemporary American belly dancing community would argue that colonial and imperial interpretations and exhibitions are gross misperceptions of the belly dance form, I argue that the authenticity and liberation claims of the contemporary movement can only be understood by contextualizing them within the history of the belly dance in the United States. As I will demonstrate, the multi-layered history of belly dancing in the United States can actually inform a current understanding of the way the dance is performed and received by contemporary U.S. audiences.

A Brief History

As most historical synopses of the American belly dance form in popular and scholarly books report, the belly dance entered the United States by way of the 1893 Chicago World's Fair. Building on a combination of ethnographic exhibits and entertainment venues from the 1889 Paris Exposition, the planners of the Chicago fair incorporated "dancing girl" exhibits and concessions into the Midway Plaisance, the site of the entertainment for the fair. Though belly dancing was staged under the auspices of ethnographic display, its ability to draw crowds and make money for concessionaires led to its replication in several exhibits on the Midway. Nevertheless, one of the most memorable examples seems to be from the "Streets of Cairo" exhibit, which may be why many of the performers are retrospectively assigned the moniker

"Little Egypt." As the English translation of the name of the dance suggests, the dancing girls at the 1893 Chicago World's Fair were primarily recognized for the ways in which they were able to move and contort their bodies, with a focus on the pelvic, or belly, region of the female body. In a Victorian social context in which idealized women's bodies were corseted and contained, the belly dancers' bodies became known for a fluidity and freedom of movement that well known commentators on the fair described as both "passionate" and "disgusting."[3]

Belly dancing, then, was introduced both as a spectacle that was a form of entertainment for its U.S. audience, and also as a means by which that audience gained coherence and definition in opposition to the exotic, romanticized, and therefore different, bodies of the belly dancers. The women who were literally imported from France and the Middle East to perform this increasingly popular dance were thus introduced into a context in which they would undergo what Rosemarie Garland Thomson has called "social process of enfreakment."[4] They were constructed as bodies of absolute difference, to which throngs of spectators were drawn despite the lack of morality associated with the gyrating and jiggling movements of the dance.

Moreover, the success of the belly dancing displays on the Midway set the stage for the incorporation of the dance into the broader arena of U.S. popular culture. In the years following the fair, belly dance performances by women calling themselves "Little Egypt" cropped up at a variety of performance venues, like amusement parks such as Coney Island and Luna Park. In this way, the debut of belly dancing in the United States was not only shaped by its status as spectacle, it was determined by its imbrication within the framework of a consumerist project. Belly dancing has been constructed, packaged, and sold since its inception in the United States. Such a framing of the dance as spectacle and commodity is crucial for understanding the future incarnations of belly dancing—as progenitor of striptease (in the 1920s), and as a revolutionary tool for reclaiming the power and beauty of the female form (from the 1970s through 2000).

The marketable qualities that made belly dancing a success at the turn of the nineteenth to the twentieth century certainly translated well in the incorporation of belly dancing into erotic dance. In fact, given the debut of the belly dance in the United States as erotic and licentious spectacle, its function as a mode of transition from the burlesque to the striptease forms is, in many ways, a logical and organic extension of its interpretation in a U.S.

context. The burlesque tradition was not associated with striptease when it debuted in the United States in the late 1860s. In fact, as demonstrated by some of its earliest performers, Lydia Thompson and her troupe, the British Blondes burlesque, functioned as an "inversion of the Victorian ideal of femininity."[5]   It offered a theatrical form and a public space in which performers like Lydia Thompson could enact masculinity by playing lead male roles and where they could implicitly question gender norms. Despite popular associations of burlesque with striptease, Robert C. Allen argues, the early burlesque performer was "not merely a mute object of sexual display."[6]   On the contrary, she was an active, speaking subject who provoked public discourse about notions of femininity and ideal womanhood.

Burlesque, then, is a rich cultural form for exploring popular notions about female sexuality precisely because, as Allen claims, its "organizing problematic is gender."[7]   In many ways, it is positioned within a tricky balance between the subversive potential inherent in a performance of masculinity and the objectifying potential inherent in the spectacle of female sexuality. It is all the more interesting, particularly given the reclamation rhetoric of the American belly dance community, that the belly dance can be credited, in part, with tipping the burlesque balance toward the side of objectification.

As variations on the belly dance were being incorporated into the performances at amusement parks, the burlesque tradition began to incorporate its own version of what Allen calls the "cooch" dance. The term "cooch" is a shortened version of "hootchy-kootchy," a term popularized by Sol Bloom (the mastermind behind the Chicago World Fair's belly dancing displays), who wrote the hootchy-kootchy song to promote the belly dance concessions on the Midway Plaisance. This incorporation of the hootchy-kootchy, which had already reduced the dance form to a set of lewd, sexualized movements, succeeded in "centering the [burlesque] form once and for all around undisguised sexual exhibitionism" in Allen's estimation.[8] The rise of the striptease form in the 1920s, then, was indebted to the cooch dance; in the transition, however, the burlesque performer "literally and figuratively lost her voice."[9]

While Allen seems to take the sexual objectification of the belly dance form as a given, the American belly dance community might consider its parallels with the subversive potential of burlesque as a worthy project of reclamation, rather than skipping over this history completely. Moreover, one might argue, as Rachel Shteir does, that striptease also offers subversive potential for the reclamation of powerful female sexuality as it has historically "tossed laughter and desire into the air, challenging conventional ideas about gender roles."[10] Ultimately, what is most interesting about the connection between belly dance and striptease is the fact that it reveals popular perceptions of both to be materially and expressly tied to the female body and to notions of female sexuality as lascivious and immoral. More interesting still is the marketability and commercial success of such licentious performances. Perhaps the American belly dance community overlooks this part of belly dance history because of the insidious parallel between the way in which both striptease and contemporary American belly dance forms appropriate the belly dance as a lucrative commodity, a connection to which I will return later.

The American belly dance movement has opposed itself to the amusement park and striptease interpretations of belly dance in that it has sought to reclaim the power of female sexuality and locate that power in the movements of the body that the belly dance incorporates. Because of the way in which language has played a role in such a reclamation, this might be a good time to explain and account for the terms I use to describe the belly dance form. Many dance communities in the United States, out of respect for the tradition and origins of the dance, use the term American oriental dance, or *danse orientale*, which are the Modern Standard English and French translations of *raqs sharqi*, or dance of the East in Arabic. The term "belly dance" is actually most likely a translation of the French term *danse du ventre*, both of which reveal a shift away from the Arabic term *raqs sharqi* in that they focus on the movement of the pelvic region of the body rather than the whole range of movements within the dance.

For this reason, most contemporary practitioners of the dance form in the United States prefer using some form of "oriental dance," arguing that it is closest to the term *raqs sharqi*. I use the term American belly dance because I argue that what we understand to be belly dance is a distinctly U.S. concept, layered with the history of the dance in its U.S. permutations, from the 1893 Chicago World's Fair through the striptease, and up to the contemporary context of belly dance as exercise and exotic performance. During the rise of the American belly dance movement in the 1970s, documented by journals such as *Habibi* and *Arabesque*, practitioners began to use the Arabic term *raqs sharqi*, or the French translation *danse orientale*, as a gesture toward reclaiming and restoring the authenticity of the dance form. The authentic claim, however, was not solely a gesture of reverence and respect for the dance form or for the culture from which it emerged. Rather, it was a means of making a grand, universalized claim for the primordial power of female sexuality. If the dance could be linked with the "earliest indications of a matriarchal dominance in society," and both the dance and evidence of female-centered power could be traced back to 25,000 B.C., then the feminist argument for women's power would gain the authority of historical evidence.[11] Given the many appropriations of the belly dance in the United States, which had clearly understood the dance as a marker of the licentiousness of female sexuality, the move to reclaim the belly dance as a celebration of female power was clearly a revolutionary project. It was also a means of encouraging women to honor their own power, as argued in an informative article in a popular publication of the women's movement: "Ultimately, *Raqs al Sharqi* [sic] is a dance of the power of women, and the dancer celebrates herself."[12] While the striptease and hootchy- kootchy traditions reveled in the lascivious eroticism of belly dancing, the revival of the 1970s and 1980s focused on the potential of the dance form to offer evidence and authority to the argument for the profound and primordial power of female sexuality.[13]

Contemporary engagements with belly dance certainly continue the 1970s fascination with its authentic origins, though a decidedly new incarnation of belly dance in the United States is its increasing popularity as a new-age form of exercise.[14] While belly dance books published in the 1970s casually mention its health benefits, a cursory survey of popular how-to books published since 2000 reveals the intentional and blatant focus on fitness and body image. Books such as *Belly Dancing for Fitness: The Sexy Art That Tones Your Abs, Butt, and Thighs* and *Belly Dancing for Fitness: The Ultimate Dance Workout That Unleashes Your Creative Spirit* indicate that the "ancient" dance form is being appropriated and deployed as a tool for women to focus on revaluing their feminine forms, rather than being heralded as a titillating spectacle for male viewing pleasure. In fact, most contemporary accounts of the history of belly dance in the United States either ignore its role in the development of striptease entirely, or dismiss its role as a distasteful misperception of what the dance is really about.

Despite these efforts, the eroticized interpretation of belly dancing has certainly not been effaced in the contemporary context. One need only look as far as the 2001 *Camel* advertising scheme that used belly dancers to promote its "7 pleasures of the exotic" series of cigarettes.[15] Nevertheless, the insistence on a complete departure from striptease and erotic dancing for contemporary and feminist belly dancers is a brilliant move. However, while I admire the desire to restore the dance to its more glorious origins, ignoring the foundations of American belly dance history is a disavowal of the way the dance has been framed in the United States. The dance form presumed to be an authentic reproduction of an ancient ritual by the American belly dance movement is actually a new world amalgamation of dance moves, based on varied elements of "Eastern" forms of dance and inevitably influenced by its historical appropriation as erotic dance form.

Despite the desire, on the part of dancers within the contemporary American belly dance movement, to see their version of the dance as profoundly different from its striptease incarnation, both appropriations of the dance operate on a perception of the belly dance as somehow naturally or organically tied to the female body. To a U.S. audience, it seems to be connected to the materiality of the body in ways that other dance forms might not. Both the striptease and American belly dance versions of the dance have emphasized the gyrating and shimmying hips of the dancer, the former for its eroticism and the latter for its association with women's power through childbirth. Therefore, both are similarly engaged with the (productive or threatening) power of female sexuality. I have argued, against the suggestion of the contemporary U.S. belly dance movement, that these two U.S. appropriations of belly dance cannot be usefully disentangled. However, in bringing these two seemingly oppositional appropriations of the belly dance in the United States together, what can one learn about the feminist claim that belly dancing can be utilized as a tool for women's liberation?

A Disruptive Dance

Mikhail Bakhtin has described the grotesque body as "a body in the act of becoming,"[16] and, in so doing, he has offered an almost irresistible framework for thinking about the possibility of reclaiming the power of bodies that have long been associated with lewdness. His own ability to reverse the powerful connotations of the word "grotesque" by turning it into a productive, useful term speaks to the parallel between his theoretical project and the goal of the American belly dance community. Because the concept of the grotesque body offers a way of thinking about bodies as fluid and dynamic as well as a way of bursting idealized images of bodies that keep them fixed within the sanitized limits of social conventions, it is an obvious application for a dance form that celebrates movement.

As opposed to a dance form like ballet, which is invested in the execution of perfected and controlled movements, the belly dance offers structure only insofar as that structure should be interpreted and transformed with each performance. It therefore opens itself up to the world in a manner that seems to identify it with the category of the grotesque body: "Eating, drinking, defecation and other elimination (sweating, blowing of the nose, sneezing), as well as copulation, pregnancy, dismemberment, swallowing up by another body—all these acts are performed on the confines of the body and the outer world."[17]   The permeable boundary between the grotesque body and the outside world is what gives it powerful (and threatening) potential to transgress the confining limits of social norms. Therefore, Bakhtin offers a way of understanding and theorizing the belly dancer's body in terms of its power to disrupt cultural assumptions about the female body. Because contemporary practitioners of the dance emphasize its ability to reclaim the power of female sexuality from patriarchal understandings of the inferiority of the female body, Bakhtin's notion of the grotesque body can offer a means of testing the viability of reclamation rhetoric.

While the belly dancer's body is not graphically grotesque (it does not perform the types of bodily functions listed by Bakhtin), it is clearly transgressive of what Bakhtin calls the classical body because of its refusal to stay still long enough to be fixed into ordered notions of womanhood. The excesses of the body, which Bakhtin describes as sweating, sneezing, and defecation (among others), are demonstrated by the belly dancer's body as an excess of lascivious movements, which ultimately signify an excess of sexuality. Joseph Smith and James Buel, both of whom wrote widely received descriptions of the dance from the 1893 Chicago World's Fair, center their comments on the "hips, stomach, and breast" or the "abdominal muscles" of the dancers rather than the dancers themselves. Such a focus further demonstrates the excess of attention that U.S. audiences brought (and bring) to that particular region of the female body, which is imaginatively linked to sexuality and procreation. The contemporary belly dance movement wants to value the sexuality and procreative function of the female body as evidence of its power, and flip the patriarchal narrative that associates female sexuality with lewd and base pleasures.

For the purposes of this essay, I am most interested in investigating this recent appropriation of the dance form to symbolize, and reclaim, the sacred aspect of female sexuality, as indicated by the way in which the American belly dance movement is quick to emphasize the dancer's role in ancient childbirth rituals. The American belly dance movement, including the latest exercise manifestation of belly dance in the United States, stresses the role of the dance in birthing rituals in "early matriarchal cultures" to "prepare young women for the physical stress of childbirth."[18] Such an assertion demonstrates the way in which reclamation rhetoric seeks to disrupt dominant narratives of female sexuality by aligning itself with the fecundity and materiality of the grotesque body. It is meant to highlight women's inherent and organic bodily power in direct opposition to a dominant script that sees her as weak and powerless.

Again, Bakhtin can offer, by way of his notion of the disruptive nature of the carnival, a method for analyzing the oppositional move of the American belly dance movement. As Robert Stam explains, carnival, in the Bakhtinian sense of the word, "is the oppositional culture of the oppressed, the official world as seen from below; not the mere disruption of etiquette but the symbolic, anticipatory overthrow of oppressive social structures."[19]   In this sense, it is a way of speaking back to, and unsettling, a dominant narrative about, in this case, female sexuality. Carnival, as a festive form of folk culture, offers a rich, fruitful venue by which, Bakhtin asserts, people "express their criticism" and "their deep distrust of official truth."[20]   The notion of the disruptive potential of carnivalesque forms maps quite usefully onto a consideration of the belly dance in the United States because of the ready link between the two. Given the history of the belly dance in the United States, it becomes clear that the relationship between the carnival and the belly dance is both metonymic and metaphoric.[21] It is metonymic because the belly dance gained fame and definition in a U.S. context through its display at fairs and amusement parks, and it is metaphoric as a folk, or festive, form that can offer critical commentary on larger cultural concerns.

Indeed, much of the rhetoric produced by the contemporary belly dance community asserts the ability and the function of the dance form to speak back to, and overturn, predominant patriarchal notions of the female body as weak, which is buttressed by subtle messages that the body is only beautiful if it remains small, slender, and devoid of fat or flesh. This rhetoric utilizes the notion of carnivalesque by capitalizing on a U.S. preoccupation with the "belly" aspect of the dance and using what Bakhtin calls the "lower bodily stratum" to upset official discourse about the female body. Instead of seeing the shimmies and gyrations as debase or immoral, as turn of the century commentators did, contemporary notions of the power of belly dancing emphasize the ambivalence of the hip and belly movements, because, as Bakhtin claims, "the lower stratum is not only a bodily grave but also the area of the genital organs, the fertilizing and generating stratum."[22] The dance is meant to provide proof of the power of female sexuality by focusing on, and reclaiming, the "fertilizing and generating" aspects of the female body. In spite of the history of belly dance in the United States as a spectacle focusing on the lascivious nature of female sexuality, both a 1970s reclamation of the cultural tradition of belly dancing and the contemporary fascination with belly dance as a booming sector of the exercise industry engage the belly dance form as carnival in the Bakhtinian sense; they reclaim the dance as a disruptive and oppositional mode of cultural communication that can topple hegemonic ideals about female sexuality and the female body.

However, in utilizing the metaphoric notion of carnival, contemporary notions of belly dance as evidence of women's creative power inadvertently invoke a metonymic relationship to its carnivalesque history in the United States. The contemporary movement wants to distance itself categorically from belly dance as erotic spectacle, ignoring the ways in which the cooch as erotic dance and the oriental dance of 1970s feminism are actually two sides of the same belly dance coin. The belly dancer's body is a "grotesque body," in Bakhtinian terms, because of the way in which it is able to signify both profane and sacred aspects of female sexuality.[23] For a striptease audience, it invokes the socially constructed notion of copulation as a base, lewd, and material desire.

The American belly dance community, on the other hand, is interested in shifting the patriarchal association of female sexuality with licentiousness toward a more woman-centered notion of female sexuality as productive and generative (as in Bakhtin's "fertilizing and generating stratum"). While patriarchal notions of female sexuality certainly recognize sacred aspects of fertility and childbirth, they do so by locating them in the idealized image of the madonna figure, which is completely desexualized. In this construction, then, the power of female sexuality is projected onto the licentious, threatening figure of the publicly sexualized woman, while the generative, life-giving power of the mother is safely contained in the chaste, desexualized figure of the privately pure woman. In focusing on the importance of the belly dance in childbirth rituals, the American belly dance community is working to disaggregate the understanding of female power with its association as threatening or lascivious, and re-couple the notion of powerful female sexuality with the act of childbirth and the concept of womanhood. However, the logic of this project sidesteps the fact that it does not question the opposition of licentious sexuality with generative sexuality — it simply wants to shift the location of power from one side to the other. Therefore, not only does the project of reclaiming the belly dance reify the framework of the mother/whore dichotomy, it depends upon the oppositional notion of female sexuality as licentious in order to stake its claim.

Given the centrality of reclamation rhetoric to contemporary understandings of the belly dance since the 1970s, as well as the persistent disavowal within the rhetoric of the dance form's erotic history, it is worth reconsidering the assertion that belly dance can upset misogynist U.S. constructions of the female body. In order to further understand the imbrication of the authenticity and liberation strands of this argument, I critically read the scholarship and literature that has been produced about the dance form since the 1970s, focusing on a cluster of sources from the 1970s and a cluster of sources in the 1990s and 2000s. Within both of these clusters, clear and re-emergent images of the ancient and authentic dance persist, giving insight into the nature of recent U.S. appropriations of belly dance.

Shedding the "Old Generation's Backward Ways"
The reclamation of the belly dance in the 1970s, and the re-naming of that dance to more particular terms such as American tribal belly dance, American oriental dance, and oriental dance,[24] have functioned within a peculiar tension between the veneration for an ancient and mystical past, and the anticipation and promise of a liberating and feminist future.

In one of the first periodicals devoted to the dance, *Arabesque*, Ibrahim Farrah explains in the introductory issue that the purpose of the periodical is "to unravel some of the mysteries of the Middle East."[25] For a "generation that is seeking its roots and origins," Farrah points to the belly dance as a way of finding purpose and grounding oneself in a "creative and unifying force."[26] Indeed, the ready association between belly dance and a "simpler" past, unadulterated by the complications of modern society, is a powerful theme in belly dance books since the 1970s. Consider the following introduction to the dance by Julie Russo Mishkin and Marta Schill:

> Since the earliest days of mankind, when movement was more natural than speech, dancing in this region of the world has been the easiest and most popular form of

communication. The Belly as Media. The Belly as Message. Why the belly? In the first place, the belly is the center of birth and sexual movement. The place of the beginnings.[27]

Mishkin and Schill not only situate the origins of the dance in the "earliest days of mankind [sic]," they construct it as more basic and natural than speech. In giving it this prelinguistic status, they are clearly engaging in a romanticized and nostalgic view of the Middle East (and the dance form) as simpler and more primitive. They also promote the dance as a way for women to reconnect with their own basic nature. Mishkin and Schill are not alone in presenting the dance in this way. Ozel, a dancer and author who presents herself as authentic by virtue of her Turkish heritage, also presents the dance as a means for U.S. women to reconnect with nature. "And there *you* are," she chides, "still hung up because thousands of years of 'civilization' have made you afraid to let loose and express your most basic desires."[28] In framing it this way, she seems to be implying that the dance, by virtue of its primitive origins, can help women "connect to [their] most basic desires" through a form that is unmediated by progress, modernity, culture, and "civilization." Similarly, Suheyla praises the dance for its "sensuousness and closeness to nature."[29] By doing so, she replicates a slippage that can be seen running through all of the aforementioned sources; belly dance, the ancient dance form, is close to nature, and therefore women, by virtue of their connection to the "sensuous" movements of the dance are also close to nature. The implication, then, is that women have an organic connection to the origins of humankind. In fact, Mishkin and Schill remind their readers that the belly is "the place of the beginnings," and, in so doing, they locate the ancient, enduring, primitive past within the female body itself.

Though these accounts necessarily associate the body with notions of the primitive past, they are not meant as debilitating representations of femininity, but rather as enabling images of women's natural, primordial power. They cast women as guarders and keepers of an otherwise inaccessible knowledge. As Ozel claims, belly–dancing "transmits a deeper, almost genetic knowledge. It says: I know what it means to be a woman. I can recreate how it was long ago, when things were simpler and it was possible to give and take pleasure freely."[30] Women, by virtue of being women, she seems to say, have access to this primordial power, and can connect to it through the quintessentially female part of the female body—the belly and hips. Where "Western man and woman have done a good job of separating themselves from their bodies,"[31] the art of belly dance, these writers claim, can reconnect them with the wisdom of their bodies. Moreover, that wisdom and ancient power is said to be embodied by the specifically female form.

What is perhaps most interesting about this construction of female power is the way in which it appropriates and invokes the authentic origins of a matriarchal past as a universal, shared history of women, while simultaneously denouncing the particularly Middle Eastern form of patriarchy from which it sprang. In her thesis about appropriations of the "gypsy" in American female oriental dance, Danielle Janessa van Dobben explains the association of belly dance with childbirth as a "strategic" connection, by which "dancers take up the category 'Woman' and give it powerful new meanings."[32] However, this kind of strategic identity formation elides the ethnic and cultural specificity within the category woman and overlooks the implicit race—whiteness—that has animated the category in relation to the American belly dance movement. Some members of the community go so far as to suggest that belly dancing needs to be rescued from the culture that produced it. Mishkin and Schill, for example, credit "American enthusiasm" with saving the dance from a worse fate: "What was in danger of becoming buried with the rest of the old generation's backward ways was redeemed from the way of the veil and the harem."[33] Here, the "old generation" is part of a Middle Eastern tradition that still engages in the so-called "backward" ways of the veil and the harem. Presumably, American women could oppose a "backward" patriarchy by reclaiming the "primitive" power of female sexuality. In a tricky opposition of backward and primitive, these writers embrace a common, matriarchal past as a means of disrupting patriarchy, both the Middle Eastern patriarchy of harems and veils as well as a seemingly monolithic patriarchy, which have functioned to contain and minimize the power of the female body.

The exploitation of the universalized rhetoric of the women's liberation movement in the 1970s is not accidental; it was an integral aspect of the marketing and framing of the belly dance in the 1970s. The promoters of the belly dance in the 1970s were, in many ways, selling the notion of a universal sisterhood, which could band together in a fight for liberation that emphasized female forms of power. As Ozel explains: "It seems to me that it's no accident belly-dancing is becoming more popular now—with more and more women doing the work that used to be reserved solely for men, it's clear we must find ways of exercising efficiently and in a way that maintains our femininity."[34] The promise of belly dancing is in its ability to revalue femininity as powerful. In fact, in order to stress its connection to power, belly dance practitioners are careful to distance the dance from its association with striptease, and trace its genealogy all the way back to a (purportedly universal) origin in the history of ancient matriarchal cultures. Mishkin and Schill demonstrate such a framing in their introductory comments: "Lest the Women's Liberation devotees misunderstand or develop mixed loyalties, let it be said that there is nothing unliberated [sic] about moving as a woman. The show girl may well be seen as a paid sex object. A woman having a good time within her body, showing her delight in motor expression, cannot be exploited."[35] Mishkin and Schill know that they must sell the dance to a liberal feminist movement, which was, in many ways, their most likely market, and they are therefore hasty to distance belly dance from its association with striptease. Though a "show girl" is clearly exploited, their logic goes, the ancient and authentic form of belly dance is inherently liberating. Here, belly dancing is celebrated as a means of asserting the power of the female body, which was intentionally oppositional to representations of the female body as erotic object. In this way, the belly dance revival within the framework of the 1970s women's liberation movement aligned itself with the progressive project of liberation by advocating a return to powerful origins.

Shimmying to the Hits

While belly dance aficionados of the 1970s had advocated the dance as a quintessentially female avenue for celebrating women's power, the contemporary belly dance exercise movement advocates it as a "total workout for the body, mind, and spirit."[36] Even so, contemporary accounts of American belly dance, including the recent explosion of it in the exercise industry, pick up on and expand upon the woman-centered reclamation rhetoric of the 1970s. Contemporary appropriations of the dance still focus on its ability to help women reclaim their own power, or, as Keti Sherif puts it, to "weave a tapestry of expression that empowers women in the West."[37] However, as opposed to enabling women to maintain their femininity while going back to work, the new liberation revolves around improving one's body image. If women of the 1970s were reclaiming their power through the glory of the ancient matriarchal origins of the dance, women in the first decade of the twenty-first century are speaking back to official discourse by revaluing their fleshier, fuller forms. Empowerment through increased self-image is a major theme in recent popular literature about American belly dance.

What is perhaps most significant about these narratives is the fact that, though the definition of liberation has shifted, the reclamation of power is still mediated through the ancient and mysterious past of the belly dance form. Laura Cooper, author of *Belly Dancing Basics*, asserts that "belly dance is a wonderful way to counteract ... negative body images and celebrate the more natural, curvaceous feminine form in all its shapes and sizes," because "in the ancient world, ... thinness was a sign of poverty."[38] Women can reclaim their voluptuous bodies, she suggests, by invoking a richer, more glorious past, in which larger bodies were a sign of wealth and success. Indeed, Rosina Fawzia al-Rawi takes the liberating claim one step further by insisting that "expressing her personality through belly dance ... enables a woman to take a new look at her somewhat negative self image ... [and] enables many a woman to reach inner freedom."[39] Here, al-Rawi seems to be taking note of the transition from a publicly expressed equal-rights oriented liberation in the 1970s to the desire to achieve "inner freedom" for the contemporary woman, who has purportedly already achieved equal rights.

One begins to suspect that the potential for women's liberation was contained within the female body all along. Keti Sherif explains that through belly dance "women begin to see and relate to their bodies differently: those with low self-image begin to honour their bodies." In fact, she informs her readers that "belly dancing is possibly one of the most liberating arts, especially for women today."[40] However, these optimistic testaments to the benefits of belly dance gloss over a disturbing shift. While the 1970s rhetoric demonstrates the need to assert women's power in opposition to outward notions of female inferiority, contemporary exercise books sell belly dance as a means for women to reassert their value in response to an inward, or self-devaluation. "After bellydancing," Dolphina encourages, "don't be surprised to find yourself bursting with newfound confidence."[41] Liberation, it seems, now comes in the form of inner freedom from one's own negative thoughts. The fight for equal rights and social justice is, therefore, insidiously displaced by the rhetoric of empowerment and inner freedom, which is buttressed and normalized by a booming self-help industry.

Though belly dancing is clearly marketed as a growing and lucrative part of the exercise industry (a quick search on the WorldCat database revealed over thirty belly dance exercise videos and DVDs from 2000 to 2005), the written sources praise it for its ability to increase self-image, without necessarily decreasing weight. While Tamalyn Dallal attests to the fact that it helped her "completely overcome anorexia," she predicts that "if you get into belly dancing for weight loss, you may well discover that the real problem was not weight but self-image."[42] Further, Dallal clearly constructs the belly dance as a way for women to resist and oppose the dominant, misogynist messages about the female body that bombard women on a daily basis. "Since belly dancing embraces all body types," she writes, "it relieves some of the pressure that is heaped on Western women from the first time they open a fashion magazine."[43] Belly dancing, in this scenario, is not really a weight loss technique or a means of sculpting one's body. On the contrary, it is hailed as a dance form that celebrates all body types and that enables women to counteract mainstream messages that encourage women to take up less space. In fact, in Hale's analysis of the contemporary belly dance community, she claims that it is constructed as a space "in which women have the freedom to express themselves creatively using their bodies, negating the oppressive and controlling influence of patriarchy."[44]

Despite Hale's own allusion to a universalized patriarchy, her observation highlights the way in which belly dancing is interpreted within the community as an oppositional tool for disrupting problematic patriarchal assumptions. Again, the problem with this line of argument is the fact that it is predicated on universalized notions of both matriarchy and patriarchy. Stavros Karayanni addresses this claim by problematizing the exclusive focus on belly dancing as evidence of matriarchal origins and childbirth rituals because it ignores the presence and influence of male dancers in the East.[45] His assertion highlights the insistence of the American belly dance movement to see only certain aspects of belly dance history as valid or authentic. However, failing to acknowledge the rich historical complexity of the dance in all its appropriations, including the U.S. feminist interpretations, ultimately dilutes the authority of the movement's own claim to authentic female power.

Anne Thomas Soffee's memoir, *Snake Hips*, is a clear demonstration of this point. Soffee, the belly dancer seeking to reclaim her Lebanese heritage, would agree with the ability of the dance to increase U.S. appreciation for "women of substance, women who are shaped like women, not waifs or twelve-year-old boys."[46] However, she shies away from pointing to a better body image as the main asset of the dance. She reveals, late in her memoir, that "the idea that belly dancing is an excuse for 'fat chicks to dress up' ... really galls me. It cheapens what we do, ...and, perhaps worst of all, it has just enough of a grain of truth in it to make it really hurt."[47] The description of belly dance as an "excuse for fat chicks to dress up" appears to be an offhand comment made on a Web list to which Soffee belongs. However, the fact that Soffee takes the disparaging comment to heart demonstrates that belly dancing is part of a larger social debate about body image. Moreover, it gives credence to the claim that belly dancing can help women to appreciate fuller, more voluptuous female forms that do not fit the mainstream ideal.

It is interesting, then, to note that Soffee's main focus on the benefits of belly dancing is on its ability to reconnect her with the essence of her ethnic heritage. She wholeheartedly engages in the strategies of dancers in the American belly dance movement to authenticate their performances. One of these tricks of the trade is to take a stage name; Dallal has even included a list of suggestions in the appendix of her belly dance how-to book. As Dallal advises: "Belly dancers commonly take on Middle Eastern names. You can, too. If you're simply dancing for exercise, this might seem a bit farfetched, but read on ... you might find a bit of yourself in one of these names."[48] Indeed, not only does Soffee find a bit of herself in her chosen name, she finds a piece of her ethnic roots, which had been lopped off in her immigration process. She changes Soffee to *al-Safi*, "wishing ... that folks at Ellis Island hadn't been so clumsy when they phoneticized [her] great-grandfather's name. *Safi* looks exotic, foreign, mysterious."[49] However, Soffee's reclamation of authentic origins seems to replicate the problematic search for authenticity within the belly dance community. It claims to simply be reviving ethnic roots, but those roots are understood, through the hazy lens of American Orientalism, as "exotic, foreign, [and] mysterious." Nevertheless, there is something curious and striking about her preoccupation with authenticity, a preoccupation that is certainly replicated within the larger American belly dance community. Moreover, the quest for authenticity goes past name, costume, and dance moves. The following revelation comes from Soffee after she has been unable to prove her ability to dance the *debke*, a popular and traditional Middle Eastern folk dance:

> I am jealous of Nadine's skin, and Samraa al-Nil's, and Tasha Banat's, and every other Arab, part-Arab, and wannabe Arab in this hotel who is darker than I am. Three years of belly dancing may have made me more comfortable in my skin, but why couldn't that skin be just a little darker?[50]

Soffee makes it clear here that belly dancing has impacted her self-image and made her "more comfortable in [her] skin"; however, it is also clear that her bigger concern is with her ability to pass as a "real" Arab. She comes to find that the ability to pass, though, is not reliant on one's genetic or ancestral evidence of Arab heritage, but on one's ability to match stereotypical notions of Arab ethnic characteristics, like "exotic" and "foreign" names and dark skin. The claim of authenticity, here, is revealed to be mediated both by stereotypical understandings of Arab culture in the United States and by the process of consumerism.

One way to understand Soffee's preoccupation with displaying real ethnic characteristics is through what bell hooks calls the "commodification of Otherness."[51] Within this construct, hooks says, "ethnicity becomes spice, seasoning that can liven up the dull dish that is mainstream white culture."[52] However, because Soffee technically already has access to ethnic "spice" by virtue of her heritage, this application needs to be pushed one step further. Soffee does not so much seek ethnicity as she does authenticity, even when that authenticity is measured by U.S. misperceptions about Middle Eastern culture. Rather than a commodification of Otherness, then, Soffee seems to be involved in a commodification of authenticity, which is replicated and affirmed in the larger American belly dance movement.

The reclamation rhetoric that threads through all of the American belly dance narratives focuses its oppositional discourse on a return to ancient, sometimes matriarchal, origins, and to times in which women's bodies were valued for their power. The strategy these narratives have employed to simultaneously invoke the power of a women-centered past and distance contemporary belly dance from its associations with striptease seems to be a viable means of disrupting dominant U.S. patriarchal understandings of female sexuality, particularly given a Bakhtinian reading of female sexuality as a generative and creative force. However, the commodification of authenticity keeps the belly dance movement trained on endlessly receding evidence of the essence and origin of female power. Ironically, the insistence on distancing American belly dancing, including the exercise belly dance movement, from its history as part of the erotic dance form serves to dehistoricize contemporary American belly dance forms, thereby eliding the close partnership between belly dancing and consumerism throughout its history in the United States. Moreover, the intense focus on authenticity funnels the potential ability of American belly dance to reclaim female power into a nonexistent past. In a movement that often measures authenticity by common misperceptions of Middle Eastern culture, or that commodifies authenticity by valuing Arabic stage names and jingly costumes from the cabaret era, the potential for liberation is ultimately undermined.

Though belly dance in the United States has clearly functioned as a tool for creative expression and as a means of rethinking the voluptuous body for scores of American women, it is not clear that the emancipatory power of belly dance has moved much past a self-help medium. While Soffee ultimately finds "true love" of self, the world of American belly dance she describes does not seem to deliver on the grand claim of liberation it implies. The focus on performing authenticity essentially encourages the dancers to both "enact the East and distance themselves from that enactment," a move that replicates Orientalist cabaret performances of belly dancing in the first half of the twentieth century.[53] In this way, American belly dancing functions as a sort of safety valve; it is an articulation of the power of female sexuality that is benignly distanced onto a romanticized and fabricated version of Middle Eastern culture. Rosina Fawzia al-Rawi's promise that "belly dance can help a woman find her inner strength ... [and] become the flying carpet on which she will move and reach her limits"[54] highlights the way in which the American belly dance movement has ultimately made gender justice seem as fantastical as a "flying carpet," leaving the goal of women's liberation from larger patriarchal structures conspicuously unaddressed.

Notes

1. Anne Thomas Soffee, *Snake Hips: Belly Dancing and How I Found True Love* (Chicago: Chicago Review Press, 2002), 42.

2. See Jana Daisy Hale, "Unveiling Belly Dance in America: A Feminist Fantasy Theme Analysis of Belly Dance Periodicals" (master's thesis, California State University at Chico, 2001); Danielle Janessa van Dobben, "Embodying the Exotic: The 'Gypsy' in American Female Oriental Dance" (master's thesis, University of California at Los Angeles, 2002); and especially Michelle Forner, "The Transmission of Oriental Dance in the United States" (master's thesis, University of California at Los Angeles, 1993), 1. See also popular belly dance Web sites such as shira.net, gildedserpent.com, bdancer.com, joyofbellydancing.com, bellydance.org, bellydancesuperstars.com, and fcbd(fat chance belly dance).com, and Stavros Stavrou Karayanni, *Dancing Fear and Desire: Race, Sexuality, and Imperial Politics in Middle Eastern Dance* (Waterloo, Canada: Wilfrid Laurier University Press, 2004), 160, 169.

3. Joseph Smith, "Within the Midway Plaisance," *Illustrated America*, Special Number (1893): 59–73, Warshaw Collection of Business Americana, Archives Center, National

Museum of American History, Smithsonian Institution, 66; James Buel, *The Magic City* (St. Louis: Historical Publishing Co., 1894.)

4. Rosemarie Garland Thomson, *Freakery: Cultural Spectacles of the Extraordinary Body* (New York: New York University Press, 1996), 10.

5. Robert C. Allen, *Horrible Prettiness: Burlesque and American Culture* (Chapel Hill: University of North Carolina Press, 1991), 138.

6. Allen, 148.

7. Allen, 27.

8. Allen, 231.

9. Allen, 240.

10. Rachel Shteir, *Striptease: The Untold History of the Girlie Show* (Oxford: Oxford University Press, 2004), 8. See also Lucinda Jarrett, *Stripping in Time: A History of Erotic Dancing* (San Francisco: Harper Collins, 1997).

11. Zarifa Aradoon, *The Oldest Dance: Origins and Philosophy of Danse Orientale* (Stanford: Dream Place, 1979), 10.

12. "*Raqs al Sharqi*: A Woman's Dance," *Connexions: An International Women's Quarterly*, no. 5 (spring 1982): 20-21.

13. For a fuller consideration of the connection between the belly dancing displays at the Chicago World's Fair and the striptease incarnation of belly dancing, see my article: A. Jarmakani, "Dancing the Hootchy-Kootchy: Belly Dance as the Embodiment of Socio-Cultural Tensions," *Arab Studies Journal* 13, no. 1 (2005): 123-39.

14. In some ways, I conflate two separate communities of dancers by insinuating that the American belly dance community and the exercise belly dance community are coterminous. I have no doubt that there are members of the American belly dance community, such as the dancers and teachers (Jamila Salimpour, Ibrahim Farrah, Dahlena) that Michelle Forner calls the "old guard" in her master's thesis; see p. 83. However, Forner also points to the fact that one of the primary means for the dispersion of belly dance in the United States is through consumerist avenues, such as performing "belly grams" for profit, and other commercial opportunities; see pp. 183-84. While some members of the professional American belly dance community would undoubtedly be offended by my implication that the exercise belly dance community is the same as the larger American belly dance community, there is a clear overlap of themes and practitioners between the two worlds.

15. "7 Pleasures of the Exotic," *CML The City Edition: Deals, Diversions and Direct Access for Camel's Coveted Customers* (2002): 13-17.

16. Mikhail Bakhtin, *Rabelais and His World*, trans. Hélène Iswolsky (Bloomington: Indiana University Press, 1984), 317.

17. Bakhtin, 317.

18. Rania Androniki Bossonis, *Bellydancing for Fitness: The Sexy Art That Tones Your Abs, Butt, and Thighs* (Gloucester, MA: Fair Winds, 2004), 24.

19. Robert Stam, "Mikhail Bakhtin and Left Cultural Critique," in *Postmodernism and Its Discontents*, ed. E. Ann Kaplan (New York: Verso, 1998), 135.

20. Bakhtin, 269.

21. I am borrowing from and building on Robert Stam's claim that the link between the carnival and cinema in the United States is both metonymic and metaphoric in *Subversive Pleasures: Bakhtin, Cultural Criticism, and Film* (Baltimore: Johns Hopkins University Press, 1989), 95.
22. Bakhtin, 148.
23. Again, see my article "Dancing the Hootchy-Kootchy" for a more developed argument about the tension between sacred and profane interpretations of female sexuality as projected onto belly dancer's bodies in a U.S. context.
24. American tribal dance actually refers to a style of belly dance developed in the United States. Its development has been credited to Jamila Salimpour, a prominent figure in American belly dance since the 1960s, and the coining of the term can be credited to Carolina Nericcio of Fat Chance Belly Dance (van Dobben, p. 98). Interestingly, the American Tribal Dance Style incorporates different forms of folk dance as it seeks to present interpretations of the dance as it was performed (authentically) in ancient times.
25. Ibrahim Farrah, "Statement of Purpose," *Arabesque*, 1 (1975): 3.
26. Farrah, 3.
27. Julie Russo Mishkin and Marta Schill, *The Compleat Belly Dancer* (Garden City, New York: Doubleday, 1973), 17.
28. Ozel Turkbas, *The Art of Belly Dancing: Fun, Exercise, Excitement* (Lido Beach, New York: El-ay Enterprises, 1977), 2.
29. Suheyla (Kate McGowan), *The Ancient and Enduring Art...Danse Orientale* (Ann Arbor: Edwards Brothers, 1977), chapter VIII (n. pag).
30. Turkbas, 12.
31. Mishkin and Schill, 19.
32. van Dobben, 175.
33. Mishkin and Schill, 16.
34. Turkbas, 3.
35. Mishkin and Schill, 16–17.
36. Dolphina, *Bellydance: Get Fit and Feel Fabulous with This Unique Workout for the Mind and Body* (New York: DK Publishing, 2005), 10.
37. Keti Sherif, *Bellydance: A Guide to Middle Eastern Dance, Its Music, Its Culture, and Costume* (Crows Nest, Australia: Allen and Unwin, 2004), 13.
38. Laura A. Cooper, *Belly Dancing Basics* (New York: Sterling, 2004), 13.
39. Rosina-Fawzia al-Rawi. *Belly Dancing: Unlock the Secret Power of Ancient Dance* (London: Robinson, 2001), 95. This book was originally published in the United States in 1999 under the title *Grandmother's Secrets*.
40. Sherif, 34.
41. Dolphina, 10.
42. Tamalyn Dallal, *Belly Dancing for Fitness: The Ultimate Dance Workout That Unleashes Your Creative Spirit* (Berkeley: Ulysses Press, 2004), 15.
43. Dallal, 15.
44. Hale, 56.

45. Karayanni, 71.
46. Soffee, 49.
47. Soffee, 227.
48. Dallal, 137
49. Soffee, 85.
50. Soffee, 179.
51. bell hooks, "Eating the Other: Desire and Resistance," in *Black Looks: Race and Representation* (Boston: South End Press, 1992), 21.
52. hooks, 21.
53. I borrow this phrasing from Amy Koritz's exploration of Maud Allan's performance of Salome. See Amy Koritz, "Dancing the Orient for England: Maud Allan's 'The Vision of Salome,'" *Theatre Journal*, no. 46 (1994): 63–78.
54. al-Rawi, 86.

Works Cited

Allen, Robert C. *Horrible Prettiness: Burlesque and American Culture.* Chapel Hill: University of North Carolina Press, 1991.

Aradoon, Zarifa. *The Oldest Dance: Origins and Philosophy of Danse Orientale.* Stanford: Dream Place, 1979.

Bakhtin, Mikhail. *Rabelais and His World*, trans. Hélène Iswolsky. Bloomington: Indiana University Press, 1984.

Bossonis, Rania Androniki. *Bellydancing for Fitness: The Sexy Art That Tones Your Abs, Butt, and Thighs.* Gloucester, MA: Fair Winds, 2004.

Buel, James. *The Magic City.* St. Louis: Historical Publishing Co., 1894.

Cooper, Laura A. *Belly Dancing Basics.* New York: Sterling, 2004.

Dallal, Tamalyn. *Belly Dancing for Fitness: The Ultimate Dance Workout That Unleashes Your Creative Spirit.* Berkeley: Ulysses Press, 2004.

Dolphina. *Bellydance: Get Fit and Feel Fabulous with This Unique Workout for the Mind and Body.* New York: DK Publishing, 2005.

Farrah, Ibrahim. "Statement of Purpose." *Arabesques* 1, no. 1 (1975): 3.

Forner, Michelle L. "The Transmission of Oriental Dance in the United States." Master's thesis, University of California Los Angeles, 1993.

Hale, Jana Daisy. "Unveiling Belly Dance in America: A Feminist Fantasy Theme Analysis of Belly Dance Periodicals." Master's thesis, California State University Chico, 2001.

hooks, bell. *Black Looks: Race and Representation.* Boston: South End Press, 1992.

Jarmakani, Amira. "Dancing the Hootchy-Kootchy: Belly Dance as the Embodiment of Socio-Cultural Tensions." *Arab Studies Journal* 13, no. 1 (2005): 123–39.

Jarrett, Lucinda. *Stripping in Time: A History of Erotic Dancing.* San Francisco: Harper Collins, 1997.

Karayanni, Stavros Stavrou. *Dancing Fear and Desire: Race, Sexuality, and Imperial Politics in Middle Eastern Dance.* Waterloo, Canada: Wilfrid Laurier University Press, 2004.

Koritz, Amy. "Dancing the Orient for England: Maud Allan's 'The Vision of Salome.'" *Theatre Journal*, no. 46 (1994): 63–78.

Mishkin, Julie Russo, and Marta Schill. *The Compleat Belly Dancer*. Garden City, NY: Doubelday, 1973.

"*Raqs Sharqi*: A Woman's Dance." *Connexions: An International Women's Quarterly*, no. 5 (1982): 20–21.

al-Rawi, Rosina Fawzia. *Belly Dancing: Unlock the Secret Power of Ancient Dance*. London: Robinson, 2001.

"7 Pleasures of the Exotic." *CML The City Edition: Deals, Diversions and Direct Access for Camel's Coveted Customers* (2002): 13–17.

Sherif, Keti. *Bellydance: A Guide to Middle Eastern Dance, Its Music, Its Culture, and Costume.* Crows Nest, Australia: Allen & Unwin, 2004.

Shteir, Rachel. *Striptease: The Untold History of the Girlie Show*. Oxford: Oxford University Press, 2004.

Smith, Joseph. "Within the Midway Plaisance." *Illustrated America*, Special number (1893): 59–73.

Soffee, Anne Thomas. *Snake Hips: Belly Dancing and How I Found True Love*. Chicago: Chicago Review Press, 2002.

Stam, Robert. *Subversive Pleasures: Bakhtin, Cultural Criticism, and Film*. Baltimore: Johns Hopkins University Press, 1989.

——. "Mikhail Bakhtin and Left Cultural Critique." In *Postmodernism and Its Discontents*, ed. E. Ann Kaplan, 116–45. New York: Verso, 1998.

Suheyla. *The Ancient and Enduring Art ... Danse Orientale*. Ann Arbor: Edwards Brothers, 1977.

Thomson, Rosemarie Garland. *Freakery: Cultural Spectacles of the Extraordinary Body*. New York: New York University Press, 1996.

Turkbas, Ozel. *The Art of Belly Dancing: Fun, Exercise, Entertainment*. Lido Beach, New York: El-ay Enterprises, 1977.

Van Dobben, Danielle Janessa. "Embodying the Exotic: The 'Gypsy' in American Female Oriental Dance." Master's thesis, University of California Los Angeles, 2002.

Not Just Disney: Destructive Stereotypes of Arabs in Children's Literature

Carolyn Speer Schmidt

Stereotyping, the anticipation of people's behavior or performance based upon widely held ideas about their ethnic, racial, or other "group" to which they belong, is a pervasive problem in American society.[1] The effect of stereotyping and other forms of racism as psychological stressors has recently begun to emerge as an area of research interest especially in their relationship to physical illness. In post-9/11 America, there is reason to view the stereotyping of Arabs and Arab Americans specifically as a particular concern.

In his influential 1994 article, "Ethnic Archetypes and the Arab Image," Ronald Stockton discusses many negative stereotypes associated with Arabs.[2] Citing many earlier studies, Stockton identifies such stereotypes as desert-dwelling, tribal, war-loving, veiled, volatile, backward, aggressive, cruel, cunning, and barbaric. In addition, such "positive" stereotypes Stockton discusses include religious, intelligent, and brave. Regardless of the "negative" or "positive" connotation of a particular stereotype, the work of Faye Cocchiara and James Campbell Quick indicates that all stereotypes are potentially destructive to the groups they attempt to describe.[3] In addition, the 2005 work of Carrie Conaway indicates that it is the most successful members of a group who are most likely to suffer psychological effects from stereotyping of any kind.[4]

Another group that is put at risk by stereotyped images is children. Cultivation theory indicates that repeated exposures to particular images leads to a distorted understanding of the object viewed. In their 2003 work, Hae-Kyong Bang and Bonnie Reece link cultivation theory to racial stereotyping and conclude that "if children are repeatedly exposed to certain portrayals of an ethnic group, they may develop corresponding beliefs about the group."[5]

This concern has led to an emergence of interest in analyzing stereotyped images in children's media including television programming and storybooks.

Stereotypes can be destructive both within groups and between groups. Between groups stereotypes lead to a distorted understanding of the unknown and can be particularly dangerous when the viewer involved lives without much contact with other groups.[6] Within groups, stereotypes can lead to a distorted sense of self which can, if unaddressed lead to poor self-concept and low self-esteem. The question is, then, what do Arab and non-Arab American children see when they open a book intended to entertain and teach them with stories and information about Arabs, Arab life, and the Arab American experience? Do the visual portrayals of Arabs betray the written content and undermine the message of tolerance and understanding?

To develop a richer understanding of the visual images of Arabs in English-language, primarily North American, children's fiction and nonfiction, fifteen books published between 1979 and 2004 were analyzed by the author for racial stereotyping. These works were identified through a review of Judith Lechner's listing "The World of Arab and Muslim Children in Children's Books," Books in Print, and suggestions made by a librarian at the University of Massachusetts at Amherst.[7] They include the following books: *The Arab Americans* by Joan Broadsky Schur, *How the Arabs Invented Algebra* by Tika Downey, *Arab Americans* by C. Ann Fitterer, *The Arab Americans* by Bob Temple, *Grandma Hekmatt Remembers* by Ann Morris, *The Arab Americans* by Alixa Naff, *The Arabs* by Penny Bateman, *Ahmad and Sarah go to Mosque* by Rashid Ahmad Chaudhry, *Lawrence of Arabia* by Richard Ebert, *An Ancient Heritage: The Arab-American Minority* by Brent Ashabranner, *The Arabs Knew* by Tillie S. Pine and Joseph Levine, *Sinbad* by Ludmila Zeman, *Aladdin and the Wonderful Lamp* by Andrew Lang and Errol Le Cain, *Arabian Nights Three Tales* by Deborah Nourse Lattimore, *Hosni the Dreamer: An Arabian Tale* by Ehud Ben-Ezer.[8] All but two of the titles are specifically North American. Bateman's book *The Arabs* represents a British viewpoint but is available in the United States.[9] Chaudhry's book *Ahmad and Sarah go to Mosque* was published in Islamabad with the intention, as stated in the introduction, of being distributed in the Western world to teach about Islam.[10] These titles were chosen because they were specifically recommended by librarians at the University of Massachusetts at Amherst.

The data were analyzed through an ethnographic lens, a process that requires a high degree of interaction between the researcher and the data in an effort to continuously verify the communication of explicit and implicit meanings.[11] A constant comparative method was used to help the researcher put the images from each work in the context of the body of Arab American children's literature.[12] The data were categorized into two distinct groupings: fiction and nonfiction, including realistic fiction, and pre-2001 and post-2001 literature. Each category was then coded with reference to a list of stereotypes derived from the work of Ronald Stockton and from the first study of Arab American women conducted in 2003 by Jen'nan Ghazal Read.[13]

This analysis uses thirteen stereotype categories, five concerning women and eight concerning men. Images of Arab women were analyzed for indications of their being "veiled Islamic traditionalists," "faceless," sexualized, pleasure-giving, and/or victimized.[14] Images of Arab men were analyzed for indications of their being tribal, intelligent, war-loving, angry, victimized, crouched and unlucky, Muslim, and/or cunning.[15] The images of Arab children were analyzed by gender with reference to the corresponding adult stereotype.

Analysis both by fiction/nonfiction and realistic fiction and by pre-2001 and post-2001 led to disturbing conclusions about the visual portrayals of Arabs in children's literature.

Fiction and Nonfiction

A striking difference in the visual portrayal of Arabs emerged when these fifteen books were separated into fiction and nonfiction/realistic fiction. Both categories presented many visual images, some of which were consistent with but not limited to the thirteen stereotypes listed above. The fiction images came from four books, all of which were printed prior to 2001. The overwhelming portrayal of Arabs was stereotypical with images consistent with most of the coding categories used in this research.

Three of the four fiction books came from the Thousand and One Nights tradition presenting the stories of Sinbad, Aladdin, The Queen of Serpents, and Ubar the lost city of brass. The fourth book told the traditional story of Hosni the dreamer. All four of these books contained images of both men and women in "traditional" dress and tribal scenes, and all four took place in the past. In two of the books, both representing tales from Thousand and One Nights, Arab men were depicted as overtly warlike wielding knives and shown in combat scenes.

The visual portrayal of Arab women in these four books relied equally heavily on stereotyped images. When women were portrayed at all, they were either overweight, covered, and secondary as in the scene from the marketplace is *Hosni the Dreamer*, covered and coyly sexual as is portrayed later in *Hosni the Dreamer*, or overtly sexualized and presented as passive pleasure-givers as in all three of the Thousand and One Nights books.

What is most striking in the images of these four books, however, is not their inclusion of stereotypes but instead their lack of inclusion both of images of children and for the most part of images of women. It is because there are so few female images in any of these books that the overt sexualization of the included images is so powerful. Clearly, these tales are overtly male, and their representation of Arab males overwhelmingly negative. In addition to the Arab male stereotypes discussed above, these books taken together portrayed Arab males as hedonistic, crouched, unlucky, victimized, sneering, sexual, poor, and deceitful/cunning. These negative images were only partly balanced by other images presenting Arab males as wise, wealthy, and resourceful.

The nonfiction/realistic fiction portrayals of Arab men, women, and children were significantly more positive than the corresponding fiction portrayals, yet the images continued to rely on stereotypes for at least some of their content. All but four volumes in this category had at least one tribal image and at least one image of a camel. Five of the eleven books in this category contained at least one image where an Arab male was presented in a warlike way including images of armed men and boys.[16] In addition to these warlike images, an additional book contained images of Arab men inflamed with anger.

In contrast to the fiction books discussed above, Arab women were rarely presented in a sexualized manner in the nonfiction/realistic fiction books. Only the cover image of Ann Fitterer's book *Arab Americans* had an arguably sexualized image. In fact, rather than being sexualized, Arab women and girls were much more likely to be presented as Read's veiled Islamic traditionalists.[17] Taken together, eight of the eleven books in this category presented a sum total of fifty-five images of women and/or girls in Muslim attire.[18] This total represents three images from Fitterer's book, two images from Schur's book, seven images from Bateman's book, six images from Ashabranner's book, eight images from Chaudhry's book, and twenty-nine images from Morris's book.

The images from Chaudhry's book are particularly interesting given that all but one of the images of females purposely obscure the face, showing only the back of the head or showing the face blocked by something else in the drawing.[19] The images in Morris's book are also work note, both for their number and type.[20] The book chronicles a day spent with Grandma Heckmatt, and given that she is presented as a covered Muslim woman, there are a number of images that were understandably coded as Muslim. What is interesting, however, is that it is only the images of Grandma Hekmatt in the United States that portray here as covered. The images of her as a younger woman in Egypt show her in Western clothing and no cover.

Arab men were also overwhelmingly imaged as Muslim in these books. In seven of the eleven works studied, Arab men or boys were overtly portrayed as Muslim, a total of forty-one separate images. In fact, it seemed as if the books' illustrators went out of their way to reinforce this image of Arab man as Muslim because almost all of the forty-one images showed Arab men entering or exiting a Mosque, praying in a Mosque, praying outside of a Mosque or studying the Koran. In addition to these images, four books contained Muslim images, Mosques or pages from the Koran, without people in them.

The images of Christian Arabs are significantly more difficult to find in these works. One obvious reason for this difference is that Christian coding is frequently less socially outward than Muslim coding can be. Nevertheless, only four of the eleven books in this category featured one or two overtly Christian images each for a total of five images. In Naff's book, three Syrian women in Red Cross uniforms are depicted along with an image of Danny Thomas in front of a statue of St. Jude.[21] Fitterer featured an image of a woman specifically designated as a Christian Syrian.[22] Ashabranner included an image of Arab boys and girls being confirmed into the Orthodox church.[23] Finally, Bob Temple depicted an image of a crowd of men and women carrying a cross through the streets of Jerusalem.[24]

Pre–and Post–9/11

Separating the works into before 2001 and after 2001 functioned as another useful lens for viewing racial stereotypes in this selection of fifteen books. There were a total of ten pre–2001 books: all four fiction books discussed above and six nonfiction/realistic fiction books.[25] These ten books represent many negative stereotypes in large measure because of the inclusion of the fiction books. Two nonfiction titles in this category deal directly with Arab

Americans. Both of these books are intended to "introduce" Arab Americans as an American minority, and both contained images of Arab men as warlike and multiple images of Arabs in Muslim attire or in overtly Muslim portrayals and other Muslim images with no people in them. Each of these books did make some attempt to "balance" the portrayal as Arabs-as-Muslims with the inclusion of a total of three overtly Christian images.[26]

The other three nonfiction/realistic fiction books in this category each brings a different set of stereotypes to the group. Ebert's book *Lawrence of Arabia* has a universally negative portrayal as Arabs as tribal and warlike, unsurprising images given the subject matter of the book. Pine and Levine's book *The Arabs Knew* is an ostensibly culturally sensitive look at the many inventions for which Arabs have been responsible for throughout time, but the lack of a single modern image of an Arab implies that Arabs are a historic, perhaps even extinct people, who were, when alive, clever, desert-dwelling, and tribal. The cartoonish depiction of Arabs contains no images of women or girls and stylized and arguably racist portrayals of Arab men with overemphasized facial and other physical features.

Bateman's book *The Arabs* is one of two non-North American books. It is filled throughout with images of Arabs-as-Muslims and also contains several images linking Arabs with oil production. Finally, Rashid Ahmad Chaudhry's 1991 book *Ahmad and Sarah go to Mosque*, contains, as is obvious from the title, many Muslim images. In addition, Chaudhry's book portrays females as secondary, veiled Islamic traditionalists with their line-drawn faces obscured in all but one image on page nine. This image shows a young girl kneeling on a prayer rug before the seated figure of her father. In this image, her mother is portrayed as a mostly hidden by the figure of the father and with her back to the artist. This portrayal is striking because each of these images is a hand sketch, not a photograph. There is no practical reason for females to be obscured in these images. Taken together, these ten pre-2001 books reinforce many stereotypes about Arabs especially the idea that Arabs are warlike and almost universally Muslim.

The post-2001 books represent an interesting shift from the earlier portrayals of Arabs. Most noticeably, the random sample studied contained no fiction books. The five books that were identified all seem to have a goal of cultural tolerance and respect. All five of the titles are part of larger series intended to teach about other cultures, especially as they exist as minority populations in the United States.[27] Interestingly, these books are replete with positive images of Arabs. Arabs are shown to be happy, hard-working, patriotic Americans. Nevertheless, even considering cultural inclusion to be an obvious goal of these books, three of the books contain Arab males in warlike portrayals, including one image that shows a young boy draped in a *kuffiyeh* and waving a gun in one hand while the other hand is clenched in an up-raised fist.[28] In addition to these warlike images the five post–2001 books studied contained a total of fifty-two overtly Muslim images and only two overtly Christian images.

Discussion

This project began with the question "What do Arab and non-Arab American children see when they read books intended to entertain and teach them something of Arabs, Arab life, and the Arab American experience?" The answer to that question is mixed but disturbing. While many of these books contained positive visual images of Arabs and interesting information about the contributions of Arabs to cultural advance, frequently these positive images are undermined either by the implication that all positive Arab contributions are historical as in the works of Downey and of Pine and Levine. Other positive images seem to be largely limited to characterizing Arabs as non-threatening citizens who are happy, patriotic Americans.

Taken as a group of fifteen works, these books overwhelmingly portray Arabs as tribal, warlike, Muslim, and in the case of women, veiled, passive, and traditional. The fact that all five of the post–2001 works studied happened to be volumes in larger series indicates that the works are intended to promote cultural inclusion and understanding, but in many cases, the visual images contained in the works undermine that message.

Conclusion

Parents and scholars alike understand that portrayals of ethnic and racial minorities in the United States become more racist as they become more mainstream. For example, Walt Disney Pictures has come under repeated fire for its portrayals of racial minorities. Nonetheless, it seems reasonable to assume that children's books would be written to be inclusive, tolerant, and balanced, especially in those few instances where the books' authors are members of the ethnic group portrayed in the stories. Even so, the review presented here indicates the racial stereotyping of Arabs and Arab Americans is still prevalent in the images presented to children in books.

What are the effects of stereotyping both within groups and between groups? For Arab Americans, it is clear that it could have a negative in-group impact to perpetuate such potentially destructive stereotypes as Arab females being either veiled Islamic traditionalists or overtly sexualized pleasure-givers while Arab males are presented as angry, warlike, and armed. The impact may be particularly destructive to second–generation immigrant Arab children who Nedim Karakayali argues are especially susceptible to problems developing a "new identity" separate from their parents' and more in line with their own cultural environment.[29]

What might be less clear is the impact that these same stereotypes have on members of out-groups. It is potentially the out-groups, however, that are even more influenced by these corrosive portrayals. The bulk of the stereotype literature finds that adolescents have strong biases based on in-group and out-group associations and that these biases affect these children's judgments about violent events. As Ronald Pitner et al. argue, "our stereotypes and preexisting beliefs can influence the ways we make judgments about violent acts" committed by others.[30] Unfortunately, holding such negative beliefs about others is pleasurable and practical because it tends to bolster an individual's self-esteem and their esteem for their own group.[31]

Post–9/11 America is a rich soil for cultivating long-held Western stereotypes regarding Arabs. As Steven Salaita argues, 9/11 took the approximately five million Arab Americans from obscurity and thrust them into the limelight.[32] The decades of obscurity did nothing to help Arab Americans counteract stereotypes. Stereotypes, Edward Said argues, have their roots in the Crusades and the subsequent conflicts between Europe and the Ottoman Turks.[33] Addressing the visual images of Arabs and Arab Americans in children's literature is a good place to start tackling the disparaging stereotypes perpetuated for so long.

Notes

1. Frank Cocchiara and James Campbell Quick, "The Negative Effects of Positive Stereotypes: Ethnicity-Related Stressors and Implications on Organizational Health," *Journal of Organizational Behavior*, 25 (2004): 781–85.
2. Ronald Stockton, "Ethnic Archetypes and the Arab Image," in *The Development of Arab-American Identity*, ed. E. McCarus (Ann Arbor: The University of Michigan Press, 1994).

3. Cocchiara and Quick, "The Negative Effects of Positive Stereotypes," 781–85.

4. Carrie Conaway, "A Psychological Effect of Stereotypes," *Regional Review–Federal Reserve Bank of Boston* 14 (2005).

5. Hae-Kyong Bang, and Bonnie Reece, "Minorities in Children's Television Commercials: New, Improved, and Stereotyped," *The Journal of Consumer Affairs* 37 (2003): para. 4.

6. Bang and Reece, para. 5.

7. Judith Lechner, "The World of Arab and Muslim Children in Children's Books," Auburn University, http://www.auburn.edu/academic/education/eflt/lechner/arabbooks.pdf (accessed November 15, 2005); University of Massachusetts, Amherst, "September 11th Resources for Educators (Print and Electronic)," University of Massachusetts, Amherst, www.library.umass.edu/sept11/education.html, (accessed November 15, 2005).

8. Joan Brodsky Schur, *The Arab Americans* (Farmington Hills, MI: Thomson Gale, 2004); Tika, Downey, *How the Arabs Invented Algebra* (New York: the Rosen Publishing Group, 2004); Ann C. Fitterer, *Arab Americans* (Chanhassen, MN: The Child's World, 2003); Bob Temple, *The Arab Americans* (Broomall, PA: Mason Crest Publishers, 2003); Ann Morris, *Grandma Hekmatt Remembers* (Brookfield, CT: The Millbrook Press, Inc., 2003); Alixa Naff, *The Arab Americans* (New York: Chelsea House Publishers, 1988); Penny Bateman, *The Arabs* (London: British Museum Publications, 1987); Rashid Ahmad Chaudhry, *Ahmad and Sarah go to Mosque* (Islamabad: Islam International Publications LTD, 1991); Richard Ebert, *Lawrence of Arabia* (Milwaukee: MacDonald-Raintree, Inc., 1979); Brent Ashabranner, *An Ancient Heritage: The Arab-American Minority* (New York: Harper Collins Publishers, 1991); Tillie Pine and Joseph Levine, *The Arabs Knew* (New York: McGraw-Hill Book Company, 1976); Ludmilla Zeman *Sinbad* (Plattsburgh, NY: Tundra Books of Northern New York, 1999); Andrew Lang and Errol Le Cain, *Aladdin and the Wonderful Lamp* (New York: The Viking Press, 1981); Deborah Nourse Lattimore *Arabian Nights Three Tales* (New York: Harper Collins Publishers, 1995); Ehud Ben-Ezer *Hosni the Dreamer: An Arabian Tale* (New York: HarperCollins, 1997).

9. Bateman, *The Arabs*.

10. Chaudhry, *Ahmad and Sarah go to Mosque*.

11. John Cresswell, *Qualitative Inquiry and Research Design*, 58 (Thousand Oaks, CA: SAGE Publications, 1998).

12. Cresswell, *Qualitative Inquiry and Research Design*, 57.

13. Ronald Stockton, "Ethnic Archetypes and the Arab Image," in *The Development of Arab-American Identity*, ed. E. McCarus (Ann Arbor: The University of Michigan Press, 1994); Jen'nan Ghazal Read, "The Source of Gender Role Attitudes Among Christian and Muslim Arab-American Women," *Sociology of Religion* 64 (2003).

14. Jen'nan Ghazal Read, "The Source of Gender Role Attitudes Among Christian and Muslim Arab-American Women," *Sociology of Religion* 64 (2003): para. 4.; Stockton, "Ethnic Archetypes and the Arab Image," 126–33.

15. Stockton, 126–27.

16. For examples, see Joan Brodsky Schur 81; Bob Temple's wholly gratuitous image on page 14, and another image on page 45; milder images in Alixa Naff's book 18, 29; images throughout Ebert's book, Ashabranner 77.

17. See Read, "The Source of Gender Role."

18. This total represents three images from Ann Fitterer's book, two images from Joan Brodsky Schur's book, seven images from Penny Bateman's book, six images from Brent Ashabranner's book, eight images from Rashid Ahmad Chaudhry's book and twenty-nine images from Ann Morris's book. The images from Rashid Ahmad Chaudhry's book are particularly interesting given that all but one of the images of females purposely obscure the face, showing only the back of the head or show the face blocked by something else in the drawing. The images in Ann Morris's book are also worth noting, both for their number and type. The book chronicles a day spent with Grandma Hekmatt, and given that she is presented as a covered Muslim woman, there are a large number of images that were coded Muslim. What is interesting, however, is that it is only the images of Grandma Hekmatt in the United States that portray her as covered. The images of her as a younger woman in Egypt show her in Western clothing and without cover.

19. Chaudhry, *Ahmad and Sarah go to Mosque.*

20. Morris, *Grandma Hekmatt Remembers.*

21. Naff, *The Arab Americans*, 67, 102.

22. Fitterer, *Arab Americans*, 8.

23. Ashabranner, *An Ancient Heritage: The Arab-American*, 132.

24. Temple, *The Arab Americans*, 20.

25. Bateman, *The Arabs*; Ashabranner, *An Ancient Heritage: The Arab-American*; Pine and Levine, *The Arabs*; Chaudhry, *Ahmad and Sarah go to Mosque*; Ebert, *Lawrence of Arabia*; Naff, *The Arab Americans.*

26. Naff, *The Arab Americans* 67, 104; Ashabranner, *An Ancient Heritage: The Arab-American Minority*, 132.

27. Downey's book *How the Arabs Invented Algebra* is part of the PowerMath series. Temple's *The Arab Americans* is a part of the We Came to America series (and is cited by Booklist as one of the best titles in the series). Fitterer's book *Arab Americans* is part of the Our Cultural Heritage series. Schur's book *The Arab Americans* is part of the Immigrants in America series. Morris's book *Grandma Hekmatt Remembers* is part of What Was It Like, Grandma? series.

28. Temple, *The Arab Americans*, 14.

29. Nedim Karakayali, "Duality and Diversity in the Lives of Immigrant Children: Rethinking the 'Problem of the Second Generation' in Light of Immigrant Autobiographies," *The Canadian Review of Sociology and Anthropology*, 42 (2005).

30. Ronald Pitner, Ron Avi Astor, Rami Benbenishty, Muhammad Haj-Yahia, and Anat Zeira, "The Effects of Group Stereotypes on Adolescents' Reasoning About Peer Retribution," *Child Development* 74 (2003): 414.

31. Pitner, et al., 421.

32. Steven Salaita, "Ethnic Identity and Imperative Patriotism: Arab Americans Before and After 9/11," *College Literature,* 32 (2005): para. 11.
33. As cited in Stockton, 126.

Works Cited

Ashabranner, Brent. *An Ancient Heritage: The Arab-American Minority.* New York: Harper Collins Publishers, 1991.

Bang, Hae-Kyong. "Minorities in Children's Television Commercials: New, Improved, and Stereotyped." *The Journal of Consumer Affairs,* 37 (2003): 42-65.

Bateman, Penny. *The Arabs.* London: British Museum Publications, 1987.

Ben-Ezer, Ehud. *Hosni the Dreamer: An Arabian Tale.* New York: HarperCollins, 1997.

Chaudhry, Rashid Ahmad. *Ahmad and Sarah go to Mosque.* Islamabad: Islam International Publications LTD, 1991.

Cocchiara, Frank K., and James Campbell Quick. "The Negative Effects of Positive Stereotypes: Ethnicity-Related Stressors and Implications on Organizational Health." *Journal of Organizational Behavior,* 25 (2004): 781-85.

Conaway, Carrie. "A Psychological Effect of Stereotypes." *Regional Review – Federal Reserve Bank of Boston* 14 (2005): 40-42.

Cresswell, John. *Qualitative Inquiry and Research Design.* Thousand Oaks, CA: SAGE Publications, 1998.

Downey, Tika. *How the Arabs Invented Algebra.* New York: The Rosen Publishing Group, 2004.

Ebert, Richard. *Lawrence of Arabia.* Milwaukee: Macdonald-Raintree, Inc.,1979.

Fitterer, C. Ann. *Arab Americans.* Chanhassen, MN: The Child's World, 2003.

Karakayali, Nedim. "Duality and Diversity in the Lives of Immigrant Children: Rethinking the 'Problem of the Second Generation' in Light of Immigrant Autobiographies." *The Canadian Review of Sociology and Anthropology,* 42 (2005): 325-44.

Lang, Andrew, and Errol Le Cain. *Aladdin and the Wonderful Lamp.* New York: The Viking Press, 1981.

Lattimore, Deborah Nourse. *Arabian Nights Three Tales.* New York: Harper Collins, 1995.

Lechner, Judith V. "The World of Arab and Muslim Children in Children's Books." Online resource available at http://www.auburn.edu/academic/education/eflt/lechner /arabbooks.pdf.

Morris, Ann. *Grandma Hekmatt Remembers.* Brookfield, CT: The Millbrook Press, Inc., 2003.

Naff, Alixa. *The Arab Americans.* New York: Chelsea House Publishers, 1988.

Pine, Tillie, and Joseph Levine. *The Arabs Knew.* New York: McGraw-Hill Book Company, 1976.

Pitner, Ronald, O., Ron Avi Astor, Rami Benbenishty, Muhammad M. Haj-Yahia, and Anat Zeira. "The Effects of Group Stereotypes on Adolescents' Reasoning About Peer Retribution." *Child Development,* 74 (2003): 413-25.

Read, Jen'nan Ghazal. "The Source of Gender Role Attitudes Among Christian and Muslim Arab-American Women." *Sociology of Religion,* 64 (2003): 207-19.

Salaita, Steven. "Ethnic Identity and Imperative Patriotism: Arab Americans Before and After 9/11." *College Literature,* 32 (2005): 146–70.

Schur, Joan Brodsky. *The Arab Americans.* Farmington Hills, MI: Thomson Gale, 2004.

Shulevitz, Uri. *Hosni the Dreamer.* New York: Farrar, Straus, and Giroux, 1997.

Stockton, Ronald. "Ethnic Archetypes and the Arab Image." *The Development of Arab-American Identity.* Ed. Ernest McCarus. Ann Arbor: The University of Michigan Press, 1994.

Temple, Bob. *The Arab Americans.* Broomall, PA: Mason Crest Publishers, 2003.

Zeman, Ludmila. *Sinbad.* Plattsburgh, NY: Tundra Books of Northern New York, 1999.

Part 4

After 9/11

10

Arab? Muslim? Canadian? A Question of Identity

Omar Alghabra

The inquiry into the actions of Canadian security agents in relation to the now infamous story of Maher Arar continues to receive attention, almost four years after his arrest.[1] Mr. Arar, a Syrian Canadian (like myself), was arrested in New York and deported in 2002 by the United States to Syria despite the fact that he is a Canadian with dual citizenship in both Canada and Syria. Born in Syria, Arar is Canadian. Over $23 million dollars have been spent trying to sort out what exactly happened to this Canadian citizen who was detained in the United States and then deported to Syria where he was tortured.[2] His story has raised many important questions about how Canada and the United States plan to pursue their investigations regarding international terrorism, specifically, questions about whether or not both the United States and Canadian governments neglected Arar's rights as a Canadian citizen to due process of law, and the legal pitfalls of dual citizenship when one of those citizenships includes that of an Arab nation.[3]

While these concerns are extremely important and deserve to be examined thoroughly, and clearly there is a need for corrective actions to be implemented swiftly, there are several other important questions to consider. This international incident raised many questions about issues of ethnicity, identity, citizenship and one's place in the larger global community when one is both of Arab origin and a citizen of a non-Arab nation. Is Arar a Syrian or a Canadian? Can he be both? If he is both, is he more of a Syrian than he is a Canadian? Who gets to decide what he is? What is his identity? What is his citizenship? Implied in all these questions for people of Arab descent living in the Arab diaspora, is the often unspoken question: What about people like me? What does it mean to be of Arab descent and live and work in North America?

I am an Arab Muslim Canadian (not in order of importance). It has taken me years to fully come to terms with what this tri-part label actually means, and stories such as that of Maher Arar make it important for me to share what I have learned about ethnicity, identity, identity politics, citizenship, and the importance of valuing and protecting a multicultural citizen-base within a country like Canada because events like that surrounding Arar negatively impact the daily lives of people of Arab descent living in the Americas and can also negatively impact a nation's views about the value of multiculturalism and how that nation participates in the global community.

Like most immigrants, when I first arrived in Canada in 1989, I brought with me excitement and hope about my new adopted home. One of my top priorities was to remove any visible or invisible signs of being a foreigner so I could belong. I wanted to get rid of my accent. I intended to assimilate. I rejected the hyphenated Canadian-Arab label; it made me feel less of a Canadian. I wanted to be like everyone else and to be treated like everyone else.

Ironically, the more I became "Canadian," the more I came to understand the seemingly confusing subject of identity. Whereas being "Arab" was at first something I wanted to make less noticeable, it eventually became an asset and a source of pride. The more confidence I gained in my Canadian identity, the more I appreciated how my other identities and experiences have positively contributed and shaped my Canadian identity. While a combination of critical thinking, self-confidence, and personal growth contributed to my new discovery, what was most important when I first came to Canada from Syria was that I found Canada to be a welcoming multicultural society, one that helped me reconcile the various aspects of my identity. That is something valuable that Canada must hold on to as it meets the contemporary political and international challenges of the twenty-first century.

Thus, one of the things that troubled me greatly about the way the Arar situation was handled was that it seemed to suggest that ethnicity determines citizenship. Ethnicity does not and should not be used to define citizenship. My ethnicity is an inherited feature, defined by the ethnicity of my parents. It does not define my citizenship or predetermine all aspects of my identity. Ethnicity is not necessarily defined by my country of origin either because countries are not composed of just one ethnicity. Additionally, ethnicity and country of birth cannot be used to determine which citizenship a dual citizen values more because, for example, I had no choice in the selection of my ethnicity or my place of birth. I am an Arab. I am Canadian. It is important to realize that identity is a much more complicated concept than ethnicity because a sense of identity is often created or defined by the experience of citizenship.

For example, many scholarly cultural studies coming from an anthropological perspective and situated in a sociological context, clearly demonstrate that collective identity is often a result of experience. Historically, national, religious, feminist, civil rights, and other types of social movements were initiated by a group of people who were brought together by their experiences. They attracted people by promoting issues that resonated with all who shared similar experiences and identities. Some of those movements eventually end up being blinded by self-interest or fanaticism causing them to lose sight of their original reason of their existence, although it was similar identities that brought them together in the first place. Scholar and field researcher Nadine Naber explains that it is often in the "aftermath" of a specific historical event and how the media respond to it that inspires a need to "articulate" identity and that the attempt at articulation actually creates or strengthens a sense of identity.[4]

Perhaps even more importantly, Naber's field research indicates that "everyday experiences" are of primary importance in identity formation because people of Arab descent must "grapple" with "multiple, competing, and often racist representations of Arabs, Middle Easterners, and Muslims and with the gendered imperatives of their immigrant parents' generation." To this I would add that there are also positive experiences that shape one's sense of identity. As Susan Marshall and Jen'nan Ghazal Read have shown, identity construction comes from both an "awareness of grievances" and a "recognition of benefits."[5] Thus, the experiences I faced throughout my life, both negative and positive, have shaped and determined my values, priorities, grievances, beliefs, and pride. My own experiences, views, aspirations, and challenges are how my identity has evolved and matured as an Arab Canadian. Ethnicity alone did not define my identity, and it is important to note that an identity can be acquired by choice as much as it can be neglected by choice.

Just as ethnicity alone does not determine identity, my citizenship is not defined by a passport, birth certificate, or citizenship card. In a recent edition of *The Canadian Review of Sociology and Anthropology*, Silma Bilge defines citizenship as more than just "an abstract way to define the limits of membership in a given political community."[6] While I cannot choose or change my ethnicity, I can choose or change my citizenship and therefore, when I say I am a Canadian citizen, I am expressing my loyalty to a system of values and government, and not to any human-made, arbitrarily drawn border. It is the commitment to values and conviction in a set of principles that makes one a citizen. I would argue that, in fact, a key part of what makes a Canadian a true Canadian citizen is his or her determination to maintain a vibrant democratic country, including a commitment to protecting a process for debating dissenting ideas. Nationhood is stronger when built on ideals and values about citizenship rather than racial or ethnic commonality. Place of birth and/or ethnicity does not create citizenship; citizenship is dependent on one's level of commitment to one's chosen nation's integrity and prosperity. That is what makes me a genuine Canadian.

As I have indicated earlier, I am an Arab Muslim Canadian (though not in any order of importance). In my experience, Canada is one of the very few countries in the world that nurtures the idea of multiculturalism in a healthy and respectful way and constructs a positive citizenship with both responsibility and pride. According to Nadine Naber, in America, for example, many young Arab American Muslims have opted for a "Muslim First" framework "by which to organize their identities," and in the United States, identifying oneself as Muslim is no longer "a religious affiliation" or "a marker of the relationship between individuals and the divine." It has instead become part of the "politics of identity." Sociologists would say that this identity politics is most likely directly a result of negative experiences in the United States in the aftermath of the September 11, 2001, attacks on New York and Washington and the rush to convict people of terrorism because of religious affiliation. It seems as if being Muslim in the United States, at least in the aftermath of September 11, was all too often equated with being a terrorist. However, as Canadian writer Jeff Sallot has said, this is "not a road Canada must follow," and religion in Canada should not be used for profiling. As Raja Khouri, a policy advisor and former president of the Canadian Federation, has explained people's religious beliefs should not be viewed as "indicators of complicity in terrorism."[7] Similarly, as Riad Saloojee, executive director for the Canadian Council on American Islamic Relations, has argued "if law-enforcement agents are going to use profiling, they should do so on the basis of behaviour, not ethnicity or religion."[8] The behavior of

Canadian Muslims does not warrant profiling. Islam is Canada's fastest growing religion, and, as Muneeb Nasir reports, it is particularly worth noting that the younger generations of Arab Canadian Muslims are "engaged in Canadian society" despite "the backlash and hate crimes against Muslims and other minorities that followed the September 11, 2001 attacks in the U.S. and the war on Iraq."[9]

My final point about identity, specifically Arab Canadian identity, Arab American identity, or any kind of Muslim identity in today's political climate, internationally and domestically, is that it is also important to remember that identity does not imply loyalty or declare convictions. It is a product of diverse real life experiences. It is this awareness of the global community that compels us to question blind loyalty to any entity such as a country or a person when instead it is imperative that one remain loyal to specific values and principles. Allegiance to the universal human values of equality, freedom, justice, acceptance, and tolerance must surpass all other loyalties.

It is this line of thinking that has helped me deconstruct any kind of perceived clash of identities that might result from my experience as a member of the Arab diaspora and a Canadian citizen with a deep and abiding respect for a homeland I have chosen to make my own. This personal journey in search of who I am, be it Canadian, Muslim, Arab, or all of the above has shown me that absolute allegiance to anything is a form of voluntary intellectual imprisonment that forces the individual to concede their right and duty to critical thinking. Critical thinking compels us all to question blind loyalty to an entity such as a country or a person rather than to the values and principles involved in being a citizen of that nation. Thus, when I am asked questions about my identity, I am sure of my answer. I am an Arab. I am a Syrian. I am a Muslim. I am a Canadian. I am an Arab Muslim Canadian. I am very comfortable and proud of my identities.

Notes

1. There are numerous newspaper articles dated 2005 that are still mulling over the implications of this 2002 event. See, for example, the *Hamilton Spectator* article from "The U.S. Won't Apologize to Maher Arar," *The Hamilton Spectator*, September 19, 2005: A09. Retrieved from Lexis Nexus Online database, January 28, 2006., or Neco Cockburn, "U.S. Offered to Return Maher Arar Inquiry Told: Demanded He Be Jailed" *The*

Gazette, June 2, 2005: A13. See also Sirma Bilge, "Citizenship in Transformation in Canada," *The Canadian Review of Sociology and Anthropology,* 41,no. 1 (2004): 91.

2. Information regarding the cost of the investigation is available from many sources. See, e.g., Lloyd Robertson, "Cost of Maher Arar Affair Soared to More than $23 million," [broadcast transcript]. February 25, 2005 CTV News, CTV Television, Inc. Retrieved from Lexis Nexus Online database, January 28, 2006.

3. See "Maher's Story in Brief," from Arar Maher's Web site. Retrieved March 10, 2006 from http: // www. maherarar.ca. See also Arar Commission, "About the Inquiry,." from the Commission of Inquiry into the Actions of Canadian Officials in Relation to Maher Arar Web site. Retrieved March 10, 2006 from http: // www.ararcommission .ca. These Web sites offer a firsthand account of Arar's story in his own words and for information pertaining to the official Canadian government's inquiry into the Arar incident.

4. To read Nadine Naber's entire argument, please see her article "Muslim First, Arab Second: A Strategic Politics of Race and Gender," *The Muslim World,* 95 no. 4 (2005): 479–96. In this essay, Naber also shows how gender plays a part in identity formation, again, not specifically because of the biological aspects of gender, but because of how gender is portrayed in the media and how people form identities is response to or against such portrayals.

5. See Susan Marshall and Jen'nan Ghazal Read, "Identity Politics among Arab-American Women," *The Social Science Quarterly,* 84 no. 4 (2003): 875. Retrieved from Proquest online Database, January 28, 2006. This article focuses on identity politics among Arab American women, but the value of their research about identity formation extends beyond the women's studies arena.

6. For more on this topic see Yvonne M. Herbert's edited collection *Citizenship in Transformation in Canada.* University of Toronto Press, 2002.

7. This interview is cited in an article by Paul Weinberg, "Anti-Terror Laws Sow Fear in Canadian Muslims," *IPS News,* February 25, 2005. Retrieved January 28, 2006. Available online at http:// www.ipsnews.net / Africa/interna.asp?idnews=27632; see also Sallot, Jeff. "Leave Religion Out of Terror Law Groups Say." *The Globe Mail,* September 21, 2005. Retrieved January 28, 2006. Available online athttp://www.theglobeandmail.com/servlet/ArticleNews/TPStory/LAC/20050921/ TERROR21/ TPNational/Canada.

8. See Weinberg, "Anti-Terror Laws Sow Fear in Canadian Muslims."

9. See Paul Weinberg, "Anti-Terror Laws Sow Fear in Canadian Muslims," and also Nasir, Muneeb. "Canadian Muslims Gain Prominence." *Amerperspective.com Online Magazine,* January 5, 2005. Retrieved January 28, 2006online from *Amerperspective.com Online Magazine,* http:// www.Amerperspective.com /html/ Canadian_ muslims_gain.html.

Works Cited

Arar, Maher. "Maher's Story in Brief." From the Arar Maher's Web site. Retrieved March 10, 2006 from http://www.maherarar.ca.

Arar Commission. "About the Inquiry." From the Commission of Inquiry into the Actions of Canadian Officials in Relation to Maher Arar Web site. Retrieved March 10, 2006 from http: // www.ararcommission.ca.

Bilge, Sirma. "Citizenship in Transformation in Canada." *The Canadian Review of Sociology and Anthropology*, 41 no. 1 (2004): .91.

Cockburn, Neco. "U.S. Offered to Return Maher Arar, Inquiry Told: Demanded He Be Jailed." *The Gazette,* June 2, 2005:. A13. Retrieved from Lexis Nexus online database, January 28, 2006.

Herbert, Yvonne. Citizenship in transformation in Canada : University of Toronto Press, 2002.

Marshall, Susan, and Jen'an Ghazal Read. "Identity Politics Among Arab-American Women." *The Social Science Quarterly*, 84 no. 4 (2003): 875. Retrieved from Proquest OnlineDatabase, January 28, 2006.

Naber, Nadine. "Muslim First, Arab Second: A Strategic Politics of Race and Gender." *The Muslim World* 95 no. 4 (2005): 479–96.

Nasir, Muneeb. "Canadian Muslims Gain Prominence." *Amerperspective.com Online Magazine*, January 5, 2005. Retrieved January 28, 2006online from*Amerperspective.com Online Magazine*,http://www.Amerperspective.com/html/Canadian muslims_gain.html.

Robertson, Lloyd. "Cost of Maher Arar Affair Soared to More than $23 million." [broadcast transcript]. February 25, 2005 CTV News, CTV Television, Inc. Retrieved from Lexis Nexus Online database, January 28, 2006.

Sallot, Jeff. "Leave Religion Out of Terror Law Groups Say." *The Globe Mail*, September 21, 2005.Retrieved January 28, 2006. Available online http://www.theglobeandmail.com /servlet/ArticleNews/TPStory /LAC/20050921/TERROR21/ TPNational/Canada.

"U.S. Won't Apologize to Maher Arar." *The Hamilton Spectator*. June 2, 2005: A9. Retrieved from Lexis Nexus online database, January 28, 2006.

Weinberg, Paul. "Anti-Terror Laws Sow Fear in Canadian Muslims." *IPS News*,February 25, 2005. Retrieved January 28, 2006. Available online at http:// www.ipsnews.net / Africa/interna.asp?idnews=27632.

11

Apologies and Amnesias: Protestant Engagement with Arab American Communities since 9/11

Deirdre King Hainsworth

In the aftermath of the attacks on September 11, 2001, members of the Arab American community in the United States were exposed to new scrutiny, suffered new discrimination, and faced new uncertainty over their ability to fully enjoy a safe place within American society. At the same time, a variety of religious organizations in the United States responded to the attacks and in many ways sought to support those in the Arab American community and defend their right to equal status and treatment. This essay begins by exploring the scope and effectiveness of one aspect of this response: that of mainline Protestant churches in the United States. I write this as a scholar on religion and rights issues who works within a mainline Protestant denomination, as well as a minister who began a pastorate two days before the September 11 attacks. As I have reflected on the response of mainline Protestant denominations, I have come to realize that like my own particular response it was shaped by our limited understanding of the religious and cultural complexities of the Arab American community. It was shaped, as well, by our limited admission of the far greater safety in which mainline denominations and largely white Christian groups function in the United States. This essay identifies the limits in relationship and common work caused by such "amnesias." My goal, though, is to go further: to identify some ways in which a greater understanding of the experiences of Arab Americans can offer vital resources to the ongoing witness of religious groups within and beyond the Arab American community in a nation still dealing with the aftermath of September 11, 2001.

The Contours of "Mainline Protestantism" and Its Response to 9/11
In the thickly wooded forest of American religious bodies, "mainline Protestantism" occupies a particular grove demarcated by both historical

longevity and common commitments. Those denominations included as "mainline churches" are the Evangelical Lutheran Church in America, the Presbyterian Church (USA), the United Church of Christ, the Episcopal Church in America, the United Methodist Church, and the American Baptist Church. These denominations vary in their liturgy, structure, and internal hierarchy (some recognize bishops and more "top down" leadership, for example), and they all place some authority in the local congregational body. They share common roots in the theologies propounded by Protestant reformers in the sixteenth century, particularly the centrality of the Bible as an authoritative text, the equal status, responsibility and calling of believers by virtue of baptism, and the centrality of faith through grace as the means of salvation. They also each share a subsequent rejection of the authority and hierarchy of the Roman Catholic Church.

While each encompasses theological and social diversity within its membership, the mainline churches have historically tended to be more "progressive" or "liberal" rather than "conservative" in their public stances on social issues. In this vein, they share, as well, similar patterns of active engagement in public life, in taking highly visible and vocal stances on a variety of social and political issues, in encouraging their members in public participation, and engaging in a broad range of social service and outreach.[1] As one example, each of these mainline denominations maintains advocacy offices for witness and lobbying in Washington, D.C.

The deep roots that these churches share in the theological and political upheavals of the sixteenth century in Europe are at the heart of another distinguishing characteristic of the mainline churches. Each traces its history in the United States back to before the country itself was independently established as a nation. Most mainline denominations were established by early settlers who emigrated from Europe pursuing particular visions of religious freedom that was seen as possible within the American context, ideas of religious freedom that in turn became intertwined with understandings of the national identity and calling of the United States. These churches, then, see their place within the United States as secure: historically important and deeply rooted. While they are open to all, and engage in intentional outreach to diverse groups (including, in at least one case, to Arab Americans), their membership is largely Caucasian, and largely middle-class to upper class in socioeconomic terms.

In the days after September 11, 2001, the responses of the various mainline Protestant churches followed similar patterns. The focus of my own ministry and my local denominational body was in many ways typical, and I will use this as one lens to highlight three main outreach emphases that attempted to create intersections between mainline churches, the issues raised by 9/11, and the lives of Arab Americans: public witness focused on security, caution, and solidarity; confrontations with war; and concern over civil liberties.

Public Witness Concerning Security, Caution, and Solidarity
Perhaps the most striking effect of the events of September 11, 2001, was the paralysis they induced in many of us not directly, physically affected. In my mid-thirties, I had grown up without the direct experience of war affecting my life or limiting my activities; I was unfamiliar with the sense of physical danger beyond my control. Along the New Jersey and Pennsylvania border that morning, however, most of us were unsure what to do: stay indoors? Stay off the roads? Act as usual? The most basic desire I experienced (after retrieving my son from his day care center) was one of wanting to be clear about when it was "safe" again: to be assured that we could safely go outside. I ventured out around 2:00 in the afternoon to open the doors of the church I had just begun to serve as a pastor, and felt an extraordinary sense of vulnerability as I drove down Route 95. The sky seemed immense; the city where I served became small.

In the days that followed, most of us serving in mainline churches had to learn how to respond in the face of insecurity and find the words to reject easy avenues to apparent security. For many of us who served as pastors, this meant explicitly preaching and speaking against the immediate identification of the September 11 perpetrators as Arab, and then speaking out against scapegoating all those of Arab descent in light of the attacks.[2] For some churches, this involved linking prejudice against Arab Americans with earlier historical episodes of prejudice, particularly racially based response in the name of security, such as the internment of Japanese Americans during World War II. For others, this involved outreach efforts to local Muslim groups, either through expressions of solidarity or offers of public accompaniment for Muslim women whose distinctive dress made them vulnerable to public attack.[3]

Confrontation with War

Soon after the September 11 attacks, the United States moved to wage war on Afghanistan as a response to the attacks and as an initial salvo in a continuing "war on terror." For mainline churches, this was familiar ground as engagement with issues of war and peace has been an ongoing emphasis for these churches. The actions of war against Afghanistan and the Taliban regime were far less of a public issue for mainline churches than the later decision to attack Iraq as a "haven" for terrorism.[4]

Here the mainline churches were far more vocal, along with other religious groups, in questioning the concept of "pre-emptive" warfare. Within Christianity more generally, war has been historically understood as a result of sin and human error (and thus a deviation from the more fundamental vision of peace under God), but churches differ on the acceptability of necessary warfare conducted by legitimately recognized governments. For some traditions, war and the use of violence is always a rejection of the teaching and example of Jesus. For others, Christians are enjoined to support even the decision to go to war as an acceptance of divinely ordained earthly authority. The mainline denominations, however, have traditionally followed some version of "just war" theory, an approach to assessing the necessity of waging war and establishing the limits of conduct within warfare guided by the goal of preventing some greater harm to those who are most vulnerable. The decision to go to war against Iraq preemptively was viewed by these churches as outside the bounds of the appropriate, just use of power.[5]

Throughout much of this engagement with the issue of war, particular issues confronting Arab Americans were largely invisible, save for growing concern over civil liberties and their limitation purportedly in the service of war.

Civil Liberties

As the scope of the "war on terror" widened in the United States, it became clear that the battlefield in view was as much a domestic one as an international one. The passage of the Patriot Act authorized what were, in effect, wartime powers of surveillance, data collection, and internal security measures with the stated goal of identifying terrorist activities as well as the potential for terrorism. As the scope of the Patriot Act became clear, so too did its impact on the Arab American community in particular, and immigrant communities more broadly, in the United States.

This scenario, too, was familiar territory for mainline churches. All the mainline denominations spoke out publicly on issues of racial profiling and the impact of the Patriot Act, connecting it again with the history of wartime racial measures such as the treatment of Japanese Americans, as well as speaking out more broadly on the historical importance of civil rights protections for the health of the country.

In my own work in the Philadelphia area, I spent the winter and spring of 2002 working with other pastors and church leaders to develop a public education session on civil liberties and the impact of the Patriot Act. Our work culminated in April with an afternoon session downtown; a national speaker in the Christian peace and justice movement addressed the crowd; I spoke on civil liberties in historical context; others led sessions on particular issues. Even so, we were largely speaking to ourselves. The audience was composed of those from mainline and Mennonite (traditionally peace-oriented) churches, as well as those in the community interested in current issues of law and justice. In addition, by then, seven months after the attacks of September 11, 2001, the public concern over civil liberties was as much over the right to dissent as it was the right to simply exist freely and safely in American society.

While the general issue of civil liberties was an important one, the stakes at hand were far higher for those in the Arab American community. Even the emphasis on civil liberties betrayed an inherent failure in our national life, serving as a remedy for harms already experienced by those in the Arab American community and other vulnerable groups. Outside of limited, early news reports and apocryphal tales, the actual impact of the American response to the September 11 events on the Arab American communities was not well understood by most in the mainline churches. More seriously, the reality was that these post-9/11 experiences were simply a continuation and intensification of larger, decades-long patterns of discrimination directed toward members of Arab American communities.

Challenges to Effective Response and Engagement on Arab American Issues

Why was this longer history and the scope of the effects on Arab Americans largely invisible to many in mainline churches that hoped to help after September 11? There were three main challenges to understanding across these cultural and religious communities, and they persist today. The first of these challenges is a set of structural barriers to ecumenical awareness within Christianity as a whole, intensified by the extraordinarily diverse character of Arab American religious life. A second challenge lies in the complexities of the classification of "Arab" itself and its ambiguity both within the Arab American community and in its treatment within the racial constructions of United States society. A third and final challenge is found in the often unexamined historical privilege which mainline Protestant churches have enjoyed in American society and the social vision which emerges from an uncriticized acceptance of overlapping categories of "American," "Protestant," "Christian," and "white."

Barriers to Ecumenical Awareness
Even within Christianity, a religion united by a common text and a common set of basic claims regarding the activity of God and the particular status of Jesus of Nazareth as the Christ, central to salvation, a remarkable diversity exists both in church organization and in the specifics of confessions of faith. In the religious life of the United States, members of different denominational strands even within the relatively narrow confines of mainline Protestantism often know that they differ in beliefs, without necessarily knowing why or how. Aspects of religious life which may be seen as "nonessentials" (from worship style to the language of prayers to the organization of lay leadership) serve as remarkably persistent dividing lines between persons and communities.

These dividing lines of understanding are drawn even more sharply between branches of Christianity that differ in understandings of sacrament, rite, and the roles of priests or ministers. Protestants and Catholics in the American context do not generally worship or participate in one another's sacramental life across the boundary that divides them, and their many strikingly common theological and social commitments are often totally obscured by differences in worship style and organization.

The diversity within Arab American Christianity as well as its overall differences from mainline Protestantism raises particular barriers for ecumenical understanding and knowledge. In many ways this reality reflects a larger historical separation within Christianity that predates the sixteenth-century Reformation. From its early centuries, debates within Christianity over the particular workings of human salvation centered on the question of the dual nature of Jesus Christ. One of the most basic claims of the Christian tradition is that in Jesus Christ God became incarnate, taking on human form while at the same time not being diminished in divinity. Divergent views of the balance and relation of these human and divine natures created different schools of thought in Christian theology, views which were debated, negotiated, and accepted or rejected as authoritative by the early councils of the church. As these theological negotiations continued, divisions over theology emerged between the "eastern" and the "western" Church, centered in Constantinople and Rome, respectively. These divisions were deepened by divergent understandings of the relationships within the Trinity of Father, Son, and Holy Spirit, as well as the relative political fortunes of the church in the east and the west with the emergence and growth of Islam from the seventh century. By the eleventh century, the church had fractured along geographic and theological lines: the church in the west claiming the title of the Catholic (or universal) Church, the church in the east becoming known as the Orthodox (literally, "right belief") church.

This theological and geographic division, as well as the eastern churches' varied negotiation of religious identity within various phases of Islamic and Ottoman rule, resulted in significant differences between the practices and leadership of Christian churches in Europe and in Arab countries, as well as between Arab Christian churches themselves. Within Arab Christianity, particular national churches' understanding of the natures of Jesus Christ as well as the understandings of sacraments shaped whether a church would join with another Orthodox church, would ultimately realign with the modern Roman Catholic Church, or would remain independent. These religious differences carried over into the immigrant settlements that émigrés from Arab countries established upon arrival in the United States. Rather than one "Arab American Christianity," then, those outside the Arab diaspora communities confront a broad diversity: the Orthodox commitments and rites of the Greek Orthodox Church, the Roman Catholic friendly Maronite Church, Syrian Orthodox, Armenian and Coptic Catholic Churches, the Syrian rooted, independent Melkite churches, the diaspora versions of Protestant missions churches established in the nineteenth century.

Adding to this are the particular role of religious organizations for those in the Arab diaspora in the United States. For many early Arab immigrants to the United States, the church and its particular rites served as a mechanism and marker of ethnic identity and solidarity. Only recently have many Arab American churches come under the leadership of a designated United States-based structure within their larger tradition, rather than the long-distance supervision of religious leadership back in their country of origin. Even with these developments and with an increasing shift to English-language worship, however, the diverse traditions within Arab American Christianity remain largely ethnically distinct due to differences in the understanding of sacrament and the rites of worship. Later immigrants, particularly those in later waves after World War II, more generally identified with Islamic traditions, creating a more complex religious picture of Arab American culture.

Issues of rites and sacrament, as well as differences in leadership and authority, create significant challenges for understanding and ecumenical relations between Arab American Christian churches and mainline Protestant churches. An exception is found in those predominantly Arab American congregations with roots in mission churches of mainline denominations, although here cultural differences, particularly in social and moral norms, create some barriers. However, in the aftermath of September 11, 2001, the greatest emphasis on religious understanding and dialogue within mainline denominations was placed on establishing relationships and dialogue with Muslim religious groups as more centrally representative of Arab American culture.[6] The Orthodox and Catholic churches and the complexity of religion within the Arab American community were given little attention.

The Challenge of Arab Identity

A second challenge for mainline Protestant engagement with the Arab American community has proven to be the enormous complexity of Arab identity, both in general and in the United States. We have quickly forgotten that the nomenclature of "Arab" is largely a construction imposed from without (although ultimately adopted from within) and that the national divisions that define Middle Eastern countries so sharply on the map are divisions established in the aftermath of colonial rule. In reality, there is no single ethnicity that can be identified as "Arabic," and the complex questions of religious identity are intertwined with the question of Arab nationalism in ways that reverberate through the Arab American community today. The identification of and claims for an "Arab" identity arose as a unifying commitment to common interests, particularly after the establishment of the state of Israel after World War II. It has since opened thorny questions for Arab and Arab American Christians: is "Arab" identity inextricably linked with Islamic identity? Will it be possible to recognize and protect diversity within the Arab community and still preserve a sense of common interests for those whose history lies in that region of the world.[7]

In the American context, this complexity of Arab and Arab American identity is largely ignored by the broader culture. "Arab" is accepted and used uncritically, often synonymously and incorrectly with "Muslim," both terms used to denote someone who is "other" even as, in a legal sense, Arab Americans are categorized along with descendents of the Mayflower voyagers and last week's arrival from Ireland as "white, non-Hispanic."[8] The frailty of this classification as "white" was rediscovered very quickly by many Arab Americans after September 11, 2001, as anger over the attacks was vented on those who seemed "foreign" and in particular upon those of Arab descent and appearance, regardless of how long or how deeply they had been participants in United States society.

The Blindness of Privilege

A third challenge for understanding and constructive relationship between the Arab American community and mainline Protestantism lies precisely within this issue of racial and national identity. For those within mainline Protestant churches, "belonging" in the United States is not a pressing issue. However, the deconstruction of the link between "American," "Christian," "Protestant," and "white," and an awareness of the problems created by the uncritical acceptance of the privilege that arises from this linkage, particularly during times of war or national stress, is a necessary basis for any meaningful understanding or relationship with the Arab American community to occur.

The scope and impact of this privilege can be subtle, or it can shout. In 2002, I moved to a Midwestern city to teach religion. In exploring my new neighborhood one day, not far from the college where I taught, I passed a house whose lawn was dominated by a sign painted on a large sheet of plywood, declaring that "America was founded by Christians." I don't know for what specific issue the owner intended to offer a counterargument or what specific claims he or she intended to pre-empt, but I found myself looking for the sign as I drove by and wondering what it would be like to look across at it every day. A year or so later, I noticed the sign was gone; had the owners thought better of the display? The mystery was solved for me soon afterward when I discovered the sign again in a neighborhood a mile or so away: same lettering, same weathered plywood, different house. The owner had apparently moved it along with other household treasures, and now had nailed it up on the front of the new house.

Statements such as "America was founded by Christians" rarely function as purely historical claims. Bound up with such statements come other claims: to be like the founders (here, white, Christian) is to be more fully, more basically American; to be Christian is to be more true to the intent and design of the nation, to merit a more authoritative voice in current affairs; that the country has a fundamentally religious identity; that the founding of the country establishes the archetype for its future identity. Arab American writers point to these and similar claims as a basis for an "us" versus "them" mentality that shapes a view of Arab Americans as "other."[9]

The historical picture of the founding of the nation, as well as the specifics of the foundational documents of the United States, point to something other than a theocracy or a Christian republic. Rather, the clearest historical scholarship we have offers a picture of settlers who at the same time sought refuge in North American colonies for the practice of their religious beliefs, as well as refuge from those who sought to dictate the scope of those beliefs. While many of the early state constitutions tend toward a recognition or requirement of religious faith for officeholders, or officially establish religious belief, in the U.S. Constitution there is explicitly no established religion for the nation. In the Declaration of Independence, the rights recognized and claimed are subject to the higher order of "nature and nature's God," a more general, deist, construction than anything specifically Christian.[10]

The challenge for mainline Protestant churches is to unravel the historical picture in understanding the privilege and safety that colors its actions. Many of the concepts that undergirded the recognition of rights and the founding of the early nation (ideas of covenant, the vocation of citizenship, and the responsibility and limits of the state) have their roots in the theological convictions of the sixteenth-century reformers.[11] These concepts, though, when applied to the public conduct of government and the shape of public life, do not yield protections intended only for those of a particular religious persuasion. Historical influence cannot be translated into present authority, except as one contributor among many concerning the ongoing negotiation and extension of rights and protections within the United States. Moreover, the fact of historical longevity cannot be translated into privilege. In fact, the challenge for mainline churches and their members is to recognize and reject the role of standard to which new immigrants must conform, recognizing the ways in which membership in United States society has historically entailed pressure for and expectations of assimilation and conformity in cultural and religious practices, with these seen as legitimate bases for moral judgments made upon new immigrants.

Such a recognition and rejection of privilege would also require a commitment to identifying the proportionate harm faced by different groups in United States society, particularly during times of war or other national crises. This differentiation was only partially achieved by mainline Protestant churches after September 11, 2001. While the recognition of racial profiling was present, the broader focus on the Muslim community lost sight of the vulnerability of all members of the Arab American community. More critical was the shift in focus to issues of war and civil liberties. With this shift, the specific issues faced by Arab Americans became lost in a more general argument over the definitions of war and its justifications, as well as a more diffuse focus on the defense of civil liberties as a check on government power in general, rather as a specific and focused protection and defense for persons endangered because of ethnically motivated suspicion or prejudice. There is a critical distinction between the possibility of a government agency invading my privacy by examining my library borrowing habits or inconveniencing me at an airport and the use of government power to summarily hold a person of Arab descent for questioning without disclosure of the sources of relevant information or recourse to family or legal council. In collapsing these into more general defenses of civil liberties and freedom those of us who spoke from places of safety squandered our voices.

For many of us who are white and who work and worship within mainline Protestant communities, despite our initial personal anxieties, September 11, 2001, largely serves as a demarcating line in our national history, a tragic day of senseless destruction that set off a new era in our nation: a "war on terrorism" without apparent end, a new understanding of the limits of privacy and security. While we grumble about longer lines at airports and continue to rightly question the impact on basic civil liberties, most white Protestants do so from a position of relative safety. For many Arab Americans, however, September 11, 2001, meant not only an awareness of a new phase of our national like, but a loss of personal safety as well. This was another shift in an ongoing and troubled negotiation of national membership that has taken different forms from the early decades of immigration, to the increased scrutiny of Arab American communities in light of Arab–Israeli relations since the late 1960s, to the negotiations and vulnerabilities of the present.[12]

One starting point for potential engagement of mainline Protestant denominations and Arab American communities would be a commitment to the recovery and broadening of memory of that process of social negotiation. The introduction to this volume highlights ways since September 11 in which Arab American communities have found themselves compelled to highlight the ways in which they contribute to American society. It would be a helpful and salutary exercise for those who do not confront this burden of "proving" their right to social membership to understand more clearly the ongoing ways in which Arab Americans face vulnerability in daily life in ways that are largely unknown to those outside the community: to take as a starting point a recognition of what life in the United States is like for those who resist assimilation or are denied full acceptance.

A second task would be to ask those in the Arab American Christian communities to help those in mainline churches to consider the negotiation of faith within culture and to help untangle the strands of Christianity, patriotism, and identity. The easy confluence of religious and national membership and reflection that most mainline Protestants experience is an overlapping relationship that has largely been unknown in the history of Arab Christianity. From the seventh century, Christians in the Eastern Church were able to maintain their religious identity under strict conditions; as *dhimmi* under Islamic law, their freedom of expression and ability to participate in public life was strictly limited. Under the Ottoman Empire and its millet system, Christians and those of other religions were largely divided into separate enclaves according to religious belief. While this separation allowed for more control over religious education and the shaping of the worshipping community, the divisions between branches of Christianity were highlighted as well. In the later twentieth century, the rise of Arab nationalism in the postcolonial era became increasingly tinged with an identification of "Arab" with Muslim identity, particularly in reaction to the religious claims involved in the battles over Israel and Palestine.

In short, to be an Arab American and to be Christian is to stand in a tradition and that has been forced to identify the essentials of the faith, the costs of public and potentially counter-cultural stances, and the work involved in the preservation and passing on of religious identity. For those beyond the Arab American Christian community, particularly those within the mainline

Protestant churches, this knowledge and memory would be a great asset in helping to reconsider the balance of roles we play as Christians and citizens, and help reveal the larger implications of being ready to say, in the terms of Reformed theology, both "yes" and "no" to the actions of government and claims of patriotic duty.

There is also work to be done in conversation and conjunction with the broader Arab American religious community, both Christian and Muslim. Two issues are central here: the common work of confronting fundamentalisms, and the task of reclaiming the language of evil.

To some extent, the efforts at dialogue between churches and Islamic groups in the aftermath of September 11, 2001, were a helpful start. An incident in my own teaching experience during that time period has illustrated for me how the dialogue inevitably leads us back to confrontation within our own traditions and the standards for faithful obedience and interpretation found there. About a year and a half after the September 11 events, I was invited to participate in a community "interreligious dialogue on peace" in a remote part of the state where I taught. The organizer of the event was a gregarious local church pastor, a man who had stopped in to visit a large urban mosque during a trip east, and who had begun an ongoing correspondence with the imam. The result was this dialogue, part of a weekend of events centered around the imam's visit to the area and sponsored by a group of local mainline church pastors and the local community college. My invitation was to serve as the "Christian" representative on the interreligious panel.

College faculty members often receive invitations like this; I agreed to participate and was kept up to date on the plans through e-mail. About an hour into my drive toward the event I stopped to ask myself an obvious question: Why did they need a "Christian" representative from two hours away for an event sponsored by so many local churches and pastors? The answer became clearer to me when I arrived for a lunch sponsored by the college's international students. One of the organizing pastors leaned over, handed me a folded page from a newspaper, and whispered, "We don't think there will be any trouble from this ... but we thought you should know."

"This" was a sizeable advertisement, similar to the commemorative ads that families place in newspapers after a loved one's death. In white letters on a black background the ad, anonymous, expressed its regret that some in the community were planning to "sup with the enemy." The pastor explained that a local conservative church had been very vocal against holding any interreligious dialogue and that church members might or might not show up. They did, walking in together and doubling the size of the crowd, and despite our efforts shifted the dialogue as soon as possible to what "you people" (e.g., Muslims) were doing to the world and especially to Christians in Islamic countries. No amount of discussion could shift the focus from the idea that every Muslim was intent on destroying Christianity, or that Christians who were involved in such dialogues were rejecting the Bible and not truly "saved."

What was unique about this event, perhaps, is that we yelled at each other about issues of faith. (I will freely admit that any claims I had to scholarly, dispassionate discourse faded relatively quickly.) This was certainly not a particularly fruitful exchange, but it was unique in that single issue or fundamentalist claims generally receive no response at all but silence within their larger faith communities. The open confrontation of fundamentalisms is a common and pressing task for those in both the Christian and Islamic communities at present. Without such engagement and challenges to more narrow views of interpretation and the demands of religious discipleship, public representations of both Christianity and Islam that pit nations and cultures against each other for survival go unchallenged.[13] Without such engagement and challenge within faith traditions, made visible beyond the boundaries of those traditions, the possibility of identifying common convictions across religions concerning justice and human needs is greatly diminished. Fundamentalisms serve simply as caricatures of faith; they reduce religious truth, mystery, and humility to a distillation of simplistic beliefs in the name of "purity," one that rarely challenges the holder of those beliefs or their views of their place in the world. Much has been written about the need to confront fundamentalist interpretations of Islam within the Arab world, yet the work is urgent as well within Christianity. Both the Arab American Muslim and Arab American Christian communities have much to contribute and teach others from the knowledge borne of the experience of diaspora.

An additional area of confrontation across religious communities after September 11, 2001, is the reclamation of the language of evil and a clear discussion of its impact. Within days of the September 11 attacks, the United States framed its military response to the attacks, the pursuit of Osama bin-Laden, and the overall "war on terror" as a battle between good and evil.[14] From the image of a battle against evil people or evil doers, to an expansive, nearly mythic conception of the battle and the identification of the United

States with the side of good, such language was used to present the movement to war as nearly unassailable. Who, after all, could reject the idea of fighting evil? On the other side, the United States was presented as satanic, demonic, infidel.

"Evil" is big language, cosmic language. For mainline Protestants, as well as for those in other religious traditions, it is a familiar concept. In Christian traditions it is present in prayers, and pervades the worldview portrayed and rejected throughout the biblical witness. We speak of injustice, lack of understanding, greed, prejudice, sin, and error—but in the most basic example of Christian prayer portrayed in Jesus' preaching, we find "deliver us from evil." Not a prayer for an easy fix or a minor adjustment in our outlook, but a prayer for deliverance from something beyond our power to wholly defeat on our own. "Evil" is irreducibly religious language.

For this reason, some within various religious traditions have criticized the use of the term for political ends in the justification of war. At its heart, to claim the role of good fighting evil, and to identify the defeat of evil with specific political or military or otherwise temporal ends, is to wholly overstep the bounds of what any government can presume or promise. It removes those identified as "good," and their tactics, from scrutiny: in such a battle, any means can be justified. It also thus helps to provide justification for a never ending war: not one objective, not one battle, but a moving target, a calling rather than a discrete and bounded task.

On a more human and urgent level, particularly for the Arab American community, the rejection of the language of good versus evil as a metaphor for war or a framing concept for life after September 11, 2001, is a critical public task for religious communities. It is a rejection that will require those who hold citizenship and religious identity in safety—those of us in mainline churches—to recognize the easy and seductive draw of such language and to reject it anyway. It must be rejected because the very abstractness and power of the concepts involved leads human beings to both be inspired by them and to wrongly attach them to particular objects, particular groups, particular people. For the Arab American community since September 11, 2001, the application of such labels has created all too real a vulnerability in public life. It contributes to a public lens that conflates suspicion with patriotic vigilance and shunning as safety, and has resulted in a gradual slide in the years since the fall of 2001 to an increasingly protracted level of "temporary" acceptance of racial profiling and suspension of ordinary civil protections for citizens and other inhabitants of Arab descent in the United States.

For these reasons, the work of ecumenical and other cross-community engagement between mainline Protestant churches and the Arab American community is essential: both for jointly and effectively confronting the increasingly institutionalized suspicion, racism, and prejudice that now marks life in the United States for many in the Arab American community. More fundamentally, those in the Arab American community have the cultural and religious memory needed for churches to reclaim a language and identity capable of such confrontation and responsible engagement within public life. In that recovered language, people of faith will need to speak beyond and break through the naiveté of privilege and open the possibility of understanding the distinct claims of religious conviction, cultural identity, and patriotism in the pursuit of meaningful rights for all.

Notes

1. Robert Wuthnow and John H. Evans, *The Quiet Hand of God: Faith Based Activism and the Public Role of Mainline Protestantism* (Berkeley: University of California Press, 2002); David Devlin-Foltz, *Finding a New Voice: The Public Role of Mainline Protestantism* (Washington, DC: The Aspen Institute, 2001).
2. Episcopal Church in America, "Seeing the Face of God in Each Other: Anti-Racism and the Episcopal Church," Episcopal Church in America, http://www.er-d.org /documents/seeing.pdf (accessed September 16, 2005); United Methodist News Service, United Methodist Church, "Basic Points about Arabs, Muslims," United Methodist Church, http://archives umc.org/umns/usnews_archive.asp?ptid =&story=6D8FA405}, September 12, 2001 (accessed September 16, 2005); General Board of Church and Society, United Methodist Church, "A Call for an End to Hate Crimes," United Methodist Church, October 13, 2001, <http://www.umc_gbcs.org /site/apps/s/content.asp?c=fsJNK0PKJrH&b=860861&ct1132636>(accessed September 16, 2005).
3. Karen S. Krueger, "D.C.-Area Congregations Work with Muslims," *The Lutheran*, November 2001, http://www.thelutheran.org/article/article.cfm?article_id=1504 (accessed October 12, 2005); Episcopal News Service. "Episcopalians Begin to Battle "Backlash Violence" against Muslim Neighbors," Episcopal Church, USA, September 20, 2001, http://www.episcopal church.org/3577 _20769_ENG_Print. html (accessed September 10, 2005); General Board of Church and Society, United Methodist Church, "A Call for an End to Hate Crimes," United Methodist Church, October 13, 2001,http://www.umc_gbcs.org/site/apps/s/content .asp ?c=fsJNK0PKJr H&b =860 861&ct1132636 (accessed September 16, 2005).

4. Episcopal News Service, "Religious Leaders Urge Caution as US, UK Launch Strikes in Afghanistan," Episcopal Church, USA, October 9, 2001, http://www.episcopal church.org/3577_20853_ENG_Print.html (accessed September 10, 2005); Women's Division Board, United Methodist Church, "Resolution on Terrorist Attacks," United Methodist Church, October, 2001. http://gbgm_umc .org/terrorism _ resolution.html (accessed September 16, 2005); United Church of Christ, "A Statement by the Collegium of Officers of the United Church of Christ," United Church of Christ, October 12, 2001. http://www.ucc.org101601b.htm (accessed October 31, 2005).

5. Women's Division Board, United Methodist Church, "Resolution on Terrorist Attacks." United Methodist Church, October, 2001. http://gbgm_umc.org/terrorism_ resolution.html (accessed September 16, 2005); Cynthia M. Campbell, "Answering the Challenge of Political Life," Presbyterian Church (USA), 2004, http://www.pcusa.org/washington/christiancitizen/newstudyguide.pdf (accessed August 24, 2005).

6. Cynthia M. Campbell, "Answering the Challenge of Political Life," Presbyterian Church (USA), 2004, http://www.pcusa.org/washington/christiancitizen/newstudyguide.pdf (accessed August 24, 2005); United Church of Christ. "Bearing our Grief and Making for Peace," United Church of Christ, September, 2001, http://www.ucc.org/911a.htm (accessed October 17, 2005); United Church of Christ, "20 Things You Can Do to Make a Difference," United Church of Christ, September, 2001, http://www.ucc.org/911e.htm (accessed September 8, 2005); Evangelical Lutheran Church in America, "Our Muslim Neighbors," Evangelical Lutheran Church in America, http://www.elca.org/globalmission/recource/muslim-print.html (accessed October 12, 2005); Karen S. Krueger, "D.C.-Area Congregations Work with Muslims," The Lutheran, November 2001, http://www.thelutheran.org/article/article.cfm?article_id=1504 (accessed October 12, 2005).

7. Joan Ferrante and Prince Brown, Jr., The Social Construction of Race and Ethnicity in the United States (New York: Longman, 1998).

8. Helen Hatab Samhan, "Not Quite White: Race Classification and the Arab-American Experience," in Arabs in America: Building a New Future, ed. Michael W Suleiman (Philadelphia: Temple University Press, 1999).

9. Amir Marvasti and Karyn D. McKinney, eds., Middle Eastern Lives in America (New York: Rowman & Littlefield, 2004); Ernest McCarus, The Development of Arab-American Identity (Ann Arbor: University of Michigan Press, 1994).

10. Thomas S. Engeman and Michael P. Zuckert, Protestantism and the American Founding (Notre Dame: University of Notre Dame Press, 2004).

11. John Witte, Jr., Religion and the American Constitutional Experiment: Essential Rights and Liberties (Boulder: Westview Press, 2000).

12. Some historical perspective on this can be found in M. C. Bassiouni, The Civil Rights of Arab Americans: "The Special Measures," Information Papers, No. 10. (North Dartmouth, MA: Association of Arab-American University Graduates, Inc., 1974), as well as in

Arab American Institute, *Healing the Nation: The Arab American Experience after September 11* (Washington, DC: Arab American Institute, 2002).

13. James Davison Hunter, *Culture Wars* (New York: BasicBooks, 1991); Mark A. Noll, *The Work We Have to Do: A History of Protestants in America* (Oxford: Oxford University Press, 2002).

14. Harvey Cox, "Religion and the War against Evil" *The Nation*, December 24, 2001; Manuel Perez Rivera, "Bush Vows to Rid the World of 'Evil-Doers,'" CNN, September 16, 2001, http://archives.cnn.com/2001/US/09/16/gen.bush.terrorism (accessed October 12, 2005).

Works Cited

Arab American Institute. *Healing the Nation: The Arab American Experience after September 11.* Washington,D.C: Arab American Institute, 2002.

Bassiouni, M.C. *The Civil Rights of Arab Americans: "The Special Measures."* Information Papers, No. 10. North Dartmouth, MA: Association of Arab-American University Graduates, Inc., 1974.

Campbell, Cynthia M. "Answering the Challenge of Political Life." Presbyterian Church (USA), 2004. http://www.pcusa.org/washington/christiancitizen/newstudyguide.pdf

Cox, Harvey. "Religion and the War against Evil." *The Nation*, December 24, 2001.

Devlin-Foltz, David. *Finding a New Voice: The Public Role of Mainline Protestantism.* Washington, DC: The Aspen Institute, 2001.

Engeman, T., and M. Zuckert. *Protestantism and the American Founding.* Notre Dame: University of Notre Dame Press, 2004.

Episcopal Church in America. "Seeing the Face of God in Each Other: Anti-Racism and the Episcopal Church." http://www.er-d.org/documents/seeing.pdf.

Episcopal News Service. "Episcopalians Begin to Battle "Backlash Violence" against Muslim Neighbors." Episcopal Church, USA, September 20, 2001. http://www.episcopalchurch .org/3577_20769_ENG_Print.html.

Episcopal News Service. "Religious Leaders Urge Caution as US, UK Launch Strikes in Afghanistan." Episcopal Church, USA, October 9, 2001. http://www .episcopalchurch.org/3577_20853_ENG_Print.html.

Evangelical Lutheran Church in America. "Our Muslim Neighbors." http://www.elca.org /globalmission/recource/muslim-print.html.

Ferrante, J., and P. Brown, Jr. *The Social Construction of Race and Ethnicity in the United States.* New York: Longman, 1998.

General Board of Church and Society, United Methodist Church. "A Call for an End to Hate Crimes." United Methodist Church, October 13, 2001. http://www.umc _gbcs.org/site/apps/s/content.asp?c=fsJNK0PKJrH&b=860861&ct1132636.

Hunter, James Davison. *Culture Wars.* New York: BasicBooks, 1991.

Krueger, Karen S. "D.C.-Area Congregations Work with Muslims." *The Lutheran.* November 2001. http://www.thelutheran.org/article/article.cfm?article_id=1504.

Marvasti, A., and K. McKinney. *Middle Eastern Lives in America.* New York: Rowman & Littlefield, 2004.

McCarus, E. *The Development of Arab-American Identity.* Ann Arbor: University of Michigan Press, 1994.

Noll, Mark A. *The Work We Have To Do: A History of Protestants in America.* Oxford: Oxford University Press, 2002.

Perez Rivera, Manuel. "Bush Vows to Rid the World of 'Evil-Doers.'" CNN, September 16, 2001. http://archives.cnn.com/2001/US/09/16/gen.bush.terrorism.

Samhan, Helen Hatab, "Not Quite White: Race Classification and the Arab-American Experience." In *Arabs in America: Building a New Future*, ed. Michael W Suleiman. Philadelphia: Temple University Press, 1999.

United Church of Christ. "20 Things You Can Do to Make a Difference." United Church of Christ, September, 2001. http://www.ucc.org/911e.htm.

United Church of Christ. "A Statement by the Collegium of Officers of the United Church of Christ." United Church of Christ, October 12, 2001. http:// www .ucc .org 101601b.htm.

United Church of Christ. "Bearing Our Grief and Making for Peace." United Church of Christ. September, 2001. http://www.ucc.org/911a.htm.

United Methodist News Service. "Basic Points about Arabs, Muslims." United Methodist Church. http://archives umc.org/umns/usnews_archive .asp? ptid=& story=6 D8FA405.

Witte, John Jr. *Religion and the American Constitutional Experiment: Essential Rights and Liberties.* Boulder: Westview Press, 2000.

Women's Division Board, United Methodist Church. "Resolution on Terrorist Attacks." United Methodist Church, October, 2001. http://gbgm_umc .org/ terrorism _resolution.html.

Wuthnow, Robert, and John H. Evans. *The Quiet Hand of God: Faith Based Activism and the Public Role of Mainline Protestantism.* Berkeley: University of California Press, 2002.

12

Being Arab: Growing up Canadian

Rula Sharkawi

Growing up as a teenager in Toronto, I never liked being an Arab. At times, you could even say I hated it. The word *Arab* always had prohibitive connotations for me, which often meant I could not do what other non-Arab kids were doing. No boys calling the house, no movies after school with friends, no school trips to other cities, no sleepovers. I didn't even have "normal" sandwiches for lunch, just *zeit wu za'atar*, a traditional Arab dish of olive oil and wild thyme spread on pita bread, which, with its very dark green, almost brown appearance, often elicited remarks from students in the cafeteria that I was eating dirt. Other times I would have *labaneh*, a pressed yogurt in mom's homemade pita bread. Repeatedly I sought an explanation for these restrictions and was given the same standard answer by my mother.

"It's because we are Arab."

It was this fact: that I was an Arab living in Canada, which led me to have to explain over and over again my identity and what it was to be an Arab.

In high school I always dreaded the horrid question, "Where are you from?" When I said I was Palestinian, I usually had to explain for those whose geography or politics were hazy, that I was from the Middle East and an Arab.

Often I would hear a surprised: "Oh...you don't look Arab. I thought you were Spanish or with a name like Rula that you were Greek." I sometimes replied with a sarcastically curious tone: "Oh, what does an Arab look like?"

I didn't know that the whole 280 million of us around the world had a "look." The idea that somehow we were generic irked me, not only for its racist connotations but also because as a shy self-conscious teenager, I internalized that and other such comments as signs of disapproval or rejection. It wasn't just my parents and our Arab "traditions" or "food" that made me feel out of place, but also my olive complexion and my brown eyes and dark hair that didn't blend in with the blue-eyed blonde-haired majority in my high school.

Once, after hearing the usual "you don't seem Arab" comment, I asked a student in high school why he didn't think I was an Arab. He said it was because I seemed "normal" and was pretty, didn't have an accent, and didn't wear a head scarf. So I explained; that for most of my life I grew up in Canada and therefore didn't have an accent, bought my jeans in the same places as everyone else, and as a Christian Arab I wouldn't wear an Islamic head scarf, but none of these realities penetrated his ignorance. He still viewed me as something alien that has managed to disguise herself to look and act "normal."

Ironically, while his image of me as "normal" was meant to be a compliment, it only reinforced the common perception that Arabs were backward, ugly, deformed, and uncivilized people. Sadly today, almost twenty years later, little of mainstream North American perceptions about Arabs have changed—except perhaps to dichotomize us as victims and villains, moderates and fundamentalists. [1] On a very dangerous level, these attitudes have pitted the "east" versus the "west" and have left many Arabs feeling that that they must fit neatly into one of U.S. President George W. Bush's basic categories of being "either with us, or you're against us."[2]

There were times in my high school days when I just got so tired of having to explain myself. I got tired of feeling that I could only be either Arab (and therefore foreign) or Canadian (and therefore "normal"). I got tired of having to demonstrate that I could be both and still be "normal." My explanation fatigue got to the point where I often decided to avoid the whole conversation by pretending to be the cousin of my best friend who was Greek, which would make me the same. Pretending to be cousins started off as a silly joke we played with some boys we met who were brothers. However, their reaction, or more accurately the lack of it, brought instant relief of a tension that automatically came to me when the "where are you from" question is asked. In the relentless déjà vu conversations and explanations about my ethnicity, the immediate acceptance and absence of follow-up questions about who I was, made it so much easier to take the "Greek" route out than to be interrogated about being an Arab.

Looking back at that period of my life, I am embarrassed and ashamed to think of the time I spent trying to be invisible, to blend, to be liked and accepted. Fortunately or unfortunately that phase didn't last long. Things abruptly changed during the 1990/1991 Gulf War. The around-the-clock coverage of this first real "media war" with its highly selective snap shots of American victories and Iraqi wickedness brought with it public hysteria and jubilation that accompanied stories of bombings in Baghdad. The killing of Iraqi civilians, children, women, and elderly alike, and the selective media coverage that highly sanitized those killings and fell short of investigating the critical questions of who, what, why, how, where, and when, brought with it such indifference to death (in some cases outright excitement) that I remember one evening having a rude awakening that made me feel really sick to my stomach.[3]

I was about 18 years old and working as a part-time receptionist during the evenings. A few of my colleagues were listening to the radio coverage of the war. The voice on the radio just announced that Baghdad had been bombed, and it was believed that many Iraqis were killed. Hands flew up in the air, shouts of hurray and screams of joy were heard. A feeling of numbness overtook my entire body as I watched them so casually flinging around phrases of encouragement; "get those rag heads," "kill those filthy bastards," "bomb the sand-niggers." It was surreal, like watching a highly charged sports game; not football or hockey, but the world series of slaughter.

I felt dizzy, nauseous, and totally invisible as I listened to them rooting for Team America. This is war, I thought: a conflict that means life or death for thousands of people, not some silly contest where the winner gets a medal or a prize. Oblivious to my presence and the fact that I am an Arab, I walked over to them and asked, "Why are you cheering? Don't you know that innocent people are being killed?"

"They are a bunch of 'dirty Arabs' who deserve to die."

"But I am an Arab too."

"Oh...but you are different."

I stood there for a moment as a surge of rage went through me. NO! I thought angrily as my eyes began to well up with tears, "I AM NOT DIFFERENT. I TOO AM AN ARAB."

Without saying anything I turned around and headed for the washroom where I had a good cry. I was disgusted with them but also angry at myself for not having the courage to tell them off. I was afraid that if we got into a discussion about politics or history, I wouldn't be able to hold my own. Realizing that I lacked the self-confidence and the knowledge made me question my high school education. We learned so much about mainstream

North American and European history in school, but I realized that I knew little of "other" histories, of the Middle East, South America, Africa, and Asia (in fact the history of the majority of humanity). The only time I recall any mention of these histories is when they intersected with the mainstream. Invariably the "other" history was mentioned merely as backdrop to the success and achievements of European expansion and the exceptionalism of North American struggles for independence. In fact that intersection was the very reason why my colleagues were listening to the radio that evening.

Regardless of my insecurity at engaging in a historical political discussion, I didn't have to doubt a very basic moral principle that human life is human life, and there was something terribly wrong with denigrating and reducing it to insignificance. I felt sick at their indifference to human life, the celebration of death, the cheering, the rooting, the inability to see Iraqis, and by extension Arabs, as anything but a seething mass of evil doers. Sophisticated communications strategies, uncritical media, selective history and a lack of desire to understand societies outside our own, make it so easy to reduce thousands of years of our history, our culture, our language, our religions, our dignity and value as human beings to a monolith of people who, in the eyes of many North Americans, end up at the wrong end of the good versus evil spectrum.

It was an evening I will never forget as the painful experience of consciousness began to set in. As the days went by and I heard a lot more of the same rhetoric, I became agonizingly aware of the world around me and my shared identity with the Iraqi people.

Being viewed by some of the Canadians I encountered as different made me reflect a lot about my family's choices and the privileges and opportunities that came with them. What makes me different? My clothes? My attitudes? My degree of integration? Would they feel the same thing about my mother who speaks English with a heavy Arab accent? Would they say the same if my parents decided to immigrate to Iraq, as many Palestinians did, instead of Canada?

This began a period of awakening in me. Throughout university and graduate school I became much more conscious of the plight of the Palestinians, Iraqis, and others' struggles for equality, justice, and self-determination. Studying journalism and mass communication and applying a critical eye to the media shed light on how public biases are formed, reinforced and further entrenched in public policy and institutions. Anyone analyzing the abysmal media coverage following the Oklahoma bombing could see that being an Arab in the media is a negative.[4] I was amazed to see how quickly terrorist experts were willing to leap to the conclusion that the bombing was the work of Middle Eastern extremists rather than home-grown fanatics. Those who follow the Palestinian-Israeli conflict know that being an Arab of Palestinian descent is a double negative. Being an Arab is bad enough in the eyes of the media. Palestinians, however, are narrowly viewed as suicide bombers and fanatics, devoid of a just cause and fundamentally opposed to peace.

A lot has changed since that evening during the first Gulf War. Today, my conversations about being Palestinian are no longer to seek a certificate of approval or even to deny, but to educate, defend, and stand in solidarity. In my sometimes-painful journey of consciousness, each layer of knowledge and insight brought with it a degree of clarity about how to advocate, protect human rights, and obtain justice. However, at critical events in my life, my naivety about the nature of justice often shattered my optimism and stripped away the clarity, leaving in its place a sense of powerlessness and insignificance.

One event in particular devastated me and my sense of justice; what it is, how to obtain it, where to get it. In 2002, my uncle Odeh died at an Israeli checkpoint when soldiers refused to allow his ambulance passage to the hospital, an event not uncommon in the occupied Palestinian territories.

I remember vividly my inability to comprehend why my uncle died so senselessly. I remember the numbness, the pain, and the guilt that riddled me and the conversation with my *Khalto* (aunt) shortly after his death.

****

It was the summer of 2002 and almost one week to the day since *Ammo* Odeh died en route to the West Bank Palestinian city of Ramallah.

I called *Khalto* to express my condolences. In the distance there was a constant sound of bullets and gunfire.

Khalto asks me if I can hear the shooting.
"Yes," I reply.
She then goes on to tell me how an Israeli bullet shot through their kitchen window the other day, just missing her youngest daughter's head. I'm

struck by how she speaks of the event so matter-of-factly. It would be like me talking about how I tripped on my shoelace and almost broke my leg, as though to say, "It's not pleasant, but these things happen."

Khalto's oldest daughter is visiting with her two young children. Her baby starts crying in the background. The loudness, the bullets, the shooting is too much for their little ears to handle. *Khalto* says the kids are terrified by the sounds of bullets, of the sight of the Israeli tanks rolling down their street, witnessing the scuttle and fear of the neighbors scrambling to get into their houses or somewhere safe, off the streets and out of sight.

When I first called, it was her eldest daughter, my cousin who answered the phone. She sounded like a zombie, no doubt numb with the sudden loss of her father and fearful of the growing sound of shooting. We have a brief conversation, she and I, but the emotional distance between us is immense. It was obvious she was mourning the loss of her father, but she also seemed resigned to the fact that he was dead.

"I'm sorry about your father. He was a wonderful joyous man and we will all miss him," I say.

"Hmmmm."

I feel awkward. I don't know what to say. I want to ask questions. I'm appalled by what I heard of his death. I'm angry and sad, but it feels inappropriate to request details somehow.

BANG-BANG-BANG-BANG-BANG-BANG-BANG. Shooting continues in the background.

"It must be very difficult for you," I mumble, as though it wasn't obvious. "And the way he died is horrible."

"Hmmm...what can we do," my cousin says in a somber depressing voice. "This is the fate of the Palestinians."

There is a dead silence on the phone. I can still hear the shooting. I feel tense and out of place. I sense a disconnect, almost as if I'm imposing on her with my phone call. She doesn't say this in words, but her silence leaves me feeling that because I don't live under occupation, I cannot possibly understand.

I ask to speak to *Khalto*. Without saying goodbye my cousin hands the phone over to her mother.

Unlike my cousin's gloominess, *Khalto* sounds strangely upbeat. "Hello dear," she greets me with a tone of warmth and familiarity.

"*Marhaba Khalto*." (Hello Aunty)

We chat for a while, but I grow restless and finally I ask about the circumstances of my uncle's death.

"They wouldn't let him through. The soldiers wouldn't let him through."

"What happened?" I ask. There is a pause on the phone. Shooting can still be heard in the background. "He was dead by the time they finally made it to the hospital."

I knew part of the story and was outraged when I heard it, but I wanted to ask more, to probe, to fill in all the blanks, but don't want to push too hard. "What happened at the checkpoint?" This time she explains in a bit of detail. He collapsed at the house around mid-morning. The local doctor, who came to the house, said he had a heart attack and should be taken to hospital urgently.

At the Surda checkpoint, manned by Israeli soldiers, on the road from the small West Bank village of Birzeit to the town of Ramallah, Odeh's ambulance was halted to a stop. At these checkpoints, Palestinians are routinely stopped, asked for their mandatory Israeli-issued identification, interrogated, left to wait hours in the rain, hot sun, or dark, before being either given "permission" or refusal to pass.

Walking over to the back of the ambulance, the soldiers swung the door open and began to interrogate my sick uncle. Barely conscious, they demanded answers from him.

Why are you in here? Where do you think you are going? You are not really sick are you? Don't play games with us. We know what you are about!

His youngest daughter began begging, hot tears rolling down her face. "Please, please. My father is sick. He must go to the hospital or else he will die."

They laughed at her. The soldiers knew how to speak in Arabic, but instead they spoke in Hebrew. Then they laughed some more.

"They just kept laughing and laughing while my father was dying in the ambulance," said my cousin. "They treated him like some criminal who had to prove he was worthy to be treated by medical professionals."

"It was so hot that day, maybe 40 degrees [104 Fahrenheit]. I was sweating and anxious and frustrated and angry but knew I had to stay calm and be nice to the soldiers. They decide who gets to pass and who doesn't."   She understands well the power of choice and the powerlessness of those who don't have it.

As my uncle was barely conscious, his son also pleaded with the soldiers to let his father's ambulance through on humanitarian grounds. By international humanitarian legal standards, the protection of the sick and dying civilian and the unobstructed access to medical care is a right, but for Israeli soldiers, it seems one more opportunity to apply their arbitrary power in decisions of life and death.

The young twenty-something soldiers, playing the roles of judge, jury, and medical experts, had decided that Odeh did not have a heart attack, despite the presence of his pale lifeless body and evidence by paramedics to the contrary.

They refused to allow his ambulance entry through the checkpoint for "security" reasons and insufficient evidence of illness. The irony is cruel. A dying 57-year old man, has his security denied and right to medical treatment violated because he, in his fragile state is deemed a "national security" threat to his occupiers.

Instead of allowing passage to his ambulance, they knocked him off the ambulance bed and insisted he walk on a dusty uneven dirt path. This was once a well-paved tarmac road, but has now been reduced to a mass of broken rubble and stone by Israeli bulldozers. It is one of many roads that are part of a destroyed Palestinian infrastructure that cripples the movement of Palestinians.

Khalto gives me more detail. "They dragged his almost lifeless body out of the ambulance. They accused him of lying. He was barely even conscious. They said he was not ill, even though the paramedics explained that he just suffered a heart attack and if he didn't' get to the hospital HE WOULD DIE," she sobs, her voice now growing louder and angrier on the telephone.

'If he wants to go to the hospital, he can walk,' said one of the soldiers to my aunt and cousins. The hospital is about 10 miles from the checkpoint.

Uncle Odeh's ambulance was never allowed to pass. The paramedics believed that he suffered another heart attack during the ordeal at the checkpoint. While being dragged around, he collapsed again. Perhaps it was at this point that he took his last painful breath, where we lost him forever, where he died. He never did regain consciousness. All the while, the soldiers stood there, watching and laughing as Odeh's unconscious body was placed on a vegetable cart and dragged for about 400 meters, his limbs dangling lifelessly across the hot dusty mountainside checkpoint where he was transferred to a civilian car and finally taken to hospital, where he was pronounced dead.

"Do you see that? Do you see how they [Israeli soldiers] have no *dameer* (conscience)," says *Khalto* who is now crying on the phone.

Shots rage in the near distance. BANG-BANG-BANG-BANG-BANG-BANG-BANG-BANG-BANG-BANG-BANG-BANG-BANG!

A hot tear silently rolls down my cheek as I sit alone in my office in Toronto with the phone to my ear. My computer beeped, indicating that someone has sent me an Email. Ignoring it, I began staring in bewilderment out the window onto a busy downtown street and saw things to which I had never really paid much attention: I see cars traveling freely on the well-paved roads. They all have the same color license plate—no white plate for Palestinians and yellow for Israelis. Here everyone has the same type of driver's license and no state-imposed identification cards, with different colors and access points for West Bankers, Jerusalemites, Gazans, and Palestinian citizens of Israel. Here no employer or state official has the right to ask you your religion, ethnicity, age, or marital status. Occupied Palestinians are routinely asked by Israeli soldiers to present this information to determine what "privileges" of passage or permits will be bestowed upon them.

The traffic light turned green and as all the cars began to move, I felt overwhelmed by a great sadness and sense of guilt. Here the movement of people and cars is controlled only by timed traffic lights, transmitting three colored signals that mean the same thing for everyone, including myself—a Palestinian. There are no soldiers, no guns, no tanks, no sniper towers, no ambulances waiting for permission, no people pleading and crying at a checkpoint.

No one was ever held to account for my uncle's death. Unfortunately it's not surprising. Palestinians suffer routine humiliation and sometimes death at Israeli checkpoints. Women are forced to give birth unaided at checkpoints when their ambulances are refused passage to hospital.[5] More than half of their babies die as a result. Young men stand hours in the heat, sun, rain, winter as soldiers conduct routine harassment via "security" checks. There are over 600 Israeli installed closure barriers, including checkpoints in the West Bank alone.[6] These represent only one mechanism of control and repression of Palestinians under occupation. My uncle's death is just one of more than 3,400 Palestinian deaths since the start of the second *Intifada*, an uprising or literally a shaking of, which began Sept 28, 2000.[7]

His death has made me rethink my ideas of justice and as a result I don't know what to make of justice anymore. As a human rights activist for many years, I thought I knew exactly what needed to be done to rectify injustice: apply laws, conduct trials, recognize crimes, official apologies, offers of compensation, and so on. However, having mechanisms to offer justice and actually implementing them are two totally different things. It is different, I think, when injustice is committed on an individual level. You clearly have a perpetrator and a victim. However, how do you obtain justice when the crimes committed are part of a larger system of oppression, where soldiers are anonymous, where repression is unofficial state policy, where the chain of command is fuzzy and almost impossible to trace? The more I think about it, the more I realize that my ideas of rectifying gross injustices are theoretical, confined to textbooks and ideologues.

It seems that every time I add a piece of knowledge to the puzzle and a bigger picture emerges, the hazier my perspective of justice becomes. When I first began advocating for justice, I always saw it as an outcome of legal proceedings against the perpetrators of crimes. Maybe it is because I live in a country where a system of laws governs our behavior as citizens and courts reinforce, punish, or offer retribution to injustices. However, when you think of world politics and modern systemic forms of injustice, especially those committed against civilian populations by states or proxy paramilitaries, so rarely is any legal system able to deliver justice or some form of retribution to the victims or their families.

Think of the thousands who went "missing" in Chile under General Pinochet's rule, and yet the legal system couldn't even manage to extradite him. In Guatemala, tens of thousands were slaughtered, mostly Mayan Indians by the Guatemalan army and paramilitaries. A truth and reconciliation commission was set up (one of the fashions of the 1990s) and none of the major generals involved has spent a day in jail. In the Rwandan genocide, more than 800,000 people were massacred and some ten years and many millions of dollars later, less than a dozen people have been tried by the International Criminal Tribunal for Rwanda (ICTR) in Arusha, Tanzania. In fact, the tribunal itself states that part of the "ICTR's relevance for peace and justice" is "NEVER AGAIN."[8]   Now after the genocide, mass killings are taking place in the Congo and the Darfur region of Sudan. These are a few of many cases where legal systems are unable to deliver justice.

I'm reminded of a memorable quote from Andre Brink, an Afrikaner writer banned during apartheid. In the movie version of his book, A *Dry White*

Season, a lawyer defending an African family commented: "Justice and the law are distant cousins, and in South Africa, they haven't spoken for years."[9]

I feel the same way about Palestine, except that law and justice is a divorced couple who not only won't speak to one another, but who seem to have abandoned any thought of ever reconciling. There is a whole litany of laws, rulings and resolutions that apply to Palestinians, but justice is not an outcome of them. For decades it seems this disconnect between law and justice is growing, even with a whole host of bodies of law that apply to Palestinians living under Israel's illegal military occupation of their lands. Article 13, paragraph 2 of the Universal Declaration of Human Rights, to which Israel is a signatory, clearly states everyone has a right to leave any country, and return to his country.[10] The right of more than 4 million Palestinian refugees to return to their lands is enshrined in Article 12, paragraph 4 of the International Covenant on Civil and Political Rights, and in UN Resolution 194 and the 49 other resolutions which refer to 194, such as Resolution 2649 (November 30, 1970) that condemns those governments that deny the right to self-determination of peoples recognized as being entitled to it, especially the peoples of South Africa and Palestine. Then of course there are the Geneva Conventions which are intended to protect the rights of civilians during war and more poignantly the 4th Geneva Convention protects the rights of people under military occupation. For decades Palestinian rights have been violated. However, time and time again, the law and its various bodies have failed to deliver even the slightest form of justice for Palestinians, let alone to preserve or protect their rights as it should.

As a Palestinian living in the "West" it is difficult for me to listen to all the modern rhetoric about "freedom and democracy" coming from the imperial powers— mainly America and Britain. Canada as the little brother next door has been eager not to offend or to make amends as it didn't join Bush's coalition of the willing, even though we sent ships to Iraq and still have soldiers in Afghanistan. Ironically it is the very countries that tout the need for "freedom and democracy" (of which a functioning legal system is part of), that continue to reward Israel, a country that has many of the trappings of a democracy, but operates above the law with impunity in its occupation.[11] Israel is rewarded with billions of dollars in U.S. military aid and weapons technology, with open free trade agreements, good diplomatic relations, and a complete unwillingness to hold Israel to account for any of its international obligations, except for the occasional meek, and empty utterances of mild and impotent condemnations.

While Canada officially opposes Israel's occupation of the West Bank, Gaza, East Jerusalem, and the Golan Heights as well as the establishment of Jewish settlements in those territories (which it considers contrary to international law and unproductive to the peace process), it rewards Israel with preferred duty-free trade status via the Canada Israel Free Trade Agreement (CIFTA). CIFTA makes absolutely no distinction between goods made in Israel and those in Jewish settlements illegally established on confiscated Palestinian land. The United States, which also opposes the settlements, has had a free trade agreement with Israel since the 1980s. Like Canada, the United States also makes no distinction between Israeli- and settlement-made goods. Neither country has any intention of amending its agreements to exclude products from settlements, thereby continuing to reward Israel's gross injustices.[12]

It is mind-boggling to reconcile the many contradictory positions Canada takes in favor of Israel. On paper, Canadian foreign policy regarding Israel and Palestine appears fair. However, in reality, Canada's actions continue to undermine the rights of Palestinians and turn a blind eye to the injustices committed against them. Imagine my dismay with Canada's position when in 2004 the Palestinians, who for years have been told to cease their violence, took the non-violent legal route to seek an advisory opinion ruling from the International Court of Justice on Israel's 620 kilometer wall in the West Bank of which 90 percent is being built on Palestinian land.[13]

The court issued an advisory opinion that the wall violates international law and that "Israel also has an obligation to put an end to the violation of its international obligations flowing from the construction of the wall in Occupied Palestinian Territories." The ICJ also concluded that Israel has an obligation to make reparation for the damage caused so far, noting the principle that "reparation must, as far as possible, wipe out all the consequences of the illegal act."[14] Canada's position that a resolution to the issue of the wall should come via a negotiated political solution and not through the ruling of the ICJ is weak and disturbing at best. Rather than back the international laws that Canada supposedly supports, it dangerously politicizes universal human rights and undermines international law. Does Canada, a country known for its reputation in peace keeping and human rights actually believe that human rights and international law are negotiable?

Even if we entertain that idea for a moment, when did anyone ever consult or "negotiate" the route of the wall with the affected Palestinian population?

In 1971, the International Court of Justice (ICJ) issued an advisory opinion ruling that apartheid South Africa's occupation of Namibia was illegal. The court's decision was not binding, but it did lead to international pressure and sanctions that eventually saw the racist regime fall. When the ICJ ruled that Israel's wall was illegal, there was no such pressure or sanctions from Canada or the international community, even though the Israeli Minister of Justice at the time anticipated there would be.[15] I found the silence that followed only revealed the hollowness of the concept of justice and left Palestinians and Arabs feeling alienated and confused about how and when, if ever, their voices will be heard and they will see any retribution at all and a just resolution to conflict.

This hypocrisy and double standard is not only witnessed in Canada's diplomatic relations with Israel, but is reinforced by equally biased media. A case in point, on October 16, 2003, the *Globe and Mail* ran a front-page news story about attacks on soldiers. Part of the story read: "Roadside bombings are an almost daily event against Israeli forces in the Palestinian territories, and against U.S. occupation troops in Iraq."[16] In a so-called factual news story, why accept the legitimacy of international law which identifies America as an occupier of Iraq, yet is unclear and willing to cast doubt on that same law when it refers to Israeli occupation of Palestinian lands.

For years, world leaders, especially those of America, have been telling the Palestinians to cease their violence, even though violence is committed against them daily and has been for the last 38 years.[17] I don't condone violence in any shape of form. However, the media obsession with suicide bombings and the killing of Israeli civilians completely eclipses all other aspects of Palestinian society— such as the large non-violent actions of civil disobedience and the flourishing music conservatory that is producing some incredible talent and the Palestine National Political Initiative which provides health care, social services, and education for the marginalized and poor. In fact, according to Harvard senior researcher Sara Roy, some 41 percent of Gazans are assessed by the World Food Programme to be "food insecure," 60 to 75 percent are impoverished, and with 80 students per class in government schools, many students are failing to pass 4th grade.[18]

This de-development of Palestinian economy and society is almost never mentioned by the media in the context of Israel's occupation which spent 38

years destroying Gazan infrastructure and making the Palestinian economy
dependent on Israel's. Instead Canadians are fed a daily diet of media bias and
selectiveness when it comes to the Palestinian-Israeli conflict or even of Arabs
in general. The media spectacle that reported on the removal of illegal Jewish
settlers from Gaza misleadingly positioned Israel and its Prime Minister Ariel
Sharon as the peacemaker, while ignoring the fact that Sharon openly
announced the expansion of settlements in the West Bank, a move that again
is contrary to international law and the so-called "road map" for peace.[19] As
well, there was little coverage of Israel's continued building of the 25-foot high
wall on and through Palestinian towns and villages and how this huge land
grab greatly diminishes prospects for a viable Palestinian state and meaningful
peace.

I conducted an analysis of one of Canada's national newspapers of all
articles that appeared in a three-month period and found that Arabs are rarely
presented in a neutral or positive manner. In fact, they are collectively
portrayed as violent, uncivilized terrorists, who are opposed to peace, culturally
deformed, lacking culture, history, or any meaningful contribution to
Canadian society, and there is almost no concept of a Canadian Arab. Arabs
in Canada are only referred to in relation to country of origin.[20]

It was no surprise to me to receive a call from a reporter of a local
television station in the aftermath of the horrific hostage taking and
subsequent killing by Chechen rebels of several hundred Russian theatre
patrons in Moscow in 2004. I was the media spokesperson for the Canadian
Arab Federation at the time. The reporter called to ask me for the
organization's reaction to the incident. Her bias and ignorance was obvious,
but I had to ask the question anyway: "Why exactly are you calling the
Canadian Arab Federation for our reaction? We have no Russian members."
She said it was because it was a terrorist attack. Ah, there it was—the local
angle. We are all terrorists!

Sometimes when I encounter average Canadians with similar views and
fears of the Arab community, I almost don't blame them. What other
perspective are they given to consider? On March 22, 2003, the *Toronto Star*,
which some consider to be a left-of-center newspaper, decided to run a full-
page spread, prominently featured with a section heading in huge fonts that
reads: "THREAT FROM WITHIN." The headline that follows reads: "THE
MURKY PICTURE OF CRIME IN CANADA." The story layout includes
photographs or sketches of 20 men, all of Arab or Muslim backgrounds who

are presented as terror threats from within Canada.[21]   To the average Canadian, it paints a frightening picture of the scary terrorist Arabs living among us. However, if you actually read the article, it says "despite persistent allegations of terrorism activity in this country...there is still no clear picture of Canada's connection." Furthermore, of the men who are profiled as terrorist threats, eight of the 20 have been exonerated, and still others have no charges or convictions. Why would they even be included in the article? Imagine police stop some twenty white men suspected of being pedophiles, and more than half of them turn out not to be. Would the newspaper still run their photos and names and profiles and label them a "threat from within"?

The incongruity between the actual facts of a story and the alarmist and misleading headlines added by editors is not uncommon of an exaggerated type of journalism in Canada that vilifies and dehumanizes Arabs. These negative stereotypes and the fear that accompanies them seep into the education system, the workplace, public places, and public perceptions. In turn, it affects every aspect of our daily lives.

The effect is so powerful that it is like déjà vu, except now it isn't just me trying to be invisible as an Arab in the post-9/11 world, but a whole host of Arabs and Muslims who fear the backlash and hope to be inconspicuous for the sake of not being singled out, at airports, at work, in the playground, by our neighbors, or even at the supermarket.

"Do you know Osama?" I was once asked by a supermarket teller who after seeing my name on my credit card asked where I was from. "Yes I do," I replied. My uncle's name is Osama, but I wasn't in the mood to explain. I just watched her eyes widen with fear as I gave her a smile and walked away.

This irrational thought process, in what is now a culture of fear, is not confined to supermarket tellers. There have been many incidents of harassment, discrimination, and plain racism in numerous professions—blue collar and white. Since 9/11, I have felt as an Arab a terrible resentment for watching our communities in the diaspora being put on the stand and incessantly interrogated about our identity, questioning our loyalties and despite our citizenship, our right to belong.

New anti-terrorism legislation has made it possible for the intelligence community to gain sweeping powers with few checks and balances and a significant margin of error. In August of 2003, 21 Muslim men were rounded up and detained in a maximum-security prison on "suspicions" of terrorism.[22] None were charged and all of them were eventually released. Many of them have become pariahs after being publicly branded terrorists, a label that is almost impossible to shake off. There is also the case of Maher Arar, a Canadian of Syrian descent, who after being fingered by security officials as a "terrorist threat" was rendered by the United States to Syria where he was tortured and held in solitary confinement for 10 months.[23] A public inquiry is now underway in an attempt to find out how Arar, a man widely believed to be innocent, was caught in the very wide net cast by Canada's "war on terror."

By far the worst policy in this new age of pre-emptive security is the use of security certificates. The certificate is issued against anyone deemed to be a national security threat to Canada by a federally elected minister. All of the certificates were issued against Arab men. Whether they are guilty or not, the public will never know as the certificate allows the state to detain an individual indefinitely, in solitary confinement, without charge, without knowing what evidence has been used to obtain the certificate, without trial, without bail, and without allowing his lawyer to examine the evidence, witnesses, or to defend him in court. Amnesty International has criticized the process of prolonged detention without charges as an abuse of human rights.[24]

Will all these measures and undoubtedly more to come, I find it very frightening to think about the future in light of the direction we are taking when it comes to Canada's security and its co-operation with other countries, mainly the United States. The concept of pre-emptive security is a dangerous one, which allows for individuals to be apprehended and treated as criminals without having committed a crime or even being charged with planning one. Rule of law and its basic principle of innocent until proven guilty are thrown out the window. Increased powers for the intelligence community are eroding civil liberties and casting a very dark shadow on entire Arab and Muslim communities, many of whom are now being treated as guilty until proven innocent.

When I think of the challenges I faced as an Arab teenager, they seem mild compared to what my one-year old son might be dealing with in 15 years' time. As a mother, who has over the years come to understand the weaknesses of Arab societies but also, more importantly, to take pride in the tremendous depth and beauty of the culture, history, language, and traditions of being a Palestinian, I worry about him growing up in an environment where as Arabs we see the daily erosion of our self-dignity, our self-confidence, and our sense of pride. Will he be able to sift through the media blizzard that sometimes succeeds in co-opting Arabs themselves into believing the negative and racist template depictions of Arabs?

Will he get tired, as I did, of defending his sense of worth, of having to prove his contribution to Canadian society, of doubting his identity, of squinting to see beauty in a society that paints pictures of ugliness? Or will that journey succeed in making him an active engaged citizen in Canadian society, so that he may bring a sense of dignity to his ancestral heritage, to educate and to dissect ignorance, and most importantly, to have pride in being of Arab descent?

While I will do my best to instill a sense of self-respect and self-solidarity in my son and hope to shelter him from some of the negative encounters of being an Arab in the West, I am certain that he will inevitably have to fend attacks on his identity and explain himself as an Arab. When he does, I hope he will have the confidence, knowledge, and sense of self-worth to know that he has nothing to apologize for or anything to be embarrassed about. On the contrary, I hope that when he is asked "where are you from?" he will speak enthusiastically about his love of food, dancing, politics, history, poetry, language, and great social gatherings among friends and family that are hallmarks of Arab culture and tradition. I hope he will boast about coming from a close-knit, very loving family where he enjoys and appreciates the best of both worlds, Canadian and Palestinian.

I hope he will dispel with confidence the propagated simplified views of the world that dichotomize societies as us and them, east and west, good and evil, civilized, and barbaric. I hope that my son's sense of obtaining justice is clearer than mine and his endeavors in life will be colored by a lens of equality for all human beings, filled with deep footsteps in the path of challenging violence, oppression, and global dominance over marginalized and impoverished societies.

Most of all, I hope that when he is a teenager there will be a shift in ideas of world threats from his olive complexion to the perspective of the great Martin Luther King who wisely said, "injustice anywhere is a threat to justice everywhere."

Notes

1. For example, see Jack G. Shaheen, *Reel Bad Arabs: How Hollywood Vilifies a People*, for a historic retrospective of Arab stereotyping.

2. Juliet O'Neill, "Civilization under Attack: Bush: President Says bin Laden Seeks 'Evil Weapons'; Tells Allies They Must Join War," *The Ottawa Citizen*, October 7, 2001: A6.

3. Eric Hoskins, "A Bloody Road to Peace," *Maclean's*, August 11, 2003: 25.

4. Mohamad Bazzi, "The Arab Menace," *The Progressive*, August 1995: 40

5. A report prepared by the United Nations High Commissioner for Human Rights, September 2005, indicates that from September 2000 to December 2004 more than 60 Palestinian women were forced to give birth unaided at Israeli checkpoints; 36 babies died as a result .BBC News "UN Fears Over Checkpoint Births," September 23, 2005, http://news.bbc.co.uk/2/hi/middle_east/4274400.stm.

6. United Nations Office for the Coordination of Humanitarian Affairs (OCHA), occupied Palestinian territory Report "West Bank Closure and Access" April 12, 2005 http://domino.un.org/unispal.nsf/0/e2294ff978610ff385256ff7005181d2?OpenDo cument.

7. BBC NEWS, "Intifada Toll Sept 2000-Sept 2005," September 30, 2005, http://news.bbc.co.uk/go/pr/fr/-/1/hi/world/middle_east/4294502.stm.

8. International Criminal Tribunal for Rwanda, "UNESCO / JIKJI Memory of the World" http://portal.unesco.org/ci/en/file_download. php/9522373b 850cbf0ec f5acf23767 7d86eTanzania.doc.

9. Andre Brink, *A Dry White Season* (London, Great Britain: Minerva, 1979).

10. For the full text of the Universal Declaration of Human Rights, please see http://www.un.org /Overview/rights.html .

11. Israel's impunity for crimes against Palestinians is widely documented by human rights organizations and repeatedly condemned by Amnesty International Public Statement August 11, 2005 "Israel/Occupied Territories: Administrative Detention cannot replace proper administration of justice." http://web.amnesty.or g/library/Index/ENGMDE150452005?open&of=ENG-ISR.

12. Scott Anderson. "Fingering the Goods: Why Does Canada Give Settlers Sweet Trade Deal?" *NOW Magazine*, August 22–28, 2002 .http://www.nowtoronto. com/issues/2002-08-22/news_story.php.

13. Amnesty International Press Release, "Israel/Occupied Territories: Dismantle the Wall Says International Court of Justice," July 7, 2004. http://web.amnesty.org /library/Index/ENGMDE150682004?open&of=ENG-ISR

14 .Ibid.

15. Dan Williams, "Israel Warned of Apartheid Boycott," *Sydney Morning Herald*, January 6, 2004, http://www.smh.com.au /articles /2004/01/05 /1073 267970184.html .Minister of Justice told Israeli radio on January 6, 2004: "There is a very serious risk the World Court (International Court of Justice in The Hague) will rule against us .... and this is liable to prompt the General Assembly into imposing all sorts of sanctions against us."

16. Paul Adams and Paul Koring, "U.S. Diplomats' Convoy Bombed in Gaza Strip; Bush Assails Arafat after Attack Kills Three," *Globe and Mail*, October 16, 2003: A1.

17. Some examples of world leaders include UN General Secretary Kofi Annan, British Prime Ministers Margaret Thatcher, John Major, and Tony Blair, U.S. Presidents Ronald Reagan, Bill Clinton, and George W. Bush, and Australian Prime Minister John Howard.

18. Sara Roy, "Praying with Their Eyes Closed: Reflections on the Disengagement from Gaza" *Journal of Palestine Studies*, 135 (2005, summer) http://palestine-studies .org/final/ en/journals/content.php?aid=6525&jid=1&iid=136&vid=XXXIV&vol=194.

19. R. Emmett Tyrrell, Jr., "Sharon's Magnanimity," *The American Spectator*, October 2005: 71.

20. Article search includes all articles from July 21, 2003 to Oct. 21, 2003 published in *The Globe and Mail* .For example, see Paul Adams and Paul Koring, "U.S. Diplomats' Convoy Bombed in Gaza Strip; Bush Assails Arafat after Attack Kills Three," *Globe and Mail*, October 16, 2003: A1.

21. Michelle Shephard, "The Murky Picture of Terrorism in Canada; CSIS Detains 23 Suspects, But Proof Is in Doubt," *The Toronto Star*, March 22, 2003: A4.

22. Carol Goar, "Canada's Dirty Little Secret," *The Toronto Star*, December 17, 2004: A36.

23. Rula Sharkawi, "Time to Return to the Rule of Law," *The Toronto Star*, December 29, 2003: A33.

24. Amnesty International Canada, "Take Action: Security Certificates Time for Reform," March 30, 2005, http://www.amnesty.ca/take_action /actions/canada_certificates .php.

Works Cited

Adams, Paul, and Paul Koring,. "U.S. Diplomats' Convoy Bombed in Gaza Strip; Bush Assails Arafat after Attack Kills Three." *Globe and Mail*, October 16, 2003.

Amnesty International Press Release. "Israel/Occupied Territories: Dismantle the Wall Says International Court of Justice." http://web.amnesty.org /library/Index/ENGMDE 150682004?open&of=ENG-ISR.

Amnesty International. "Israel/Occupied Territories: Administrative Detention cannot Replace Proper Administration of Justice." http://web.amnesty.org/ library /Index/ENGMDE150452005?open&of=ENG-ISR.

Amnesty International Canada. "Take Action: Security Certificates Time for Reform." http://www.amnesty.ca/take_action/actions/canada_certificates.php .

Anderson, Scott. "Fingering the Goods: Why Does Canada Give Settlers Sweet Trade Deal?" *NOW Magazine*, August 22–28, 2002 .http://www.nowtoronto.com/issues/2002-08-22/news_story.php.

Bazzi, Mohamad. "The Arab Menace." *The Progressive*, August 1995 .

BBC News. "Intifada Toll Sept 2000-Sept 2005." http://news.bbc.co.uk/go/pr/fr/-/1/hi/world/middle_east/4294502.stm.

BBC News. "UN Fears Over Checkpoint Births." September 23, 2005, http://news. bbc. co.uk/2/hi/middle_east/4274400.stm.

Brink, Andre. *A Dry White Season*. London, Great Britain: Minerva, 1979.

Goar, Carol. "Canada's Dirty Little Secret." *The Toronto Star*, December 17, 2004.

Hoskins, Eric. "A Bloody Road to Peace." *Maclean's*, August 11, 2003 .

International Criminal Tribunal for Rwanda. "UNESCO / JIKJI MEMORY OF THE WORLD." http://portal.unesco.org/ci/en/file_download.php /9522373b850cbf0ec f5acf237 677d86 eTanzan ia.doc.

O'Neill, Juliet. "Civilization under Attack: Bush: President Says bin Laden Seeks 'Evil Weapons'; Tells Allies They Must Join War." *The Ottawa Citizen*, October 7, 2001.

Roy, Sara."Praying with Their Eyes Closed: Reflections on the Disengagement from Gaza. *Journal of Palestine Studies*, 135 (Summer 2005) http://palestine- studies .org/final/en/journals/content.php?aid=6525&jid=1&iid=136&vid=XXXIV&vol=4

Shaheen, Jack. *Reel Bad Arabs: How Hollywood Vilifies a People*. Thousand Oaks: July 2003.

Sharkawi, Rula. "Time to Return to the Rule of Law." *The Toronto Star*, December 29, 2003.

Shephard, Michelle. "The Murky Picture of Terrorism in Canada, CSIS Detains 23 Suspects, but Proof Is in Doubt." *The Toronto Star*, March 22, 2003 .*The Toronto Star*, http://www.thestar.com.

Tyrrell, R. Emmett, Jr. "Sharon's Magnanimity." *The American Spectator*, October 2005 .

United Nations Office for the Coordination of Humanitarian Affairs (OCHA), Occupied Palestinian Territory Report "West Bank Closure and Access." http://domino .un.org /unispal.nsf/0/e2294ff978610ff385256ff7005181d2?OpenDocument.

Williams, Dan. "Israel Warned of Apartheid Boycott." *Sydney Morning Herald*, http://www.smh .com.au/articles/2004/01/05/1073267970184.html.

ಐContributors ಐ

Omar Alghabra is a founding member and past chair of the Canadian Arab Political Action Committee (CAPAC), 2003–2004, and also a former National President of the Canadian Arab Federation. Representing the riding of Mississauga–Erindale, in 2006 Alghabra was elected a member of Canada's Federal Parliament. Mr. Alghabra earned his bachelor's of Engineering at Ryerson Polytechnic University and his master's of Business Administration from York University with specializations in finance, entrepreneurial studies, and strategic management. A winner of the 1991 Robotics International and Society of Manufacturing Engineers Award, Alghabra works for a multinational industrial corporation in Canada where he specializes in sales, commercial strategies, and global business management. A freelance writer for the *Toronto Star* and also *Globe and Mail*, Alghabra has published many articles on Arab Canadians including "A Chance to Lift the Veil of Ignorance about Arabs," (2003) and "Al-Jazeera in Canada" (2004).

Nader Ayish earned his bachelor's degree from Ohio State University, his master's degree from the University of Houston, and his Ph.D. in Education with a specialization in multicultural and multilingual education from George Mason University. His international professional experience includes work with the Palestine Children's Relief Fund in the West Bank, Gaza Strip, and Washington, DC. A skilled researcher, teacher, and interculturalist with over 17 years of professional experience in education, Dr. Ayish is a frequent presenter on the topic of multiculturalism and education. Currently, Dr. Ayish works for the Fairfax County Public Schools in Virginia, U.S.A., where he teaches a variety of subjects from English and Reading to English for Speakers of Other Languages and Creative Writing. He also teaches as an adjunct professor at George Mason University and George Washington University, and consults as a cross-cultural sensitivity trainer.

Hani Ismaeal Elayyan earned his bachelor's and master's degrees from the University of Jordan and his Ph.D. from the University of Southern Illinois at Carbondale in the United States with a specialization in twentieth century American Literature. An Assistant Professor at the University of

Jordan in Amman, Jordan, Dr. Ismaeal currently teaches courses in American Studies. Dr. Ismaeal has won numerous awards and appointments including a grant from the School of Criticism and Theory at Cornell University (1999) and a Fulbright Scholarship (1998–2000). He has also participated in the New Jersey Scholars 2004 Program *Jerusalem at the Crossroads*.

Carol N. Fadda–Conrey is a Ph.D. candidate in American literature at Purdue University where she is finishing a dissertation on Arab American literature entitled "Racially White But Culturally Colored: Defining Contemporary Arab-American Literature and its Transnational Connections." Fadda-Conrey grew up in Beirut, Lebanon, where she earned both her bachelor's and master's degrees from the American University of Beirut. Her research interests include ethnic and postcolonial literatures and women's literature. Fadda-Conrey served as an instructor of English at the English Language Center at the University of Sharjah in the United Arab Emirates, and has also taught literature and composition courses in the English Department at Purdue University. A recipient of Purdue's Bilsland Fellowship (2005–06), her previous published work has appeared in *Al-Jadid Magazine*, *Studies in the Humanities*, and Greenwood Press's *Encyclopedia of Multiethnic American Literature*.

Deirdre King Hainsworth serves as an Assistant Professor of Christian Ethics and the director of the Center for Business, Religion, and Public Life at Pittsburgh Theological Seminary. An ordained minister in the United Church of Christ, Hainsworth has experience as a church educator and pastor as well as experience in urban ministry and civil rights advocacy for persons with disabilities. Dr. Hainsworth received her bachelor's degree from Harvard and her master's of divinity degree and a Ph.D. in social ethics from Princeton Theological Seminary. Hainsworth's research and scholarly presentations focus on issues of religion and human rights, religious concepts of vocation and professional responsibility, and the global and ethical implications of information technologies and technological change. She is currently working on a book entitled *Digital Personas, Human Lives: Christian Ethics and the Uses of New Technologies* as well as an ethics primer centered on vocation and social justice.

Amira Jarmakani is an Assistant Professor of Women's Studies at Georgia State University. She earned her Ph.D. from Emory University and her areas of specialization include transnational feminisms, visual culture, Arab American studies, as well as literatures of representation and the body. Dr. Jarmakani has served as a conference coordinator for the National Coalition Against Domestic Violence in Denver, Colorado, and a volunteer and translator for Tapestri, an immigrant and refugee coalition in Decatur, Georgia, U.S.A. Currently, she is a core organizer for AMWAJ: Arab Movement of Women Arising for Justice. Recent publications and presentations include an article on "Mobilizing the Politics of Invisibility in Arab American Feminist Discourse," and a presentation on "The Commodification of Arab Female Sexuality in the Early Twentieth Century U.S. Advertising Industry." Currently, she is at work on a book entitled *Disorienting America: The Nostalgic Allure of Veils, Harems, and Belly Dancers in U.S. Popular Culture.*

John Tofik Karam, a graduate of the University of Rochester, earned his Ph.D. in Anthropology from Syracuse University and served as a 2005 Sultan Postdoctoral Fellow at the Center for Middle Eastern Studies at the University of California at Berkeley. An Assistant Professor in the Latin American and Latino Studies Program at DePaul University, Chicago, Karam's teaching interests include ethnicity, nationalism, globalization, Brazil, and the Arab Americas. Karam's current research, funded by the Center for Middle Eastern Studies at the University of California, Berkeley; the Center for Latin American Studies at the University of Florida, Gainesville; and the U.S. Department of Education, includes a comparative study of Arab immigrants and descendents in Brazil, Argentina, and the United States. His previous published work has appeared in *PoLAR: Political and Legal Anthropology Review* and *The Journal of Latin American Anthropology.*

Sharon Lopez is an accomplished foreign language instructor and translator with over seventeen years of teaching experience at both the high school and university level. Ms. Lopez earned her bachelor's degree from Ohio Dominican College in Columbus, Ohio, and her master's degree in Spanish Language and Literature at Tulane University in New Orleans, Louisiana. Professionally active in the field of foreign language instruction, Lopez serves as a member of the American Council on the Teaching of

Foreign Languages (ACTFL), a member of the American Association of Teachers of Spanish and Portuguese (AATSP), and as Treasurer of the Kansas World Language Teachers Association (KSWLA). Lopez has also served as Treasurer for the Louisiana Foreign Language Teacher's Association. Currently, Sharon Lopez is a Lecturer in French and Spanish at Friends University in Wichita, Kansas, where she also co-coordinates the Spanish Education program.

Steven Salaita currently serves as Executive Director of RAWI, the Radius of Arab American Writers, Inc., a professional organization designed to encourage Arab youth to write, to urge members to publish their works in mainstream publications, to support sister and brother writers in the Arab world, and to encourage both established writers and also writers beginning their careers to represent a progressive voice in the American community, and to be a voice for justice in the United States and abroad. Salaita is an Assistant Professor of English at Virginia Tech. He is also the author of *Anti-Arab Racism in the USA: Where It Comes from and What It Means for Politics Today* and of two forthcoming books *The Holy Land in Transit: Colonialism and the Quest for Canaan* and *Arab American Literary Fictions, Cultures, and Politics.*

Carolyn Speer Schmidt earned her bachelor's degree from the University of Kansas, her master's degree from the University of Iowa, and her Ph.D. in Adult Education from Kansas State University. For thirteen years, Dr. Schmidt worked at Friends University in Wichita, Kansas as a political science professor, history professor, and English professor in both the traditional day-time undergraduate program and in an innovative adult night program for which she became the Social Science Coordinator and Faculty Chair for the College of Adult and Professional Studies. Today, Dr. Schmidt specializes in teaching and developing online courses for college students.

Kirk Scott earned a master's in History from Wichita State University in Kansas where he specialized in the study of political theatre and the public spectacle of martyrdom. The 1999 Editor of the *Fairmont Folio*, he has also been an adjunct instructor of history at Friends University and Cowley County Community College, and an instructor of guitar at Bethel College. He also served a term as the Artist-in-Residence for Jazz and Classical guitar at Hutchinson Community College. Since 1999, Kirk Scott has served as the

Senior College Textbook Representative for the Midwest Region in the College Division of Houghton Mifflin publishing located in Boston, Massachusetts.

Rula Sharkawi is an Executive Committee Member for the Canadian Arab Federation, and a media and communications consultant for organizations working on social justice issues who require assistance with lobbying, media training, communications strategies and media relations. Ms. Sharkawi earned her honours bachelor's degree, from the University of Toronto and her master's degree in Journalism and Mass Communication for the University of Western Ontario. A 2001 recipient of the Deputy Minister's Award for Outstanding Achievement, Ms. Sharkawi has held a number of senior positions with the Ontario Government. She has also, previously, worked as a media and public relations consultant for the United Nations in Jerusalem, a freelance journalist writing on Middle East affairs, and a Lecturer of Journalism at Birzeit University in the West Bank where her students produced radio broadcast documentaries, several of which were later aired on the *BBC World Service in Arabic*.

Katharine S. Speer graduated Phi Beta Kappa, summa cum laude from the University of Kansas with a double-major in Anthropology and Latin American Studies. A former project director for *Amigos de las Américas*, Speer has served in Michoacán, Mexico; La Esperanza, Honduras; Tarija, Bolivia; and San José, Costa Rica where Speer later interned with the Department of Archeology of Costa Rica's National Museum working on projects related both to the geography of Latin America and the global history of migration. Interested in international development law and ethics, Speer's research projects include the relationship between field agriculture and social structure in northern South America, and also crop cultivation on the shores of pre-Columbian Lake Titicaca. Her thesis "Los Inmigrantes Italianos de San Vito, Costa Rica: La Transformación de una Colonia" compared the adaptive experience of Italian immigrants to urban areas with that of Italian immigrants to the Costa Rican rain forest. Currently, Speer is pursuing advanced studies in law at the University of Denver.

Darcy A. Zabel is a Phi Beta Kappa cum laude graduate of Mount Holyoke College. Zabel earned her master's and Ph.D. from the University of

Connecticut where she was the English coordinator for the Center for Academic Programs' Student Support Services Pre-Collegiate experience, a program designed to increase access to higher education for high-potential students who come from underrepresented ethnic or economic backgrounds and/or are first-generation college students. Zabel's research and publication interests include world literature in translation, women's literature, and the multi-ethnic literature of the United States. Zabel is currently an Associate Professor of English at Friends University where she also serves as the Vice Chair for the Religion and Humanities Division.